UNDER MY THUMB

UNDER MY THUMB

SONGS THAT HATE WOMEN
AND
THE WOMEN WHO LOVE THEM

Edited by Rhian E. Jones and Eli Davies

Published by Repeater Books
An imprint of Watkins Media Ltd

19-21 Cecil Court
London
WC2N 4EZ
UK
www.repeaterbooks.com
A Repeater Books paperback original 2017
2
Printed and bound in Malta
Distributed in the United States by Random House, Inc., New York.

Cover design: Johnny Bull
Typography and typesetting: JCS Publishing Services Ltd
Typefaces: Chaparral Pro and Corbel

ISBN: 9781910924617
Ebook ISBN: 9781910924686

Contents

Introduction

Rhian E. Jones and Eli Davies

While women have always been offered songs that love, defend and celebrate them, there is an equally long tradition of music that does the opposite. In lyrics, videos, album artwork and the music industry's everyday operations, women see themselves attacked, excluded, stereotyped, fetishised and viewed purely through their impact on the male ego. But this hasn't stopped generations of women from loving, being moved by and critically appreciating this kind of music — no matter how that music may feel about them.

Being a woman and a music fan can feel like hard work at times. Back in 1970, a writer named Arlene Brown expressed her disappointment with the contemporary rock scene in a piece entitled "Has anyone reading this article met a woman bass player". At one point, she recounts her experience at a Grateful Dead concert:

> Something inside me went boom. There I was digging this beautiful voice, beautiful guitar, but with words about some woman's box [...] I felt pretty sullen

for the rest of the concert [...] I think that rock music has changed a lot of things, released a lot of energy, created some good images for young people, emphasized enjoyment, sensual pleasure, relaxation, freaking out, looking weird, turning on, etc. But I also think as far as the male-female relationship goes, as far as women's liberation goes, and the image a woman should have of herself, it is totally reactionary, and must be changed.[1]

Here, Brown describes the contradictions that can still confront women invested in music today. The visceral thrills, exhilaration and anti-establishment kicks — they're there for us as well as the boys, but so often there's an undercurrent to our appreciation that whispers: "this music doesn't like me" or "this music doesn't even acknowledge that I exist". When stories are told about bands, artists and gigs, women are either completely written out of them or featured only in relation to men — as delicate muses, insatiable groupies or a swarm of faceless fangirls — meaning that our own experiences, ideas and arguments about the music we love are marginalised or glossed over. Traditionally, the boys not only do music, they also criticise, analyse and canonise music. The girls? We're just there to applaud and appreciate.

Men's experiences — and men's experiences of women — have structured so much of the music we listen to. If this is ever noticed by male fans and listeners, many will see it as "just the way it is", barely worthy of comment or deserving of challenge. Among other things, this highlights how the ability to consume "problematic" media often relates to your real-life proximity to it. Men do not face the same threat of sexual violence, harassment and objectification that women do, and so will necessarily have a different reaction to hearing music which is predicated on the subordination, exploitation or exclusion of women. But being a female music fan affects your physical experience when out in the world — at gigs, at clubs, on the dancefloor, in conversations, at the bar, on your journey home — and can change the ways you feel able to relate to an artist, band, scene or subculture.

Over forty years after Arlene Brown wrote her article, Jessica Hopper published *The First Collection of Criticism by a Living Female Rock Critic*. Although, as she acknowledges, the accuracy of the book's title is up for debate, its intention was to highlight a broader lack of awareness and acknowledgement of women as music fans, listeners, critics and writers. In the essay "Emo: Where the Girls Aren't", Hopper observed that sections of the alternative music scene were no more immune than the mainstream to regurgitating reactionary values of male chauvinism. Her objections to this fit into a long tradition of how women relate to the music they love:

> [T]he well-worn narrative of the boy rebel's broken heart, as exemplified by the last 50-plus years of blues-based music [...] men writing songs about women is practically the definition of rock 'n' roll. And as a woman, as a music critic, as someone who lives and dies for music, there is a rift within, a struggle of how much deference you can afford, and

how much you are willing to ignore what happens in these songs simply because you like the music.[2]

The sexism and misogyny which often attaches to music also influences mainstream music journalism, both in its relative lack of writing by women and in the attitudes of male writers to performers and fans. Classically, a musician's credibility is judged by the nature of their fanbase, with a following of "screaming teenage girls" or "frustrated housewives" cited as reasons not to take a band or artist seriously. The same attitudes are present in the wider culture surrounding music: in documentaries, articles, panel discussions, interviews and autobiographies. Some of these areas have seen signs of improvement, particularly since the rise of women writing about music themselves — whether memoirs by musicians like Pauline Black, Viv Albertine and Kim Gordon, or works of criticism and celebration by writers like Ellen Willis, Laina Dawes, Sylvia Patterson and Lavinia Greenlaw. But despite this evolution in music writing, and the increase in alternative media sources providing space for women to write on popular culture, there is still a lot of ground to cover in reflecting the range of identities and experiences women can have. Articles like that by former musician Emma Jackson, on "retrospective sexism" when looking back on Nineties music[3], describe a music industry and cultural history still submerged in sexist assumptions that enable the unthinking erasure of women's contributions and perspectives.

Partly inspired by Jackson's piece, Eli wrote about her own experience as a music fan in the Nineties, from a viewpoint she felt had been resolutely ignored by the critical consensus.[4] The response to this article on social media and elsewhere, from other women who felt similarly, is part of what pushed us to put this book together. We wanted to collect these stories and experiences not only in order to assert some balance, but also to explore specifically the messy, complex and confusing — and at the same time thrilling, fulfilling and life-changing — relationships that women can have with music and musicians.

***

There is, of course, no single definitive female identity or one way to experience music, which is something we were keen for this collection to emphasise. This book's contributors cover a variety of music, subjects, styles and opinions. The essays are grouped loosely by chronological order and their references to songs and bands beyond their central subject mean that many of them have points of incidental but illuminating crossover with each other. The book's connecting thread is that all the beloved bands, artists and songs discussed here might be found off-putting, politically troubling, ridiculous or even dangerous from other perspectives. In recognising the dubious aspects of the music and musicians they love, writers variously critique them, denounce them, laugh about them, or find ways to positively channel them, fashioning subversive or empowering lessons from often unpromising material. Throughout this process, gender interacts with class, race, sexuality and other aspects of an individual's identity.

While there has been no shortage of women capable of expressing themselves through music, it has taken decades for them to achieve mainstream visibility and to be taken seriously on their own terms. However, as many of these essays show, women have always been able to sing along with the male voices made available to us, even though we know we aren't singing from exactly the same hymn-sheet. Needing an outlet for a deeply-felt but unarticulated anger, disaffection or rejection of the status quo and the social roles imposed on us, many women found affinity and solidarity with the resistance and resentment expressed by male artists, even while recognising its limits and flaws. Writers who identify with or admire a whole array of male misfits, male rebels and angry young men — from Tupac to Jarvis, Elvis Costello to Eminem, Kanye to Rivers Cuomo — can also regret that women seldom see themselves represented in the same terms or allowed the same indulgences.

Throughout this book, writers consider the social and cultural imperatives, and the personal histories, that allow them to align themselves with the emotions expressed by male artists, and to overlook or even embrace the misogyny that often informs them. Some essays observe how different generations of women bring different attitudes to bear on the same music, revisiting bands or songs of their youth with a wiser and more jaundiced eye, or seeing them have an unexpected or instructive effect on a younger generation. Many pieces demonstrate the importance of adolescence as a time when young women engage most intensely and intently with music. "First bands" can be as memorable and influential as first boyfriends or girlfriends, often acting as a gateway to the sexuality and politics of the adult world and how they impact on girls growing up. Writers discuss the contradictions and complexities of their relationship with femininity, with feminism, and with stereotypes or assumptions about female music fans, and explore how this has helped them to manage their encounters with misogyny in music. In particular, a number of writers reflect on the ways — not always conscious or deliberate — in which it's possible to accept or ignore negative or troubling representations of women by thinking of yourself as somehow "not like the other girls", as somehow intrinsically different from the kinds of women mocked, exploited or resented in the music you love. This absence of automatic solidarity was a tendency that the rock critic Ellen Willis identified in 1967, noting that she herself "did not question the idea that women were guardians of oppressive conventional values: I only thought of myself as an exception [...] I understood men's need to go on the road because I was, spiritually speaking, on the road myself. That, at least, was my fantasy."[5] Like Willis, however, many of us would go on to discover that the distance between fantasy and reality can never be completely maintained.

Several writers recount their frustrations with supposedly alternative scenes which can end up reinforcing mainstream values and gender dynamics. A song as classic as Bob Dylan's "Like a Rolling Stone", now over fifty years old, still reflects some fundamental and enduring problems with the idea of rebellion through rock 'n' roll. In a depressingly large amount of Sixties subcultures, opposition to capitalism and commitment to a male-by-default model of liberation did not prevent the reproduction of gendered divisions of labour or the objectification of women. Although challenged by successive waves of intersectional liberation movements, later musical subcultures — even punk, and right up to twenty-first-century indie, industrial and emo — have not been immune to blindspots around gender, race and class either. It's a very old story, whereby allegedly revolutionary art, politics or social movements in fact shore up reactionary conventions. The deeper you've invested, the more betrayed you may feel. As Marissa Chen writes in her essay on Weezer's *Pinkerton*: "I realised I'd been pledging membership to a club I didn't even have permission to be part of".

Having realised this, is it possible to enjoy the "club" regardless — to stop pledging membership but still carry on dancing? This book argues that it is. For all our authors, music has been and remains a physical and emotional pleasure and a lifelong source of excitement, comfort, identification, escapism and inspiration. As female music fans we are more than capable of forming our own stories, emotions and solidarities around the songs that we love, even if the song's content may be suggesting otherwise. This book is a small part of a huge and ongoing conversation, in which nuance and subtlety are too often absent, and it's perhaps more important that the conversation is had than that any side "wins". Discovery happens in the spaces between disagreement.

Notes

1 Brown, Arlene. "Has anyone reading this article met a woman bass player". *International Times*, 13, 27 August – 10 September 1970.

2 Hopper, Jessica. "Emo: Where the Girls Aren't". *Punk Planet* 56. http://www.rookiemag.com/2015/07/where-the-girls-arent/

3 Jackson, Emma. "Indie Music's Women Problem and Retrospective Sexism". *Huffington Post*, 19 October 2015. http://www.huffingtonpost.co.uk/emma-jackson/sexism-in-music_b_8330178.html

4 Davies, Eli. "Retrospective Sexism: How Women Are Written Out of British Indie Music History". *Vice*, 4 November 2015. https://noisey.vice.com/en_us/article/revisiting-pulps-different-class-and-how-indie-writes-women-from-history

5 Willis, Ellen. *Beginning to See the Light: Sex, Hope and Rock-and-Roll*. (Wesleyan University Press, 1992), p.12 fn.

Bibliography

Albertine, Viv. Clothes, *Clothes, Clothes. Music, Music, Music. Boys, Boys, Boys.* (Faber and Faber, 2014)

Aronowitz, Nona Willis. *Out of the Vinyl Deeps: Ellen Willis on Rock Music.* (University of Minnesota Press, 2011)

Black, Pauline. *Black By Design: A 2-Tone Memoir.* (Serpent's Tail, 2012)

Dawes, Laina. *What Are You Doing Here?: A Black Woman's Life and Liberation in Heavy Metal.* (Bazillion Points Press, 2013)

Gordon, Kim. *Girl in a Band: A Memoir.* (Dey Street Books, 2015)

Greenlaw, Lavinia. *The Importance of Music to Girls* (Faber and Faber, 2007)

Hopper, Jessica. *The First Collection of Criticism by a Living Female Rock Critic.* (Featherproof Books, 2015)

Patterson, Sylvia. *I'm Not With the Band: A Writer's Life Lost in Music* (Little, Brown, 2016)

Dion, Frankie and Me

Christina Newland

To Charles, who first gave me the gift of Dion and the Belmonts. All this time and I'm still a teenager in love.

The author of "Runaround Sue" — the jangly doo-wop cornerstone for spurned boyfriends everywhere — seemed to have really suffered the vagaries of love. Of course, pop songs about heartbreak aren't exactly unusual. But Dion DiMucci, lead vocalist of Dion and the Belmonts, had more than his fair share of romantic cataclysm. From a tear-shedding teenager in love to a womanising "wanderer", he just never seemed to have much luck with women.

In 1957, DiMucci and his teenage friends — all Bronx natives — would harmonise on street corners. They soon grew popular enough to need a name. It seemed like a logical conclusion to call themselves after the place where they lived and sang — Belmont Avenue. Signing to Laurie Records, the group hammered out doo-wop hits like "I Wonder Why" and "A Teenager in Love". Dion went solo in the early Sixties, maintaining a career full of hits until the middle of the decade, when fast-changing tastes dented his popularity.

But Dion's buttery tones and poppy compositions belie a real sting of bitterness toward the opposite sex. Occasionally, beneath that sugary woosh, there's even a hint of seething condescension. In "Donna the Prima Donna", he scathingly remarks on a neighbourhood girl's airs and graces after she has rejected him: "She always wears diamonds and pearls galore / She buys 'em at the five and ten cent store / She wants to be just like Zsa Zsa Gabor / Even though she's the girl next door".[1]

This resentment only grows in 1963 track "This Little Girl", where Dion talks about "taming" a girlfriend, showing her the "way to behave" and "cutting her down to size".[2] The paternalism that's nearly ever-present in the rock 'n' roll of this era — constant references to "little girls" and child-like women — is one of its most pernicious habits. The underlying and patronising belief is that women, much like children, need firm guidance and discipline, or they're liable to misbehave. To his credit, DiMucci later remarked on the song: "When I listen to it now, it sounds like I had a lot of resentment in me toward women. I guess I did. When you're young and frustrated trying to understand yourself and the opposite sex, this is how it comes out."

Similar traits — not to mention origins — can be attributed to Frankie Valli and the Four Seasons, another Italian-American doo-wop group. The first iteration was Valli's group the Four Lovers, forming sometime in 1953. When the falsetto-voiced singer met producer Bob Crewe and superstar lyricist Bob Gaudio in 1959, the foundations were laid for the Four Seasons.

Still, they had only moderate success for several years, shopping their songs around until the release of their first album in 1962. Hit single "Sherry" changed everything. From that point until early 1964, no other musical group — except the Beach Boys — released as many chart-toppers.

But Bob Gaudio's songs for Valli seemed to share Dion's attitudes toward women. The Four Seasons are known and loved for their distinctive and joyful pop songs — but on close inspection, some of the subjects therein are less cheerful. The group's songbook touches on male egotism ("no woman's worth / crawling on the earth / so walk like a man, my son"[3]), emotional cruelty ("I used to love to make you cry / It made me feel like a man inside"[4]) and a wandering eye ("Shoulda told you I can't linger / There's a wedding ring on my finger"[5]).

Despite such ample evidence of misogyny, critiquing this genre — and period — of music proves difficult. Songs like "Runaround Sue" or "Walk Like a Man" are couched in wholesome catchiness, making it easy for their undercurrents to be ignored. And both of their respective recording artists signify a particular "sweet spot" in American history. Before the Beatles led the British Invasion or President Kennedy was assassinated, doo-wop ruled the airwaves. It was an innocent time in popular music, forever forsaken on that November afternoon in 1963. So even now, those songs evoke a certain era. Both Frankie Valli and Dion DiMucci hailed from the Tri-State area, the former from Newark and the latter from the Bronx. These groups recall the memory of mid-century blue-collar NYC, of baseball games and finned, wide-bumper cars.

These impressions are reinforced by the types of films where Dion or Frankie have been featured on the soundtrack. *Goodfellas*, *Back to the Future*, *A Bronx Tale*, *Jersey Boys* and the like all share a certain degree of nostalgia.

Doo-wop music is deeply associated with American cultural memory, and nostalgia for the late Fifties and early Sixties has been a part of our national DNA for a long time. Nostalgia is very powerful. It can eclipse all kinds of darker memories — racism, segregation, oppressive sexism, domestic violence. All of these things were woven into the fabric of the Fifties and Sixties, but it's both easy and tempting to yield to the *Happy Days* sitcom version of history. In many ways, that's what Dion or Frankie's brand of honeyed doo-wop has become a part of: a collective set of rose-tinted blinders about the era it came from. The unpleasant elements often get lost along the way.

What's undeniable is that this type of selective nostalgia has always been harder for women and people of colour. For pretty obvious reasons, we are mostly excluded from the luxury of reminiscing about the past. So how do I justify my taste for anachronistic oldies? What could Dion and the Belmonts et al possibly have to offer a modern feminist listener?

Part of it — on a gut level — is because I can afford to be blasé about the music's content. The courtship rituals and attitudes of doo-wop are so antiquated as to seem a little bit quaint. It's hard to feel especially ambivalent about dancing around to this music while I get ready to go out. The world's changed an awful lot since 1963 — and transporting yourself back to that time via music is a striking way to discover that. To quote the old advertising slogan — "You've come a long way, baby."

And yet, if you're after one-sided macho rambling about romance, there's still plenty to choose from in 2016. In spite of the Beyoncés of the world, for many male musicians the obsession with "good girls" is as prevalent as ever. Whether it's Kanye's "one good girl is worth a thousand bitches" or Drake's "you used to always stay at home/be a good girl"[6], the dichotomy is clear. In truth, the Sandys, Dianes and Sues who backstab their way through Dion's world aren't too different from pop music's current conception of women — still too often seen as untrustworthy snakes or malleable playthings. Maybe that old saying is true: the more things change, the more they stay the same.

At the same time, Dion and Frankie offer insights into what romance and womanhood meant at a specific moment in history. This may be indirect, or camouflaged by dulcet tones, but it's still present. In the same way that a show like *Mad Men* did, it offers us a window into the recent past and displays the subtleties of gender relations in a time of widespread, mainstream misogyny. It's not pretty, but it is a valuable learning experience.

Both artists reveal expectations of female behaviour; showcase the rampant chauvinism of the age; and even hint at domestic violence, as with Dion's "Little Diane": "I want to pack and leave / And slap your face / Bad girls like you are a disgrace"[7], he snarls on the 1963 track.

Threats of violence sadly don't end there. They could occasionally be found in other popular music from the time — most notoriously in a 1962 song by the Crystals entitled "He Hit Me (And It Felt Like a Kiss)". Dion and the Crystals actually share a curious link — the stellar songwriting duo of Carole King and Gerry Goffin. The pair had penned hundreds of songs and several dozen solid gold hits, including Dion's "This Little Girl".

"He Hit Me" was immediately unpopular and received little radio play. It was intended to document the masochistic mentality of an abused woman — "He hit me and I knew he loved me".[8] Goffin and King were said to have based it on singer Little Eva, who once justified a beating from her boyfriend to them in a similar way. Nonetheless, Phil Spector's forbidding, ambiguous production of the song — combined with his reputation as a homicidal misogynist — make it a difficult song to feel comfortable with, even if it was intended as critique.

Still, the frank nastiness of "He Hit Me (And It Felt Like a Kiss)" does achieve one thing that neither Dion nor Frankie ever did; it's impossible to be nostalgic about it. We can defang the others, but the Crystals make certain we can't forget the endgame of the era's misogyny.

It's interesting that Carole King was a major creative force in these songs. She's an avowed voice for the rights and talents of women — and a beacon for female subjectivity in music. She transcended prettiness or saleable sexuality to become the first female solo artist to have a record go diamond, selling more than ten million copies. And even before all that, she was integral to the culture of doo-wop and early Sixties pop through her songwriting. She moved from being the co-writer of "He Hit Me (And It Felt Like a Kiss)" to the masterpiece of confessional womanhood that was *Tapestry*. Her career offers a poetic corrective to the macho culture where she first worked.

That macho culture undeniably produced great music — Dion and the Belmonts, Frankie Valli and the Four Seasons, and the like — that, on a personal level, I will never stop loving. It's still joyous, charming stuff. Maybe it's the benefit of hindsight that can make the ugly parts tolerable. Doo-wop says "you're no good", and Carole King answers, "you're as beautiful as you feel". It's that sprinkle of modern wisdom that makes Dion and Frankie OK in my book.

Notes

1 Dion and the Belmonts, "Donna the Prima Donna", *Donna the Prima Donna*, (1963), Columbia Records. Copyright Dion DiMucci, Enest Maresca, Bronx Soul Music Inc. (1963).

2 Dion and the Belmonts, "This Little Girl", *Donna the Prima Donna*, (1963), Columbia Records. Copyright Carole King, Gerald Goffin, Screen Gems-EMI Music Ltd (1963).

3 The Four Seasons, "Walk Like a Man", *Big Girls Don't Cry and Twelve Others*, (1963), Vee-Jay Records. Copyright Bob Crewe, Robert Gaudio, Gavadima Music, MPL Communications Inc. (1963).

4 The Four Seasons, "Working My Way Back To You", *Working My Way Back To You*, (1966), Philips. Copyright Denny Randell, Sally Linzer (1966).

5 The Four Seasons, "Bye Bye Baby", *The Four Seasons Entertain You*, (1965), Vee-Jay Records. Copyright Robert Gaudio, MPL Music Publishing Inc. (1965).

6 Drake, "Hotline Bling", *Views* (2015), Ovo Sound/Cash Money/Young Money/Republic. Copyright Aubrey Drake Graham, Anthony Paul Jefferies, Timmy Thomas, EMI April Music Inc, EMI April Music Canada Ltd, EMI Longitude Music, EMI Music Publishing Ltd, Is Love And Above, Nyankingmusic and Sandra Gale (2015).

7 Dion and the Belmonts, "Little Diane", *Lovers Who Wander*, (1962), Laurie Records. Copyright Don DiMucci, Bronx Soul Music (1962).

8 The Crystals, "He Hit Me (And it Felt Like a Kiss)", (1962), Philles Records. Copyright Carole King, Gerald Goffin, Screen Gems-EMI Music Ltd (1962).

The Two Sides of Phil Spector

Stephanie Phillips

Every now and again, when my day-to-day tasks aren't enough to prevent me from drifting into a particularly captivating day dream, I wonder what it would be like to be in a girl group in the Sixties. How big would my hair be — a classy Supremes curled bob or a sky-scraper, bad girl beehive? Would I hang out with the Beatles or the Stones? Most importantly, how long could I cope with the racism and sexism that permeated every aspect of the decade?

The one question I regularly pose to myself is how would I react when a certain slight, dapper man in his mid-twenties, wearing an Edwardian suit with an ego triple the size of his small stature, walked in the room. Would I be friends with him? Would I follow him? Would I be offended by his attitude or try and put him in his place? Knowing the stories I've heard about legendary music producer Phil Spector, it's hard to know how I'd react to his, let's call it, extreme personality.

There really needs to be a whole book about the undeniable mental strength of the people who had to put up with the mad genius of Phil Spector. Known for his innovative wall of sound technique that propelled pop songs to Wagnerian heights, he was the genius behind the Sixties sound, creating hits such as the Crystals "He's a Rebel", the Ronettes "Be My Baby" and the Righteous Brothers "You've Lost that Loving Feeling".

After Spector had his first number one hit at nineteen with his own group the Teddy Bears, he began perfecting his formula for pop magic. In 1961, he partnered with Lester Sill to form the label Philles Records, which became a hit factory throughout the Sixties. His reputation attracted the attention of bands and artists such as George Harrison, John Lennon, the Beatles and the Ramones, who all wanted Spector to produce their albums.

From the beginning of his fame he was the focus of the press, who claimed he was a mad genius, something Spector played up to constantly as his ego grew bigger and bigger. He is known for being difficult and volatile both at work and in his personal life. His ex-wife and star of the Ronettes, Ronnie Spector, has spoken out about her marriage to Spector, claiming she was subject to constant emotional abuse. Ronnie also said he was insecure and obsessive about her, and kept her a near prisoner in their LA mansion.

Spector also had a dangerous fixation with guns, and regularly brought them into the recording studios to the horror of anyone around him, including John Lennon who was stunned when Spector fired a shot into the ceiling during a heated recording session. His abusive behaviour, violent tendencies and obsessions with firearms led to the inevitable. In 2009, he was convicted of the murder of actress Lana Clarkson, who was killed in his LA home in 2003.

A convicted murderer isn't really someone you'd expect to look up to, but, alas, here I am, two hours into a Phil Spector compilation, belting out the words to "Da Do Ron Ron" and trying to figure out why these teenage love songs mean so much to me. To break it down, first of all, you can't listen to the Crystals, Darlene Love or Tina Turner without feeling ecstatic. The songs Spector and his team gave them were songs of joy and rebellion that seemed to burst out of the speakers and come to life. Though it is not surprising that they cannot be contained, as Spector packed each song with numerous guitars, strings, pianos and percussion to create his famed wall of sound. Compared to the normal song productions of the time, which featured four or five elements, Spector's orchestral approach blew people away.

Many of his most famous songs dealt with teenage love and heartbreak. Even though it's safe to say I wasn't a teenager when I first heard his songs, I still connected with the sentiment and related to it. But the main reason I love Spector's work, especially his early work, is because it captures the voices of young black women, a segment of society that were rarely heard at the time. As a black woman, it's reaffirming to know some of the greatest hits were made with the talent, youth and spirit of people like me.

And it is because I connect so deeply with these young black women that it hurts even more to acknowledge the reality of who Spector was and how he treated his stars. To be both a feminist and a Spector lover is to be constantly at odds with oneself, as his aggressive personality is integral to the quality of the music he made. In *He's a Rebel*, the 1982 documentary about Spector's life, musician Nino Tempo made his thoughts about Spector clear: "I don't think he could have made the records he made if he didn't have quite an ego. I think they go hand in hand."

In 1962, when Spector wanted to record Gene Pitney's song "He's a Rebel", he planned for it to be a Crystals release, but the band were touring the East Coast at the time. As Spector got word another record label wanted to record the song, he quickly brought in Darlene Love and the Blossoms so his version would be out first. Although Love's trademark vocals are easy to hear, Spector still labelled the release as the Crystals.

Spector's love of switching around singers happened often at the label, he even made Love sing another song, "He's Sure the Boy I Love", that was again released as the Crystals. I always wondered why Spector did this, as it's not like he didn't care about the vocals. Realistically the reason why he would swap around singers so much was because he did care deeply.

In a *Saturday Night Live* sketch about Old Hollywood, Kate McKinnon plays a former Hollywood actress whose tales of the mistreatment of women by studios grow increasingly more depressing and perplexing. In one sketch, she recalls that actresses were literal objects and were part of the props budget: "When I wasn't filming I'd have to sit on a table next to a piece of masking tape that said woman. Then one of the union guys would pick me up, show me to Alfred Hitchcock and say sorry this is all they have."

It's a hilarious take on Old Hollywood misogyny and also an appropriate depiction of Spector's approach to his artists. The Crystals were already stars and would be able to sell a big hit better than a new group would. Love, on the other hand, had more experience and depth as a singer than others on the Philles roster. Spector picked the parts of his singers he liked and put them in one package — to him, artists were interchangeable props in the Phil Spector show. He was always looking for the right singer for the track and if that singer didn't happen to be in the group, it was tough luck.

It can't be overlooked that the majority of his singers were young women of colour, straight out of high school, with little experience in the world. They were easy to manipulate and take advantage of. Though Spector treated his artists as if they were disposable, he couldn't make the music he made without them.

In *Twenty Feet from Stardom*, the 2013 documentary about the lives and losses of the industry's most famous backing singers, Bruce Springsteen acknowledged that he could never replicate the Spector sound fully because the key missing ingredient was youth. It's also important to acknowledge that the rock 'n' roll sound everyone craved in the Sixties was based on rhythm and blues. To get that authentic sound, these women had to channel something that a white singer never could — the black experience. It's heart-breaking to know that black women were treated as if their talent was not important, not knowing at the time that they were the cherry on top of the whole production.

There's no real way to come to terms with Phil Spector's legacy and the things he has done. I want to separate them to opposite sides of my brain. The Spector that instantly brings a smile to my face when I hear "Be My Baby" and brought me my heroines in the form of Darlene Love and Ronnie Spector stays with me most often. The Spector that is a violent, abusive, gun-obsessed murderer visits less frequently, but perhaps I need to think about the latter version of Spector.

The two sides of Spector have to be taken as one. He needs to be recognised for everything he is, both so his legacy can live on but also so we can remind ourselves that his behaviour was not normal and should not be tolerated or dismissed. When I listen to his back catalogue now, I want to appreciate the music he was part of whilst also being aware of the pain he brought to the lives of others. It's a difficult lot to balance but, for the sake of his victims, it's not too much to ask for.

You Shouldn't Take It So Personal: Bob Dylan and the Boundaries of Rebellion

Rhian E. Jones

Bob Dylan is both a master-storyteller and the hero of his own stories. Abrasive, contrary and often absurd, a permanent revolutionary, a shape-shifting blend of Guthrie, Garbo, Chaplin and Christ, he has spent his life shedding stylistic skins and compulsively travelling on. This essay is less about Dylan himself than about how the idea of Dylan as prototypical rock-rebel — although this is only one of many roles he plays — demonstrates the complications and frustrations of a certain idea of rebellion. Dylan's 1965 single "Like a Rolling Stone" is explosive and exhilarating, pioneering in its length and lyrical complexity, and acknowledged even by his detractors as one of the greatest in rock. But this song of individual agency, liberation and escape is also built around a woman's downfall. For me, loving this song meant discovering how class and gender solidarity complicate each other, and that while the male rebel has readymade roles to step into, women drawn to the same parts cannot play them with quite the same ease and abandon. How do we square this eternal circle?

***

I grew up with the kind of politics that meant I should have liked folk music, but I didn't. I thought the revolutionary efforts of the Sixties deserved a better soundtrack. The strained and plodding authenticity of folk's over-earnest luminaries, Joan Baez's stiff crystalline piety, bored me to tears — Dylan included. When I left my ex-mining town and escaped to university in London, in the middle of my cultural adjustment from the dark satanic mills to the city's bright lights I met half-absurd, half-intimidating hip middle-class boys who accorded Dylan — seemingly a wholly different Dylan from his folk incarnation — the status of revered single-name recognition, like you'd speak of Madonna, or Cher, or Beyoncé. But they always seemed to talk of him as a received-wisdom icon — someone you had to talk about, especially if girls who liked musicians were talking to you — and they had very little use for talking about his music. Intrigued, and since these were the early, dodgy days of streaming and filesharing, I had to seek his post-folk, proto-pop music out myself.

Before I fell in love with the contents of *Blonde on Blonde*, I was in love with how he looked on the album cover: timelessly sexy and effortlessly significant, a New York icon forever frozen with that unruly halo of curls. As you do when you fall in love, I wanted to discover everything at once. For the next year or so — these were also the days just before YouTube — I spent the spare time and money I had on acquiring the rest of his back catalogue. After YouTube, I discovered him onstage and in interviews: old-man curmudgeonly at not even twenty-five, or urchin-capped and (playing at) achingly earnest in his even-younger folk days, or proto-trolling the world's press from behind his cigarette in massive indoor sunglasses. I liked his insouciant obnoxiousness, his *chutzpah*, his insistence on existing, as I was trying to do, just as he was in a world where he didn't altogether belong.

London in the early 2000s was not 1960s New York, but, in the self-absorbed irony soup of East London's indie scene, Dylan's scene-sceptical songs like "Positively 4th Street" or "To Ramona" still resonated with me. *Blonde on Blonde*, a hazy, rich, hallucinatory album partly about the self-conscious construction of identity, was also a record of urban alienation, capturing that feeling of being alone in a crowded room ("We sit here stranded, though we're all doing our best to deny it"[1]; "Ain't it clear that I just don't fit?"[2]). It skewered both the tedious pseudo-bohemia coagulating around me and the feeling of standing outside it, awkward but ablaze with the self-righteous relief that rejection can bring. I identified with Dylan as deliberate outsider, in love with what the city could offer but reliant on wits and resourcefulness in contrast to those who, despite their class advantages, were still "helpless like a rich man's child"[3]. While still growing into my own identity, I drew self-confidence and strength from (consciously and subconsciously) play-acting as the young Dylan — or rather, trying on the same masks that Dylan had chosen to wear, even though they didn't always fit entirely comfortably.

Again, as you do when you fall in love, I overlooked his doubtful aspects and adored him. Even through discovering his later swerve into evangelical Christianity, his political trajectory best described as idiosyncratic, and his bad-to-wretched Eighties albums, my love was fixed and unstinting. I even read his novel, once.

And, of course, I loved "Like a Rolling Stone". From its pistol-crack kick-off to the whirlwind catharsis of its final chorus, the song is a diamond-hard anthem of autonomy and independence. Its definitive version emerged from the crucible of Dylan's 1966 UK tour, which consolidated his switch of style from folk to electric in perhaps the most spectacular example of divisive art since the riots at Victor Hugo's *Hernani*. That anti-electric outrage, and Dylan's denouncing by former musical comrades, was fuelled by both personal and ideological betrayal, a sense of being played for fools, at seeing folk's worthy communalism abandoned for rock's commercial glitter. (Guess which side I was on.) To look back on the 1966 Manchester Free Trade Hall gig, to see and hear music carrying a now-unbelievable emotional and political charge, is extraordinary: the slow-clapping and strategic walk-outs, audience members arguing amongst themselves and relentlessly heckling, baiting and insulting Dylan between songs. That climactic shout of "Judas!" is so perfectly attuned to the show's legendary status — and, from today's less invested perspective, so ridiculously over-the-top — that it seems like part of the performance. As does the shot of another offended folkie, staring down the barrel of a camera-lens after storming out and stating, with flat Stalinist conviction: "He's a traitor. He wants shooting".[4] Dylan — fishbowl-eyed, sharp-suited and slight in the centre of this storm — responds to the crowd's hostility by whipping the band into a scourging, set-closing version of "Like a Rolling Stone" that is a singular performance of grace under fire and victory in defeat. Its core of absolute steely defiance seems to render its performer bulletproof, as if, like all the best wind-up artists, he draws strength from attracting antipathy. Even four decades later, the song still sounded to me like inspiration, aspiration and possibility. Its declaration of independence showed how shaking off the obligations and responsibilities of former identities could offer freedom in the middle of free-falling terror.

Was there anything I didn't love? Sure. Isn't there always?

One could argue that exasperated frustration is just the default state of any Dylan fan who engages with the variety and intricacy of his work. The number of things I found, and still find, to admire about his music have always outweighed its more questionable underpinnings. One could argue that misanthropy defines him more than male chauvinism: if his conduct in relationships has sometimes been difficult to defend, his lyrics are more often generally or self-critical than specifically directed at women. The targets of memorably caustic kiss-offs like "Positively 4th Street" are guessable but not specified by gender. Aside from the markedly ungracious "Ballad in Plain D" — which he himself later acknowledged as the work of "a real *schmuck*" — Dylan's break-up songs, at once intensely personal and universally relatable, are concerned more with the articulation of pain than with apportioning blame or guilt.

But, for someone so endlessly surprising and inventive, so easily revolutionary, with such a gift for conjuring the profound from the prosaic and making the old sound new, Dylan's sexual politics can be drearily retrograde. For all the wry sincerity of "One Too Many Mornings" or "If You See Her, Say Hello" — and for all the arch, glorious bitchiness and feline snark in his own presentation — his work is also studded with casually crushing disdain and incomprehension towards women who appear as figures of ridicule and pity or as unreliable, grasping, withholding, malicious, hysterical. At the other end of the scale, women are set on pedestals but also stuck there: earth-mother goddesses selflessly giving shelter from the storm, putting a blanket on your bed, and speaking — in sharp distinction to their Sixties male contemporaries — "without ideals or violence"[5]. At its worst, this results in m'lady-ing condescension like "a woman like you should be at home, that's where you belong / Taking care for somebody nice who don't know how to do you wrong" or the (surely parodic) lyrical catastrophe that is "Can you cook and sew, make flowers grow? / Do you understand my pain?".[6]

This unreconstructed outlook is in some ways just a product of its time and place. It reflects both Dylan's mid-century Midwest upbringing and the plaintive hippie-manchild demand that women not only share the burden of making the world anew but also provide as much pleasure, nurture, support and understanding as they did in the old world. But you can also find a more nuanced breakdown of gender relations in his lyrics, based around the willing or unwilling exchange of power, trust and intimacy and its potential to corrupt, diminish and humiliate men as much as women ("You will start out standing, proud to steal her anything she sees / But you will wind up peeking through her keyhole down upon your knees"[7]). In *Blonde on Blonde*'s druggy scenester decadence, this power-play, both subtle and overt, is particularly apparent. Through the byzantine skirmishing of "4th Time Around", the giddy chase of "Absolutely Sweet Marie", and the aching, frustrated "Temporary Like Achilles", strength, control and self-assurance constantly swing between partners. Women in "Visions of Johanna" or "Sad-Eyed Lady of the Lowlands" are still idealised repositories of comfort or inspiration, but elsewhere they demonstrate an eroticised aggression towards men who must struggle, connive or plead for the upper hand, even if this mutually calculating performance ends in misjudged disaster ("And I told you as you clawed out my eyes / I never really meant to do you any harm"[8]).

A distinctly New York album despite its Nashville recording, *Blonde on Blonde* is full of sexually-charged bargaining and competition in which big-city sophistication equals advantage. In this game, Dylan plays his wide-eyed outsider act, his little-boy-lost styling, as both an initial shortcoming and a strategy of seduction: the classy, glossy debutantes who populate the album may have the in-group credibility the narrator needs, but he has what they want. Over four decades later, lost in the often underexamined privileges of millennial hipsterdom, this was a game I still felt just about able to play myself, up to a point.

From this perspective, "Just Like a Woman" — a song heavily criticised as misogynist, though I've never found it substantial enough to take any real offence — is just another score-sheet in this battle of the sexes. Its rules of engagement are made clear in the pay-off line, "Please don't let on that you knew me when / I was hungry and it was your world". A bleakly mercenary view of how sex and social position interact, maybe, but hardly an inaccurate one and certainly one I could relate to — up to a point. Whether or not Edie Sedgwick inspired "Just Like a Woman", she is typical of women in hip Sixties circles — bored, thrill-seeking It Girls and heiresses — who possessed power through wealth and social status. And, as though this power is a kind of provocation, many songs of the period identify sex as a point of vulnerability through which socially superior women can be brought down to the male narrator's level or destroyed completely.

This trope, the ruin of a spoilt female socialite, is part of what "Like a Rolling Stone" revels in. Despite the narrator's occasional flashes of sympathy — of identification, even — with his subject, the song's *schadenfreude* is centred on the social descent of this fallen princess and its expression through submission ("go to him now he calls you; you can't refuse"9), and this can make it an uncomfortable listen. When I first heard it, Dylan's vitriol towards "Miss Lonely" was alive with the electric class rage that I was learning how much I wanted to express. The song's critique, after all, is not simply of a woman but of one who has squandered the opportunities her status affords and who has, until now, experienced life's lower reaches safely and vicariously.

Like the slumming-it anti-heroine of Pulp's "Common People", if she called her dad I'm sure he could stop it all. As someone conscious that I too hadn't gone to the finest schools, that I would never be a debutante, I could sing along until my throat was raw. But I also found it impossible to ignore that my identification with the singer — and more broadly with Dylan as hero-rebel-outsider — could only shakily translate into reality. It was difficult to imagine the song's story working with the genders reversed, in a world where sexuality is still seen as a weapon for men but a point of weakness for women.

Now, I don't receive this as some ideological betrayal of the sort that so antagonised his anti-electric audiences. Dylan has never had a shred of feminist credibility to lose (and he knows it). It's really only by virtue of Dylan's association with rebellion that I presumed his most definitive work must or should be more progressive than it is. And this presumption of a link between male rebellion and broader liberation can be, and has been, endlessly disproved. Early rock 'n' roll, provoking unease and hostility among the establishment on both sides of the Atlantic, established itself as quintessentially rebellious, a vague but definite threat to the status quo. But its oppositional status didn't mean it wasn't masculinist — indeed, as with rebellious subcultures from the Beats to the Angry Young Men, the two things often went together. While rock allowed women a measure of empowerment and escapism as fans and consumers, it had little space for women to tell their own stories or become their own creations.

Literature, stage, screen and song have seen a long and deep tradition of male rage against the disappointments and restrictions of their expected roles. In this tradition, women can be fertile ground over which men fight righteous battles, but can rarely fight on our own terms. For men to rebel against the status quo was to rebel against social conventions and stifling domesticity, and these things were usually represented by women: the girlfriend hell-bent on marriage, the smothering mother, the pram in the hall. But if women themselves rejected conventional values and expectations, what role models could we look to in popular culture and what ready-made paths could we follow: where were the angry young women? Is a working-class heroine something to be? What can a poor girl do when she can't even sing for a rock 'n' roll band?

Dylan's hierophant-in-chief Greil Marcus described "Like a Rolling Stone", somewhat counter-intuitively, as "the story of a woman attempting to escape into a life of her own and continually finding herself imprisoned by the life she was born to". Mike Marqusee, in another straightforwardly generous reading, sees the song as "stripping bare the illusions that once upheld an individual's life and a milieu's lifestyle. Its high-school rage seethes into a broader critique of all aristocracies". Well, sure it does. That's part of why I love it. But why make a woman, yet again, the default face of objectionable ruling-class privilege and the cautionary tale of its vulnerability and fragility? A classical artistic device, maybe, but, in life as in art, it's a line I'm tired of hearing.

Where Dylan can perhaps be excused is that his work sits at the start of this spectrum, rather than its supposedly more enlightened later stages. "Like a Rolling

Stone" poses less of a problem than another Pulp effort of thirty years later, "I-Spy" — a song with whose class-war narrative I also longed to fully identify, but in which a woman with social power is inescapably reduced to an object, a trophy, a means by which the male hero can be validated or his male enemy hurt. ("I-Spy" also hints more sharply at the nastier implications of this: that the glamour and gloss of social superiority is what makes a woman worth desiring, and that women without those class attributes might barely expect to figure on an angry young man's radar at all.) But both songs are marked by this tradition of reactionary rebellion, with women automatically part of bourgeois convention to be disrupted or subverted, rather than potential allies or rebels ourselves. It's hard to fight a class war if you only take aim at gender.

These aspects of "Like a Rolling Stone" may be hard to swallow, but they're easily washed down by the song's taste of world-shaking catharsis, adventure and reckless abandon, which can intoxicate women as much as men. "Like a Rolling Stone" makes it possible to forget yourself and to transcend your place in the world, even if it's on the understanding that this transcendence is a momentary fantasy. In fact, stepping out of the song's escapist vortex and returning to reality, with the consciousness of restrictive social roles clanging back into place, can even strengthen the resolve to slip these coils. Under current political conditions I could never quite be the defiantly independent, liberated narrator of "Like a Rolling Stone"'s story, but I still aspire to be.

Acknowledging and exploring the tension between existing as a woman and identifying with male creators or narrators is just that — recognition, not resignation or acceptance. It's an eternal journey with no comfortable destination in sight. Songs like this remind us why we need to change the world, and why the ways in which we try to change it need adjustment too.

Notes

1 Bob Dylan, "Visions of Johanna", *Blonde on Blonde* (1966), Columbia Records. Copyright Robert Dylan, Dwarf Music, Sony ATV Music Publishing (1966).

2 Bob Dylan, "Just Like a Woman", *Blonde on Blonde* (1966), Columbia Records. Columbia Records. Copyright Robert Dylan, Dwarf Music, Sony ATV Music Publishing (1966).

3 Bob Dylan, "Temporary Like Achilles", *Blonde on Blonde* (1966), Columbia Records. Columbia Records. Copyright Robert Dylan, Dwarf Music, Sony ATV Music Publishing (1966).

4 See http://www.bbc.co.uk/news/entertainment-arts-36211789. On the complex politics behind audience hostility on the tour, see Jones, Michael. "Judas and the Many 'Betrayals' of Bob Dylan" in Bouchner and Browning (2009).

5 Bob Dylan, "Love Minus Zero, No Limit", *Bringing It All Back Home* (1965), Columbia Records. Copyright Robert Dylan, Special Rider Music, Sony ATV Music Publishing (1965).

6 Bob Dylan, "Sweetheart Like You", *Infidels*, (1983), Columbia Records. Copyright Robert Dylan, Special Rider Music, Sony ATV Music Publishing (1983). Bob Dylan, "Is Your Love In Vain?" *Street-Legal* (1978), Columbia Records. Copyright Robert Dylan, Special Rider Music, Sony ATV Music Publishing (1978).

7 Bob Dylan, "She Belongs to Me", *Bringing It All Back Home* (1965), Columbia Records. Copyright Robert Dylan, Special Rider Music, Sony ATV Music Publishing (1965).

8 Bob Dylan, "One of Us Must Know (Sooner or Later)", *Blonde on Blonde* (1966), Columbia Records. Copyright Robert Dylan, Dwarf Music, Sony ATV Music Publishing (1966).

9 Bob Dylan, "Like a Rolling Stone", *Highway 61 Revisited* (1965), Columbia Records. Copyright Robert Dylan, Special Rider Music, Sony ATV Music Publishing (1965).

Bibliography

Bouchner, David and Browning, Gary (eds.). *The Political Art of Bob Dylan*. (Imprint Academic, 2009).

Gray, Michael. *Song and Dance Man III: The Art of Bob Dylan*. (Continuum, 2002).

Marcus, Greil. *Bob Dylan by Greil Marcus: Writings 1968-2010*. (Faber, 2010).

Marqusee, Mike. "Review: *Like a Rolling Stone* by Greil Marcus", *The Guardian*, 28 May 2005. https://www.theguardian.com/books/2005/may/28/highereducation.news

O'Dair, Barbara, "Dylan and Gender Politics". In Dettmar, Kevin J. H. (ed.) *The Cambridge Companion to Bob Dylan*. (Cambridge University Press, 2009) pp. 80–86.

Willis, Ellen. "Dylan", in *Beginning to See the Light: Sex, Hope and Rock-and-Roll*. (Wesleyan University Press, 1992), pp. 3-25.

Discography

Dylan, Bob. "She Belongs to Me", "Love Minus Zero/No Limit" from *Bringing It All Back Home*. (Columbia Records, 1965).

_____. "Like a Rolling Stone" from *Highway 61 Revisited*. (Columbia Records, 1965).

_____. "Visions of Johanna", "One of Us Must Know (Sooner or Later)", "Just Like a Woman", "Absolutely Sweet Marie", "Temporary Like Achilles" from *Blonde on Blonde*. (Columbia Records, 1966).

_____. "Is Your Love in Vain?" from *Street-Legal*. (Columbia Records, 1978).

_____. "Sweetheart Like You" from *Infidels*. (Columbia Records, 1983).

Pulp. "Common People", "I-Spy" from *Different Class*. (Island Records, 1995).

And Now It Hurts to Know the Truth: On "Young Girl"

Nina Power

Youth, so it's said, is wasted on the young. Unaware of the brevity of life, the transience of beauty (or at least the fleeting quality of relative health) and the crushing reality of mortality, youth is that most confusingly fetishised of conditions. The youth of the Young Girl is doubly "wasted" because it is always youth for another, at the time and in the future — the Young Girl does not get to enjoy her youth, because others are always ready to enjoy it for her, or mourn its loss later on her behalf. The Young Girl is a repository of projection. Whoever speaks of the Young Girl usually isn't one. Whenever the Young Girl does speak, she is ignored.

"Young Girl"[1] is a song written by Jerry Fuller, performed by Gary Puckett & the Union Gap and released by Columbia records in 1968. It got to number one in the UK and number two in the US, behind Otis Redding's "(Sittin' On) The Dock of the Bay". It is sung from the standpoint of a lovelorn, or lusty, man who has somehow come to learn that the object of his affections (the nameless "young girl") is under the age of consent. It is, in turn, angry ("And now it hurts to know the truth"), obsessive ("Get out of my mind"), victim-blaming ("And though you know / That it's wrong to be / Alone with me / That come-on look is in your eyes") and threatening ("Get out of here / Before I have the time / To change my mind", and also, from the famous chorus, "You better run girl"). It has been alternately read as an open admission of paedophilia from a more "permissive" (or abusive) age, but also as a cry of responsibility from someone who has been tricked by an underage girl lying about her age and is doing the right thing by sending her home. However you read it, it is a deeply creepy thing. These days, it makes people feel uneasy.

It is also a song I adore, and have played many times, for many people, in pubs and flats and on my own, pretending that I am the singer and wondering if I could ever get away with doing a karaoke version.

"Young Girl" is, without doubt, a deeply misogynistic song, reinforcing the idea that neither men nor women can be trusted (she has tricked him with a "disguise" of perfume and make-up and her womanly "charms"; he cannot be trusted not to have sex with her unless she manages to escape). There is a double-meaning in the line "You've kept the secret of your youth", as her youth is both an actual secret, as well as one of those phrases that you say positively whenever someone older happens to look a bit younger than we might imagine someone of that age would look. It is this line that reveals something of the truth of the song, and its context: to be a young girl is to be the pinnacle of heterosexual desire — it is to be, in fantasy at least, the most desirable kind of person.

Everything — from TV to films to tabloids to both men and women's magazines to pop music to porn — is "about" the young girl. Everyone, including some men (or even more complexly, all masculinity), is supposed to want to "be" the young girl, as it is in her desirability that power lies. Of course, this is not actual power, in the form of political decision-making, or money, or property, or respect or a platform, but it is some other, ineffable kind of authority. The mysticism of girlishness, that supposed kernel of unknowability — forbidden even to the young girl herself, because all the interference just doesn't give her a fucking chance.

A decade later, ABBA singer Anni-Frid Lyngstad attempted to redeem the song, keeping the tune and replacing the lyrics with those by Marie Bergman. In this version, the song is sung from the perspective, not of the anguished man, nor the young girl herself, but from the standpoint of an older woman looking back — the former young girl herself, perhaps, or maybe another woman giving advice:

Slowly, I become accustomed / To arranging the day so that it goes (on) without you / I'm by myself now I am myself now / You stepped straight into my inside / I became so small in your hand / But you were smaller when your mask fell off / From everything you gave / You live in a wonderland / Slowly, I become accustomed / To arranging the day so that it goes (on) without you / I'm by myself now I am myself now / Beneath your cultured surface / You are surely more than a sea

/ When you grow older, you can ask me / And I shall answer you / About how to give and how to take / Slowly, I become accustomed / To arranging the day so that it goes (on) without you / I'm by myself now I am myself now.[2]

The original tune so haunts Lyngstad's version that any space the lyrics attempt to carve out is quite overwhelmed, despite the reflective lyrics and oddly jaunty guitar. Yet there is an aloneness here not over-coded by the fantasies of others, and their violent interjections ("You stepped straight into my inside ... You live in a wonderland"), and the idea that being by oneself is not loneliness but rather being oneself ("I am myself now"). It is only, thus, when one becomes "invisible" that one can have any peace as a woman.

The young girl is, despite all the attempts to save her, a power without depth, yet culpable, blameable. As the French theorist collective Tiqqun put it in 1999, though careful at the outset to state that their theory of the Young Girl is "obviously not a gendered concept":

All the unquestionable character of [the Young Girl's] power, all the crushing self-confidence of this blueprint-person, comprised exclusively of the conventions, codes, and representations fleetingly in force, all the authority that the least of her gestures contains — all that is immediately cross-indexed to her absolute transparency to 'society'. And precisely because of her nothingness, each of her judgements has the imperative weight of the whole organization of society — and she knows it.

The young girl, everything screams, is nothing, despite her "authority". Why, then, do I find the original song so appealing, so alluring despite (or, psychoanalytically, of course, because) the fact that it is so, so terribly wrong? Do I imagine myself in the position of the young girl, possessed of the ability to bewitch this man so he can barely contain himself? Is it Gary Puckett's wolf-like croon-howl as he warns the young girl to run home "before it's too late"? Do I imagine myself in the position of the man, as sexual predator? Do I imagine singing it to myself as a young girl, from the standpoint of an older woman, as Lyngstad did? Is it merely a great pop song, three minutes of heaven, a message from a more, or less, innocent time?

I think it is all of these, something in between all of this mess, in a world in which those who are most vulnerable are used as a cover-story for those with actual power. A world in which victims are blamed for the violence imposed upon them. The Young Girl is an omnipresent fantasy we are encouraged to believe in, a kind of religion of eternal desire and object-hood that of course tells us nothing about actual girlhood.

Would the young girl in the song tell the guy to fuck off for being a creep, or would she stand up for the right to be a sexual being, consent laws be damned? Unless misogyny, both externally imposed and internally reproduced, never has a chance to thrive, how could we ever know? In the meantime, probably best to *keep running*.

Notes

1 Gary Puckett & The Union Gap, "Young Girl", *Young Girl*, (1968), Columbia Records. Copyright Jerry Fuller, Warner-Tamerlane Publishing Corp (1968).

2 Many thanks to Anna Gumucio Ramberg who, at very short notice, translated the lyrics to the song "Jag Är Mej Själv Nu", and helped me to understand the perspective of the narrator, as well as Anni-Frid Lyngstad's broader interest in often singing from the standpoint of a strong/vulnerable female perspective. Anni-Frid Lyngstad, "Jag Är Mej Själv Nu", *Frida ensam*, (1975), Polar Music/Universal.

Betwixt and Between:
The Travesties of Mick Jagger

Manon Steiner

Showgirl and domina, devilish fiend and heroic leader of a revolution, sex object and objectifier of women: Mick Jagger has had many faces over the long period of his career and yet, his role as womaniser remains undefeated — being played out until this day.

What is it that women love about this scanty man with his ridiculously large lips and the flamboyant makeup? Certainly, he is a rock star and a gifted dancer, pouring out male sexuality with an ability to move the masses. Yet, the lead singer of the Rolling Stones sings about objectifying women and, if one believes the press, books, and several ex-girlfriends, treats them accordingly. And he is in good company: with his behaviour, he is only representing the archetypical example of a male rock star. So why, ask the editors of this anthology, do women love the very men and their music that turn them into hot sex symbols at the least and dumb playthings at the worst?

Music — The Catalyst for Unsatisfied Desires?

In the early Sixties, youth in the Western world was fed up with old rules and traditions. For the first time, teenagers in America and Great Britain had spare time and, through the expanding economy, money to spend. However, postwar society provided little entertainment for them. The new wealth tasted of boredom. Through the distribution of the radio and the growing mass media, music soon became the only source of entertainment. While white rock 'n' roll developed with musicians such as Jerry Lee Lewis and Elvis, the blues found a new popularity among white youth in Great Britain. Music provided a catalyst for their frustration. As a result, British youth — often members of the working class — formed their own skiffle or beat bands — derivations of Afro-American music. Still, only a very few venues played the actual blues. The Crawdaddy Club was one of the only bars that featured black musicians. The scene was wilder and stood in contrast to the prevailing trad jazz bars with people dancing until late. It was there that the Rolling Stones celebrated their first success. They were loud, wild and obscene. The Rolling Stones provoked because they were the first band to discard the symbols of manliness — suit, collar, tie and neatly kept hair. Instead, they turned them into a caricature in a game of mix and match and wore the traditional suit with tight trousers, flamboyant shirts, and obscenely long hair. Simon Reynolds and Joy Press write in *The Sex Revolts: Gender, Rebellion, and Rock 'n' Roll*:

> [...] in the beginning, it wasn't the Stones' clothes that mattered; it was their hair, and the murder in their

faces, peeping out through the jungle. [...] hair used as a kick in the teeth, as insult and ridicule heaped on every drabness of the system; hair as symbolic of sex, of energy; hair almost as religion. The kids loved them, parents hated them and the government soon proclaimed the Rolling Stones as enemies to the state.

Mick Jagger, the Drag Queen

Their rebellion against the stereotypical male image earned the Rolling Stones respect among their peers. On the back of their single, "Have You Seen Your Mother, Baby, Standing In The Shadow?" (1966), the members of the Rolling Stones presented themselves in drag. But this didn't necessary imply that they respected women: "The blurring of sexual lines was part of the creative mix of the era, but it also had its dark side. The homoerotic subculture had a virulent strain of misogyny to it as a nasty by-product", explains Mick Jagger's then-girlfriend and singer Marianne Faithfull.

In *Gender Trouble: Feminism and the Subversion of Identity*, the American theorist and philosopher Judith Butler differentiates between a travesty within a theatrical setting and lived travesty in public spaces. According to her, the act on stage can be "derealised" and interpreted as play. That way, the borders between life and performance remain. However, that was no longer the case with the Rolling Stones, and particularly Mick Jagger. While the album cover, as well as the shows, were an act, Jagger was seen in silk and ruffles on as well as off the stage: "He often used deliberate bad taste, either kitsch or pornographic, and he clashed silks with denims, velvets with satins, colours thrown together in orgies", rock critic Nik Cohn writes of Jagger's getup.

Butler's theory about the performativity of gender was written in 1990 — yet Mick Jagger had already given it substance almost twenty years earlier: "What I'm doing is a sexual thing. I dance, and all dancing is a replacement for sex [...] What I do is very much the same as a girl's striptease dance", a twenty-three-year-old Jagger said in 1966. While the lead singer of the Rolling Stones has a reputation of being a misogynist, he was and still is also a charming ladies' man. By putting his body on display and, in a way representing the very women he sings about, he suggests a certain level of empathy. It leads to thinking that this man, so unafraid of showing his effeminate side when old school masculinity was still the norm, understands women. In the process, he questioned the societal roles of gender as a whole. According to feminist writer Sheila Whiteley, an entirely new definition had to be developed for Jagger's stage persona.

Jagger's performance style is provocative and it could be argued that the conventional body-image of the male (muscle, tension, posture, feel and texture of the body) was subverted by his stage performance. There is muscle, but somehow it is transformed by an emphasis on preening narcissism which can be read as a sense of "otherness". The play between similarity and difference which is crucial to role definition is blurred to be replaced by a fantasy of eroticism which challenges the traditional sense of masculine-feminine dualism.

Jagger could be man and woman at once and thus attract both genders: "It was that dual sexuality that was to emerge later on when Mick performed with the band, and it probably accounted for the fact that Mick became a sexual turn-on for both the female and male members of audience", writes novelist A.E. Hotchner in *Blown Away*, his portrait of the Rolling Stones' early success and its entailing escapades. Jagger turned the band's stage show into his own performance — loaded with sexual innuendo, vulgarity and showmanship, as Cohn describes:

> When he came on out, he went bang. He'd shake his hair all down in his eyes and he danced like a whitewash James Brown, he flapped those tarpaulin lips and, grotesque, he was all sex. [...] And he was outrageous: he spun himself blind, he smashed himself and he'd turn his back on the audience, jack-knife from the waist, so that his arse stuck straight up in the air, and then he'd shake himself, he'd vibrate like a motor, and he'd reach the hand mike through his legs at you, he'd push it right in your face. Well, he was obscene, he was excessive.

This sudden confrontation with blunt and raw sexuality led to a frenzy among young women and men who often couldn't handle the sexual pressure. On several occasions, shows of the Beatles and later the Rolling Stones had to be broken off because mostly female fans climbed the stage and tore it apart. Talking about their early concerts in 1964 in England, Keith Richards compares the scene to the Western front in his autobiography *Life*: "These chicks were coming out there, bleeding, clothes torn off, pissed panties, and you took that for granted every night." To some extent, it is understandable then, that young male musicians started viewing girls as objects, waiting to fulfill their sexual desires, while not fully understanding these desires themselves.

Before the Aftermath

This becomes particularly evident in their fourth studio album, *Aftermath* (1966). It provides an example of the Rolling Stones' mixed stance on women, at the same time making them internationally famous. Their hit single "Under my Thumb" has one of the most sexist lyrics in rock 'n' roll. It was one of the first songs in which the band expressed their contemptuous view of women and has been interpreted as Mick Jagger's final conquest of his first girlfriend Chrissie Shrimpton. Triumphantly he sings: "The way she does just what she's told / Down to me the change has come / She's under my thumb".[1]

On the record, the song is preceded by "Mother's Little Helper", "Stupid Girl" and "Lady Jane". The anti-housewife's anthem "Mother's Little Helper" deals with the ordeals of an ordinary mother's daily life in the 1960s and turns the core values of a traditional suburban family around. The stay-at-home-mom becomes an addict, bored with life at home, considering "cooking fresh food for a husband [...] a drag"[2], grabbing the bottle of pills instead. The song reflects the frustration of the Sixties youth with their parent's generation and the growing abuse of prescription drugs among their mothers. This can be either read as a criticism of women having lost interest in pleasing men or as a call for women's liberation. "Stupid Girl" on the other hand, is a direct attack on young women of the bands' own generation. In an interview with *Rolling Stone* in 1971, Keith Richards commented on the song: "It was all a spin-off from our environment... hotels, and too many dumb chicks. Not all dumb, not by any means, but that's how one got. When you're canned up — half the time it's impossible to go out — it was to go through a whole sort of football match."

While this doesn't justify the Stones' attitude towards women, it does provide an explanation. To them, most female fans meant either being violently torn off stage or being offered sexual favours. The albums' third single, "Lady Jane", in turn seems to reverse that image. It appears as a sweet ballad to a loved one in which the singer offers himself as her humble servant. There are many interpretations of this song, one claiming "Lady Jane" is the result of Jagger's literary exploration into D.H. Lawrence's *Lady Chatterley's Lover*, others seeing it as an ode to a mysterious affair, and yet another suggesting it is simply a synonym for the female genitals. However, it does seem to generate uncertainty among songwriters Mick Jagger and Keith Richards. In the years following *Aftermath*, it was mostly Mick Jagger who carried his youthful arrogance to an extreme. In 1995, he still commented on "Stupid Girl": "I had so many girlfriends at that point. None of them seemed to care they weren't pleasing me very much. I was obviously in with the wrong group." This is representative for who Jagger cares about most and what role a woman defines for him.

Cock Rock

For the sociologist Simon Frith and the cultural critic Angela McRobbie, Jagger's performance amounted to something termed Cock Rock — aggressive, dominating, arrogant and most of all, controlling: "Their stance is obvious in live shows; male bodies on display, plunging shirts and tight trousers, a visual emphasis on chest hair and genitals". On stage, Jagger played an exaggerated version of himself: "Thus it is suggested that Jagger's role as a singer is analogous to that of a complex character in an unfolding drama. He was, is Little Red Rooster, Jumping Jack Flash, Lucifer, the Midnight Rambler." *Melody Maker*'s article of 1964, "Would You Let Your Sister Go with a Rolling Stone?", solidified his image of the "bad" man, seducing innocent girls. Originally it was staged by Rolling Stones' manager Andrew Loog Oldham, but its content soon rang true and many saw in Jagger and the Stones the reincarnation of the lustrous devil and the embodiment of sin. Seth Vannatta compares the consumption of rock music even with the taste of the devilish apple from the tree of knowledge. By peeling off his (male) clothing, snakelike and diabolic, offering sex as a product free for consumption, Mick Jagger and the Rolling Stones questioned its taboo status in society. In prude America, people in San Francisco, Berkley, New York or LA had taken to the streets to free themselves of old puritan ethics with miniskirts, rock 'n' roll and mind altering substances such as marijuana and LSD.

The Rolling Stones too were very much a product of their time. Young men were sexually frustrated but able to let that frustration out for the first time. Young women also experienced somewhat of a sexual revolution, but the leftovers of the post-war society still held them back in regards to sex and independence. Songs like "Stupid Girl", "Get Off Of My Cloud" or "I Can't Get No Satisfaction" were never just about sexual frustration. They must be seen in a broader spectrum of generational revolt. As rock stars became the new role models in a world where teenagers no longer looked up to parents and teachers and the Sunday walk to church had become redundant, boys and girls alike encountered undiscovered territories. But since women's liberation in the early Sixties was still in its infant shoes and the early rock stars mainly consisted of young men, girls' only means of getting close to their idols was through sex. For the first time, girls were not only allowed to be sexual but encouraged by the musicians.

Archaic Desires

To me, the Rolling Stones will always be one of the best rock 'n' roll bands in the world — especially in their early years. Had I lived during the peak of their success, I, like thousands of other girls, would have fallen for the effeminate and provocative frontman. As illustrated in this essay, Mick Jagger doesn't represent the classical image of a masculine man. He is an androgynous figure filled with sex, lust and violence providing temptations for both, male and female. Up to this day, he enters the show in women's clothes, struts and flits across the stage, buttocks in tight jeans and hips swinging lascivious: violently homoerotic in his act, yet unmistakably straight. Despite the Rolling Stones' misogynist stance, represented through their songs and actions, they remain a band women love. It is exactly that raging sexuality, combined with the demeaning arrogance that attracts our gender to the world of rock 'n' roll. When somebody like Jagger enters the stage, the outline of his cock visible in tight trousers, swinging hips and lustful lips, we can't help but desire. At the bottom lies an archaic desire to be dominated, that no longer has a place in modern Western society. Before rap music, rock 'n' roll has provided an allowed substitute to live out animalistic instincts of female submission. Rock music started in the prime of the sexual revolution and helped free both men and women from sexual stagnation. But, as Faithfull suggested, its by-products were primal male instincts of extreme domination.

Without question, the Rolling Stones have written many songs that can be interpreted as sexist or even misogynist. *Aftermath* was followed by singles such as "Brown Sugar" and "Some Girls", which aren't only sexist but racist. Listening close to lyrics like "Brown sugar, how come you taste so good / Brown sugar, just like a black girl should"[3] and "Black girls just wanna get fucked all night"[4], it is hard to show sympathy for this particular devil.

Yet, the Rolling Stones have published at least as many love songs and ballads as they have sexist rock anthems and murder songs ("Midnight Rambler", "Gimme Shelter"). "Ruby Tuesday", "Angie" and "Wild Horses" are just the most popular examples. In "Miss You" Jagger even expresses his complicated relationship with his lovers in lines such as, "I guess I'm lying to myself / It's just you and no one else"[5], while trying to convince himself that he won't miss his lover in the next. After all, Mick Jagger is just another lonely man, expressing his frustration with failed love through the only means he knows — music. As Marianne Faithfull once said, his love/hate relationship with women stems from nothing but the need to be loved: "It's just the desire, a very strong desire, to have people be in love with you." While she described her own relationship with Jagger as difficult and painful, she portrayed him as a deeply sensitive and emotional man at the same time, in need of a release from the daily pressure of fame. Instead of drugs, he turned to women and subsequently abused himself and those around him.

You can say and think of Mick Jagger and the Rolling Stones what you like. But to me, what it comes down to is a raw but healthy outlet for all too human emotions, be it anger, lust, violence or joy. That is why even today, without the political meaning of the Sixties and staged to perfection, their shows can still make people feel, dance and let loose. This book has asked us why women love rock 'n' roll music, and I reply: why the hell not?

Notes

1 The Rolling Stones, "Under My Thumb", *Aftermath*, (1966), Decca. Copyright Mick Jagger, Keith Richards, Abkco Music Inc. (1966).

2 The Rolling Stones, "Mother's Little Helper", *Aftermath*, (1966), Decca. Copyright Mick Jagger, Keith Richards, Abkco Music Inc. (1966).

3 The Rolling Stones, "Brown Sugar", *Sticky Fingers*, (1971), Decca. Copyright Mick Jagger, Keith Richards, Abkco Music Inc. (1971).

4 The Rolling Stones, "Some Girls", *Some Girls*, (1978), Columbia Records. Copyright Mick Jagger, Keith Richards, Colgems EMI Music Inc. (1978).

5 The Rolling Stones, "Miss You", *Some Girls*, (1978), Columbia Records. Copyright Mick Jagger, Keith Richards, EMI Music Publishing Ltd (1978).

Bibliography

Butler, Judith. *Gender Trouble: Feminism and the Subversion of Identity*. (Routledge, 1990).

Cohn, Nik. *Awopbopaloobop Alopbamboom: Pop from the Beginning*. (Weidenfeld & Nicolson, 1969).

Coleman, Ray. "Would You Let Your Sister Go with a Rolling Stone?". *Melody Maker*, 14 March 1964.

Egan, Sean. *Keith Richards on Keith Richards: Interviews and Encounters*. (Review Press, 2013).

Faithfull, Marianne and Dalton, David. *Faithfull*. (Penguin Books, 1995).

Frith, Simon and McRobbie, Angela. "Rock and Sexuality", in: Frith, Simon and Goodwin, Andrew, *On Record: Rock, Pop and the Written Word*. (Routledge, 1990).

Hotchner, A. E. *Blown Away: "Rolling Stones" and the Death of the Sixties*. (Simon & Schuster Ltd, 1994).

Reynolds, Simon and Press, Joy. *The Sex Revolts: Gender, Rebellion, and Rock 'n' Roll*. (Harvard University, 1995).

Richards, Keith. *Life*. (Hachette Book Group, 2010).

Sanchez, Tony. *Up and Down with the Rolling Stones*. (New American Library, 1979).

Vannatta, Seth. "The Most Dangerous Rock 'n' Roll Band in the World", in Dick, Luke and Reisch, George A. (eds.) *Rolling Stones and Philosophy: It's Just a Thought Away*. (Open Court, 2011) pp. 187–199.

Whiteley, Sheila. "Satanic Verses: Lucifer, Literature and the Rise of the Rock Rebel". University of Salfold 2004. http://www.popmatters.com/chapter/04win/.html

Wenner, Jann S. "Mick Jagger Remembers". *Rolling Stone*. 14 December 1995. http://www.rollingstone.com/music/news/mick-jagger-remembers-19951214

"It was a different time": Negotiating with the Misogyny of Heroes

Em Smith

The conversation surrounding misogyny in music might have been given a clearer voice in recent times, a more visible platform, a discourse armed with potent evidence and justifiable vitriol and an army of articulate, gutsy women. But the topics of these conversations are not new. Woman-hating being soundtracked by a catchy melody is not a twenty-first-century hobby or a recent phenomenon.

Though we slowly wade through tar in our progression towards parity, the discussion around sexism in music gains momentum daily. It highlights what was previously buried, recognises that which before was hidden, and makes us redefine as unacceptable what for so many decades has been normalised. The conversation has been led by women who have finally had enough: enough of silent resignation, of quiet indignance, of passive frustration and of being told it's "just the way it is". Of course, anger does not necessarily act alone as the impetus for turning the wheels of change, but by continuing the discussion, we offer a warning to the men who formerly spewed misogyny: you will now be held to account.

However, there are double standards around those who get away with open misogyny and those who don't and I — even as someone who has identified as a hardline feminist since the age of sixteen — am guilty of falling into these traps too. There is a hypocrisy in the tolerance of misogynistic behaviour and lyrics from our legendary rock artists, from those certified National Treasures and immovable heroes whose past indiscretions are quietly pardoned because their artistic currency is considered too great to discount.

When it comes to musical stalwarts who have all been card-carrying misogynists, the list of culprits reads uncomfortably like a catalogue of my heroes: Lou Reed, Iggy Pop, David Bowie, Mick Jagger. In short: the Sixties and Seventies could be a pretty damn hostile time for women. However, these men often get a free pass because, rather than considering their sometimes appalling attitudes, we instead say "What a legacy, what a body of work!".

It was in my teens and early twenties that I properly began my musical exploration of these men. The Velvet Underground found me around the age of fifteen, via bands I already loved who bore their influence, like the Strokes and the Flaming Lips. I couldn't believe a band could sound so timeless and yet seem so unmistakably woven into their era. Their world appeared so impossibly glamorous, aspirational, art-house. It possessed a knowledge of things you could never hope to be let in on. I remember commenting to a friend — in charac-teristically ill-conceived fashion — that listening to the Velvet Underground was the one thing that gave heroin an appeal to me. Their songs were self-destructive and beautiful. Nico especially cut such an intriguing figure to me, another tragic Sixties beauty, a lonely notion, which, as a navel-gazing adolescent, I was very seduced by. Oh, to be Nico! The likes of "Candy Says" and "Pale Blue Eyes" held a gorgeous sadness for me. All this glamorised fem-inine tragedy seems even more problematic when put in the context of Lou Reed's history of abuse to women, something I was unaware of. Lines like "You'd better hit her" in the song "There She Goes Again"[1] hinted at these violent impulses. (The song referred to a female prosti-tute who Reed seems keen to openly abuse.)

When I found out about this, though, I kept right on listening. Well, how was I supposed to use my feminist ideals to fight the art which had already penetrated my core? The Velvet Underground's appeal was already entrenched in so much of what I loved, so then came the tricky business of separating my feelings about the treatment of women and my feelings about the creation of great art. The latter couldn't outweigh the former, but it did mean I could neatly tidy my principles away for the duration of "White Light/White Heat".

The Rolling Stones, meanwhile, represented a hazy, halcyon image of the Sixties. Everything about them was like a portal to a musical culture lightyears away from where I was, characterised by hedonistic excess, nihilistic thrills, a world of doe-eyed muses, unabashed sexuality, mountains of narcotics. God, it sounded like it would only end in death — how beguiling! The Stones were the outlaws of the era, a public menace. Jagger's beautiful face, huge cartoonish mouth, the knowing self-possessing air of an absolute rogue, the Sixties equivalent of the millennial Fuck Boy; undeniable in their draw. Their music, borne from blues, steeped in history and psychedelia, spiky and cocksure, was a constant source of intrigue. How could a band who riffed through the illegal highs of "Brown Sugar" have the emotional insight to write "Wild Horses"?

As a band who have eternally buckled to male rock star stereotype #1 by repeatedly dating women several decades their junior, perhaps it's unsurprising that the Stones' anthology and bad-boy sexuality is bound up with an approach to gender that is far from progressive. As I listen to the likes of *Aftermath* I wince at the lyrics: "She's the worst thing in this world / Well, look at that stupid girl" ("Stupid Girl"[2]), or those well-known lyrics of male domination in "Under My Thumb". Responding to the accusations of sexism in the latter song, Jagger commented that it was "Not really an anti-feminist song any more than any of the others"; he wasn't arguing with the idea that the song was anti-women, rather he was just saying it wasn't an anomaly. It was a narrative of a certain, not unusual, kind of heterosexual relationship in which women were subjugated. These songs didn't exist in a vacuum; they were produced within the context of a society — and moreover a music industry — that abused women systematically and without fear of reproach.

In spite all of this, "Under My Thumb" remains one of my all-time favourite songs. I cannot resist its pop credentials — the casually brilliant hooks, Jagger's swaggering delivery. I return to it time and time again; I lose myself to it in dark corners of nightclubs. But its pull remains troubling to me as a narrative of an abusive relationship which I can't square with my love of the song. In order to embrace the music, I need to detach myself from the words, even as I sing along to them; I want to give a disclaimer to anyone who sees or hears me enjoying this song: "Everything he's saying is terrible!" I don't want anyone to assume that my enjoyment is tantamount to condoning, I feel the need to let people know I vehemently oppose the lyrical message, while adoring the music.

Bowie is another of my Seventies rock star heroes, an untouchable entity, a figure of undying love and regard and sorely missed by many including myself. As a figure, he represented those resolutely on the fringes, acting as a conduit through which the collective misfit spirit flowed. He flitted between identities in a way that seemed a natural reflection of his curiosity and passion, never appearing contrived or cynical and always pushing the edges outwards of any genre he cared to grace. He remained a mystery and an enigma until the end. His absence has made me reflect on just how crucial a part of my consciousness he had been, soundtracking every trajectory in my own adult narrative and seemingly forever poised in the shadows of popular culture, waiting to unleash his latest incarnation.

He also slept with underage girls. Notorious "baby groupie", Lori Maddox, lost her virginity to him at the age of fifteen, reflecting what Jia Lolentino calls "a sexual norm that has always appallingly favoured men, and the abuse that stems from and surpasses even that". Though Maddox recalls the tale in a positive way and some retain an ambivalence towards the issue of consent and choice with underage girls, the fact remains her experiences are judged through rose-tinted lenses in relation to this musical hero, as part of a wild supposedly liberal sexual revolution — and as the result of a culture which awards sexual agency to young women only when the behaviour of the man could be called in to question, when actually the inclusion of young women in this was more often to their disadvantage and exploitation.

Bowie's androgynous beauty sung to my nixing of gender constraints, his stance as the outsider a celebratory mirror to all my own oddities as a frequenter of the periphery. His death galvanised my feelings to the realisation that, it turns out, he had meant everything, and his passing led me to *Station to Station*. In particular, "Word On A Wing" struck a reverberating chord, his words "Trying hard to fit among your scheme of things"[3] those of the perennial outsider looking in. When he died, it was hard to fathom his death because he didn't feel like a real, tangible human being but an otherworldly figure who could never been victim to the whims of something as banal as human mortality.

Only in the past year did I read about Bowie and Maddox. As a figure who seemed so subversive, who up until the end of his life was so vocally supportive of female artists and of women, it seemed so utterly at odds for him to be very much ingrained in a mentality, however era-defining, that treated girls as disposable and allowed men to sleep with vulnerable young women without fear of consequence. It's something I've almost compartmentalised within my own principles so that I can continue to love him and his music. The thought of a life without Bowie is unbearable, so I rewrite the significance of Maddox's experiences in the context of Bowie as a whole. I don't buy the arguments of the "time dependent" context that fuels the defence of the "baby groupie" era, but I almost level them with my own conscience.

Iggy Pop, meanwhile, wrote "Look Away" with regards to his sexual tryst with a known figure on the gig circuit, thirteen-year-old Sable Starr — "I slept with Sable when she was thirteen / Her parents were too rich to do anything".[4] Such an admittance in 2017 would lead to Yewtree-scale investigations and at least a blotch on one's record, but Iggy is more popular and mainstream a figure now than he ever was, and is held in the ultimate esteem. In later years, he is quoted as saying "Well, I hate women. I mean, why do I even have to have a reason for that? It's like, why are people repelled by insects?"

Pop reduced his misogyny to a level of insignificance comparable to a hatred of bugs — a stance he's since 180'd on, but still absolutely indicative of his previous conduct towards women. I listen to the Stooges and Iggy's solo records uneasily with this full knowledge and yet I can't deny their pull. Knowing that he brazenly slept with underage girls does not stop me marvelling at the thrilling, carnal buzz of *Raw Power*. Remembering his open contempt for women does not negate the value of "The Idiot". There is something in the music, in what we perceive as great art, which allows us to view these men through a lens that skews the borders of our usual firmly held moral codes.

But time does not appease an injustice, history does not erase itself, and pop has never had to face up to his past. Now known as the Godfather of Punk, it seems that old punk sensibility was happy to exist in a framework that was happy not to challenge the idea that women could be tossed aside like garbage. Somehow these artists are awarded an era-dependent dispensation, their acts pardoned by the sheer fact that they were so commonly and openly practised at the time. That they did actually pursue these girls, that they knew their ages, that they were in total control of their own actions — these facts fall happily by the wayside. It often feels as if these discussions are met with a side-eye of suspicion, that they are the arguments usually reserved for the sexually repressed moral majority.

I rationalise my continuing love of these artists by remembering their music took root before the stories did, and perhaps the adulation I gift them would have been different had that not been the case, but it's kind of a feeble moral standpoint to take.

Context is crucial, but the context simply hasn't changed. Women were often treated like dirt and they make up the dirt that these men are allowed to stand on, their lives and experiences deemed inconsequential and paling in comparison to genius. That's the message we give out: the great art of the male simply must take precedent. To reason with what we know, maybe all we can do is separate the music from the individual and try and appreciate it in a void of meaning. We listen to it on its own terms, imagining a distant world of chauvinism that existed unchecked, as opposed to how we would now kick back against it. We try and wash away the implications and strip away the morality that we know it is tied into, render it less inextricable. This becomes a difficult task when we remember these songs are not fictitious narratives, rather they are embedded in the realities of the lives of real women, then and now. There are women all around us being told to keep their eyes to themselves, who only talk when they're spoken to, whose sexual agency is not allowed to be their own, who are being stamped out like insects. Compartmentalising our feelings becomes an even more impossible tactic when it is not only the music we love, but the men themselves. When hero-worship enters the picture, there is only room for so many indiscretions that we can comfortably acknowledge, lest we topple their God-like status and have to turn inwards to question the validity of our own double standards.

There is no neat resolve to these observations, no pleasing arc of morality. The music industry reflects the deep hostility to women in society, whether that's attacking them onstage or the more insidious — but just as dangerous — side of it, where women have to play twice as well as men to "prove" themselves and earn their worthiness. Have you ever noticed how many men in the crowd immediately pick up on how physically attractive a girl is onstage, thus reducing her most important value — as mirrored by society — to her appearance primarily? Or heard the stories of how many girls experience sexual assault at gigs and don't say anything because they've come to expect it now? Or clocked how women — professional, actual musicians and artists — face sexually aggressive yells on a stage? Or read about the endless sexual assault women in the music industry are subjected to?

The male musical heroes of mine offering moral conflict occupy the same space in my mind and my heart. Though their attitudes to women and young girls were deeply troubling, I have to witness them through a lens which was the product of an attitude that ran unchecked. Though it still very much abounds, is much less likely to be tolerated. The voices of subversion now call out these attitudes, rather than act as part of the problem, and I guess that's the solace we now can take in order to deal with the dichotomy between music and moral code.

Notes

1 The Velvet Underground, "There She Goes Again", *The Velvet Underground and Nico*, (1967), Verve Records. Copyright Lou Reed, Oakfield Avenue Music Ltd (1967).

2 Rolling Stones, "Stupid Girl", *Aftermath*, (1966), Decca. Copyright Mick Jagger, Keith Richards, Abkco Music Inc. (1966).

3 David Bowie, "Word on a Wing", *Station to Station,* (1976), RCA. Copyright David Bowie, Chrysalis Music Ltd, Tintoretto Music, Fleur Music (1976).

4 Iggy Pop, "Look Away", *Naughty Little Doggie*, (1996), Virgin. Copyright Iggy Pop, James Osterberg Music, BMG Rights Management (1996).

Bibliography

"Lou Reed Biographer Alleges History of Violence Against Women". *The Guardian*, October 2015. https://www.theguardian.com/music/2015/oct/13/lou-reed-new-biography-domestic-violence-abuse-women

Almeida, Rachel Grace. "Swimming with Sharks: Sexual Predators in The Music Industry". *Vice*, 5 October 2015. https://broadly.vice.com/en_us/article/swimming-with-sharks-sexual-predators-in-the-music-industry

Ambrose, Joe. *Gimme Danger: The Story of Iggy Pop*. (Omnibus, 2004).

Brassington, Jessica. "Women In The Music Industry: A Call For Equal Profiling And Stronger Representation". *Impakter*, 25 June 2015. http://impakter.com/women-music-industry-call-equal-profiling-stronger-representation/

Oyler, Lauren. "Lou Reed Was a Jealous, Misogynistic 'Prick' Who Acted Obnoxious to Sell Records". *Vice*, October 2015. https://broadly.vice.com/en_us/article/lou-reed-was-a-jealous-misogynistic-prick-who-acted-obnoxious-to-sell-records

Tolentino, Jia. "What Should We Say About David Bowie and Lori Maddox?". *Jezebel*, 16 February 2016. http://jezebel.com/what-should-we-say-about-david-bowie-and-lori-maddox-1754533894

Webb, Joanna. "Feminist punk band who play topless blasted as 'sluts and have fake blood thrown on them during gig'". *The Mirror*, 6 September 2016. http://www.mirror.co.uk/news/uk-news/feminist-punk-band-who-play-8779195

Wenner, Jann. S. "Mick Jagger Remembers". *Rolling Stone*, 14 December 1995. http://www.rollingstone.com/music/news/mick-jagger-remembers-19951214

Country Songs and the Deflection of Moral Labour

Elizabeth Newton

"All the things we thought weren't proper could be right in time"[1], sings the hopeful narrator of "Amie", a 1973 hit by country rock group Pure Prairie League. The song, from their album *Bustin' Out*, fits into a long line of country tunes obsessed with the difference between right and wrong, in which men find themselves morally astray but forever hopeful that tomorrow they might find themselves redeemed. All they need is one good woman to show them the light.

Throughout the history of popular music, men have posed themselves as morally weak in contrast to the women they use and abuse, denying women agency while still managing to blame them for their own moral failings. Country stories always hinge on morality, as well as on rigidly gendered roles by which a poor white man fails to aspire to rich men's standards of success and to satisfy women's moral expectations — but it's never the poor white man's fault. If country is the music of the working class, the only labour the men seem to perform is the work of shifting their problems onto somebody else.

In a tradition that includes Hank Williams and Merle Haggard (what Barbara Ching calls "hard country" music), men's moral uncertainty and ineptitude often leads them to collapse into utter abject failure. These failures collectively tell a history of *burlesque abjection*: "an immediately recognizable tradition that allows the wretched white man to emerge from the spectacle of failure with a hard country star's inglorious name". What permits them this redemptive transformation, in spite of all their failings?

My interest is in a particular phenomenon within moralising country: the deflection of affective moral labour — the invisible work of making moral decisions — onto women. This is a narrative move by which male subjects of country songs profess a desire for moral righteousness that they then transfer to a woman, placing morality upon her as a burden. It is a shift of weight by a man from himself onto his mother, lover, sister or wife, whose job it becomes to right his wrongs.

This feels familiar: a man just can't pull himself together, so he finds a woman to do it for him. At best, the men admit to their reliance on, and appreciation for, women's labour. This is the case on Merle Haggard's "Mama Tried" (1968):

> Dear old Daddy, rest his soul,
> Left my Mom a heavy load,
> She tried so very hard to fill his shoes.
> Working hours without rest,

Wanted me to have the best.
She tried to raise me right but I refused.[2]

At worst, though, the subject positions of men in country music are, in Barbara Ching's words, "crudely Freudian: this psychopathic mama's boy is 'not responsible for what he's doing; his mother made him what he is'."

In these songs, sometimes the female saviour refuses to show the man the light. She holds him accountable, or leaves, or fails to appear at all, morally absent. On "Good Woman", a modern-day alt-country tune, Cat Power sings that she wants to be a "good woman"[3] — but also that she wants him to be a good man. Knowing that won't happen if they stay together, she tells him she's leaving. Throughout country music history, women's refusal to be exploited has prompted male country stars to sing songs of mourning, grieving over what Pamela Fox calls a "loss of women as the embodiment of that mythologized 'home' place", which forces men to confront their pitiful state of being all by their lonesome, without any moral guidance.

Maybe for this reason, outlaw country of the mid-twentieth century grew increasingly un-endearing, devolving into what Benjamin Nugent calls "disavowals of vice and caustic self-portraits". The era's biggest star, Johnny Cash, came to represent this "'hard-bodied masculinity' of the working-class country music patriarch", embodying (if occasionally resisting) the trope of the abject failure who, although he achieves some redemption through his songs, nonetheless finds his chances nearly used up.

The song "Amie" has roots in this long tradition of country morality, but it departs from convention: its narrator does not simply confess his shortcomings and plea for pardon. He actually tries to do the work of righting them. The song exemplifies the emergence of an affably abject variation on Seventies country in which male humility helps to compensate for their moral failures.

By the end of the Eighties, no wave, disco and hair metal would render masculinity unrecognisable, a queered and emasculated rendition of its former self. In the Seventies, the gender stereotypes still held for the most part; the men are men and the women are women. But singers were starting to push up against those bounds, exploring gender and morality differently. When compared to the pitiful cowardice of earlier outlaw country tunes — featuring an anti-hero either deflecting his problems onto a woman or drowning them in lonely oblivion — the moral gradations of Seventies country heroes are more subtle, less haggard and harder to despise.

In what Travis Stimeling calls the "progressive country movement" of the Seventies, music was used to convey shifting ideas about masculinity, as exemplified by artists like Waylon Jennings; Crosby, Stills, Nash and Young; Big Star; and the Byrds. Waylon Jennings, on his 1972 song "To Beat the Devil", contemplates and critiques men's moral failures: "The things that they complain about / are things they could be changing"[4], he sings, referring partly to himself. These men might be as miserable as they ever were, but they confront their shortcomings in a respectable way, using a musical style borrowed from the light, soft, smooth sensibilities of folk and pop. As a result, their narrators are engaging, almost sweet.

Through this aesthetic of hi-fi humility, the men of the Seventies manage to land their self-pity on just the right side of endearing. Accepting moral responsibility, they are affable, self-aware, effeminate in sensibility, nonchalantly non-committal and therefore less threatening — at least on the surface.

***

"Amie", the 1973 song by Pure Prairie League, exemplifies country music's transformation from outright abjection to a subtler, more insidious expression of moral shortcomings. In some ways, "Amie" describes a classic country situation, in which the narrator is preoccupied by past wrongs waiting to be righted. He sings an admission of moral blindness and begs for a good woman to help him calibrate his ethical compass. "Amie, what you wanna do? Can't you see? I can never see what's right or what is wrong", he sings. He requests that Amie show him the light — a classic deflection of moral labour.

But "Amie" departs from earlier moralising lyrics, in a way that is typical of this newer Seventies country. Whereas the traditional country narrative comes off as an extended explanation, excuse or complaint, "Amie" seems aware of the problems with the history it comes from. The classic move of moral deflection is to force a decision on a woman. But this is the Seventies, and the narrator has been taught by women's liberation that Amie doesn't want to be told what to do. This right to choose is arguably the most basic of women's rights;

in 1973, the year the song was released, the landmark United States Supreme Court decision Roe v. Wade gave women the right to end a pregnancy. Here, the narrator tenderly expresses awareness of moral ambiguity rather than gruffly demanding moral assistance. Rather than extracting moral labour from Amie, the narrator offers it to her instead, disguising a burden as a gift. The narrator asks politely: "Amie, what you wanna do?"

Our ability to love him depends entirely on whether we view this deflection as a trick — a refusal to work — or, instead, as a gracious refusal of power, an invitation for Amie to act within a tradition in which action was so often denied to women. The narrator tries to endear us to his moral deflection, presenting his lack of moral clarity and dependence on a woman as a feminist move that gives Amie power.

Of course, a woman's right to choose is ultimately granted by a *him*, and therefore always able to be taken away. In the song, immediately after asking Amie for help telling right from wrong, the narrator reasserts his power, adding a snide expression of moral righteousness: "Doesn't take too long to see", he sings. This quip arrives as an afterthought, snuck into the end of the phrase, sung under his breath. He's winking when he sings it because his earlier humility turns out to have been a front, pure performance. The real choice is clear: Amie, be with me.

And yet, while at this point the narrator claims that he knows what he wants, he then reverses again, collapsing back into confusion. The song closes with an introspective monologue that rivals the most abject of failures: "Don't know what I'm gonna do", he finally admits as the song fades out, deciding only on indecision. "I keep fallin' in and out of love with you. Don't know what I'm gonna do."

Only in the end do we realise that he's not only a classic deadbeat, but a sweet-talking liar — a self-absorbed, backpedalling mess. At first, he professed conventional moral confusion that he then ironised as a performance, distancing himself from his outlaw predecessors, only to eventually undo that performative distance by rendering his initial confusion real. He doesn't actually have his shit together, and he has no idea what he wants.

After all this, we still give him credit for trying, and we're still willing to listen to his song. Maybe it's the way he sings so sweetly; maybe it's that hi-fi country sheen. Maybe it's simply that the song, as an exploration of moral confusion, expresses the height of ambivalence, which is far more forgivable than a glib admission of wrongdoing. While the latter comes off as a childish evasion, the former enacts a genuine concern for moral problems.

Whatever it is, the responsibility of making moral decisions emerges intact as something forever desired but forever deflected on to somewhere and somebody else. The song fades out, and we're left wondering what to do. If this endless burden of compensating for men's moral lack is a labour women sometimes welcome, it's also one whose weight we continue to struggle beneath.

Notes

1 Pure Prairie League, "Amie", *Bustin' Out*, (1972), RCA. Copyright Craig Lee Fuller, Unchappell Music Inc. (1972).

2 Merle Haggard, "Mama Tried", *Mama Tried*, (1968), Capitol Records. Copyright Merle Haggard, Blue Book Music, Gold Book Music, Sony ATV Publishing (1968).

3 Cat Power, "Good Woman", *You Are Free*, (2003), Matador Records. Copyright Charlyn Marshall, Doorman Music (2003).

4 Waylon Jennings, "To Beat the Devil", *Good Hearted Woman*, (1972), RCA. Copyright Kris Kristofferson, Universal Music Careers (1972).

Bibliography

Ching, Barbara. "The Possum, the Hag, and the Rhinestone Cowboy". In Hill, Mike (ed.) *Whiteness: A Critical Reader.* (New York University Press, 1997).

Edwards, Leigh E. *Johnny Cash and the Paradox of American Identity.* (Indiana University Press, 2009).

Fox, Pamela. *Natural Acts: Gender, Race, and Rusticity in Country Music.* (University of Michigan Press, 2009).

Nugent, Benjamin. *Elliott Smith and the Big Nothing.* (Da Capo Press, 2004).

Sutton, Matthew D. "Charley Pride, Autobiography, and the 'Accidental Career'". In Pecknold, Diane and McCusker, Kristine M. (eds.) *Country Boys and Redneck Women: New Essays in Gender and Country Music.* (University of Mississippi Press, 2016).

Stay With Me: Subcultures, Sexism, Siouxsie and Rod Stewart

Jacey Lamerton

Growing up as a late-to-the-party punk kid, I didn't have to think much about sexism in music. I had Siouxsie, Viv and Poly bellowing in my ear. I had the anarcho-punk heroes of Conflict, Crass and Subhumans forming my delicate little sensibilities. They didn't give a shit about cars and girls. They were into revolution, no matter what bits you had in your pants.

Dad had briefly been the frontman for amateur Margate band the Secrets and was therefore the barometer of musical taste in our house. And he was contemptuous of the noddy-headed Beatles. Never mind that Mum had screamed enthusiastically at George Harrison when they played Margate Winter Gardens in 1963. Mum wasn't the boss of the stereo. She only owned four records and one of them was by Leo Sayer. (It must be noted though that even Mum despised the likes of John Denver, who was dismissed with a shudder as "wet".)

No surprise then that my own musical tastes developed in a robust direction. Transfixed weekly in front of *Top of the Pops*, I was baffled by the adulation shown towards two artists in particular — David Bowie and Rod Stewart. Bowie was scary and weird. Having been in nappies at the time, I missed his early glory days. My young parents missed them too, being too tired and busy earning a living to get their heads around this new space oddity. By the time Bowie was no longer scary and weird, he was gracing the charts with music that I considered risible. "Let's Dance" and "China Girl" certainly failed to explain his god-like status to the teenage me.

The other enigma, Rod, was the warty man who wailed that tedious dirge "Sailing", released in 1975, when I was five years old. I watched, increasingly horrified, as he turned into a Spandex-clad, leopard-spotted, poodle-haired, faux-camp preener strutting around a cavernous stage and demanding "Do Ya Think I'm Sexy?". By December 1978, even an eight-year-old girl in Margate knew that a new wind was blowing through pop and this kind of dial-it-in soft-rock-goes-disco posturing wasn't going to cut it. For god's sake, this loser was older than my dad.

"Do Ya Think I'm Sexy?" shared a chart with fresh music and new ideas; "Rat Trap", Bob Geldof's operatic yarn about a young couple escaping dead-end futures in a provincial town; "Tommy Gun" by the Clash, a commentary on terrorism in which Topper Headon hammers the drums to create a sound like gunfire while Joe Strummer screams out sarcastic lyrics; and "Hit Me With Your Rhythm Stick", which comes in with a soft, soulful bassline, before being joined by Ian Dury's clear cockney accent. Dury was the inverse of Stewart's transatlantic lechery and I knew which I preferred.

Rod had kicked off the year with "Hot Legs", an eye-wateringly offensive ditty that I knew was out of order, even as a child to whom crotch shots of Legs & Co (anyone spot a lower limb objectification theme here?) was presented as perfectly acceptable on an almost weekly basis.

The lyrics of "Hot Legs" are pretty shocking when read with today's sensibilities:

Imagine how my daddy felt
In your jet black suspender belt
Seventeen years old
He's touching sixty-four.[1]

These are lyrics written by a thirty-two-year-old man, joyfully discussing energetic sex with a teenage girl and mentioning his "Daddy".

But back in 1978, the troubling teenage exploitation left me largely unmoved. It was the video that struck me as puzzlingly uncomfortable.

In it, Rod — coquettish and wearing dungarees — cavorts laddishly with his band around a dusty farmyard somewhere in America. Much of his performance is shot through the fishnet-clad legs of a woman. We see her legs in a couple of different poses and at one point we are treated to a full-length back view. But we never see her face and she never moves. Rod and the boys, by contrast, enjoy a right rollicking time, visibly cracking up while cruising about on the roof of a pickup truck and playing rock god on some old railway tracks.

Rod's string of late Seventies self-indulgent adverts for his own sexual prowess probably did a lot to drive me directly into the black-clad arms of Siouxsie Sioux and the buck-toothed charms of Poly Styrene. Here were women who resisted objectification and lived life on their own terms. So they were the women I emulated, with lashings of black eyeliner atop Barry M white foundation. The eyeliner served as lipstick too. Bargain. I bought crimpers, joined CND and actively protested against vivisection and fox hunting.

While I was getting a political education from the hard-hitting record sleeves issued by anarcho-punk bands, I also pinched a few of my dad's albums. With the relentless enthusiasm Dad had shown towards Hank Williams, my heavy rotation playlist comprised early Stones, the Kinks' *Greatest Hits* (rather prematurely released in 1966) and Eddie Cochran. A heady mix, then, of down and dirty British rhythm & blues and US rockabilly.

By the time I was old enough to drive, my then boyfriend and I were involved in the skinhead scene, dancing at all-nighters to Jamaican ska acts such as Laurel Aitken or revved-up British bands like the Hotknives and the Riffs. He bought me my first Lambretta and with it, freedom. For a while our backwater seaside resort resisted the worst of the National Front's senseless infiltration of skinhead, a subculture with its entire identity firmly and joyfully rooted in London's Jamaican immigrant culture.

The racism, when it came, drove me away from skinhead culture for many years, but not before its association with mod led me to the Faces. Scooter skins vociferously claim to have little in common with mods. They clash on stylistic, cultural and musical issues, not least the mod idea that if one mirror on your scooter is good, fifty-seven of them must be better. But the cropped headed, boot-clad skins often find themselves rubbing shoulders and sharing a bar with their longer-haired, Parka-wearing cousins. (Back in the Eighties, the physical contact was often a lot more violent than rubbing shoulders.)

It was at one such gig, sniggering in the corner with the skins, that I first heard "Stay With Me" by the Faces. The tight, exuberant British R&B musicianship obviously shared a lineage with my beloved Kinks, but this was pure energy distilled into four-and-a-half minutes of fun.

"Stay With Me" kicks off at a fair old lick. In fact, the intro smacks you in the face like walking into the wildest amphetamine-fuelled party a teenage rebel could dream of. Guitars race at breakneck speed, joined by a pumping piano, huge drum sound and actual whooping... before slowing into a much dirtier, more rhythmic pace. As the beat clops along, the lead singer's voice soars above it — an incredible, rasping, bluesy instrument, blasting out lyrics that I instantly found equally sexist and sexy. It begins:

In the morning
Don't say you love me
Cos I'll only kick you out of the door

And he carries on hurling abuse at this poor woman:

You won't need too much persuading
I don't mean to sound degrading

But with a face like that you got nothing to laugh
   about[2]

Somehow though, the song oozed a tongue-in-cheek, youthful honesty that was refreshing, amusing and life-affirming.

I'd heard of the Faces. Dad had sometimes played the Small Faces at home and I liked the distant, evocative harmonies of "All or Nothing" and "Itchycoo Park", as well as the quirky music-hall Englishness of "Lazy Sunday". But even the almost anthemic "All or Nothing" couldn't come close to the raw sexuality of what I was listening to now. But, this wasn't the Small Faces, this was the Faces. Were they a different band? They definitely sounded different. It was all very confusing.

Eventually, my musical education caught up and I discovered that when Small Faces frontman Steve Marriott left to form Humble Pie, the remainder of the band — Ian McLagan, Ronnie Lane and Kenney Jones — teamed up with Ronnie Wood and Rod Stewart from the Jeff Beck Group to form the Faces.

Even more confusing. This rasping, energetic, life-affirming frontman was *Rod Stewart*? And yes, I did think he was sexy.

Rod and Ronnie Wood wrote "Stay With Me" in 1971. It featured on the Faces third album, *A Nod is as Good as a Wink... to a Blind Horse*, and was released as a single on the first day of 1972.[1] The Faces' searing zenith lasted only months really, before the energy and zest for life blew up in their faces and Rod's ego took him on a different, more lycra-filled, path.

So why has "Stay With Me" remained one of my favourite songs of all time? Why can I forgive Rod the lyrics to this but not "Hot Legs"? It's not an easy — or comfortable — question to answer. Youthful brass neck has a lot to do with it. When he created "Stay With Me", he was twenty-six and Wood just twenty-four. The song is misogynistic and perpetrates the worst of groupie culture, but it's somehow less sinister than Rod at thirty-two pretending to be worn out by the energetic demands of a teenage girl.

Another saving grace is its place in the fine heritage of the rock-star bad boy. My beloved Elvis Presley covered "Shake, Rattle and Roll", urging his partner to get out in the kitchen and make his breakfast. He gleefully objectified women in a string of hits and films, including *Girls! Girls! Girls!*. Even lovely, tragic Eddie Cochran recorded "My Way", featuring the charming exhortation:

Don't let me hear you argue, when I say frog you jump
Cause a woman ain't been born yet
That can play me for a chump
Oh little girl, better hear what I say
Yeah, I'm a easy goin' guy, but I always gotta have my
    way.[3]

Presley, Johnny Cash, Gene Vincent, Keith Richards, Jim Morrison, Ozzy Osborne, John Lydon, Liam Gallagher... the list is long and oestrogen-soaked of men who've capitalised on the sex-sells image of the sneering rock rebel. Isn't that what rock stars are *for*? Don't they exist to be cartoon personas, burning bright and briefly in 3D technicolour, inspiring us out of the humdrum — at least for three minutes? What would most men still recovering from puberty do if they suddenly found themselves rich, famous and successful, with women falling over themselves to sleep with them? The posturing cock rocker may be a pretty vile role model for our sons, but there's a kind of honesty to him that's lacking in the musicians who build a honey trap of sensitive songs when in fact they're getting just as many blow jobs from groupies in the back of the tour bus.

So "Stay With Me" remains a thing of joy to me. It's a slice of unbridled carousing from the dawn of the Seventies, created by a band packed with outstanding musicians, all at the top of their game at that very moment. It's a brief flash of exuberance before the whole sex and drugs and rock 'n' roll life imploded around them and they sank backwards into the gilded puffiness of their own overblown success. Even at the time, "Stay With Me" was a hard and fast musical orgasm in a chart that was beginning to take itself very seriously. The real world was a grey and gloomy place too, despite the purple loon pants. The UK news in January 1972 was dominated by a crippling miners' strike, Bloody Sunday, escalating unemployment and growing tension around nuclear weapons that would lead to the Aldermaston demonstration in March. It was the kids growing up in this bleak Britain that burst through in 1976 to rip the flesh from the indulgences that Stewart and his ilk had settled into. The punk message was that it was the energy and attitude that mattered, not how many chords you could play.

I don't want to sanitise rock. Music is about freedom, excess, pushing the boundaries. It's about letting talent fly and creating idols out of talented, messed-up, beautiful adolescents who sometimes write exquisite poetry that communes with your soul and sometimes choke on their own vomit in the bath. Time passes and the flaws beneath the make up and airbrushing reveal a less heroic truth. In Rod's case, warts and all.

Notes

1 Rod Stewart, "Hot Legs", *Foot Loose and Fancy Free*, (1977), Riva Records. Copyright David Roderick Stewart, Rod Stewart Publishing (1977).

2 The Faces, "Stay With Me", *A Nod is as Good as a Wink... To a Blind Horse*, (1971), Warner Bros. Copyright Bobby Byrd, Jean-Luc Ponty, Mark DeBarge, Rod Stewart, Ronny Wood. (1971).

3 Eddie Cochran, "My Way", *My Way*, (1964), Liberty. Copyright Eddie Cochran, Jerry N Capeheart, Unchappell Music Inc., Warner-Tamerlane Publishing Corp. (1964).

Dirty Deeds: Mischief, Misogyny and Why Mother Knows Best

Fiona Sturges

AC/DC are the worst. This much I know. They are preposterously smutty, hopelessly unsophisticated, and pretty much every one of their songs sounds the same. Their singer wears a vest and flat cap while their lead guitarist, who's well into his sixties, favours a Fifties-style schoolboy outfit completely with cap and short trousers. As well as big riffs, they are defined by casual sexism and oafish double entendres. When not extolling the delights of fighting, gambling, drinking and fast cars, their songs are about getting laid or hoping to get laid. Their songs are populated by strippers, prostitutes and young men with apparently unvanquishable erections. They really are appalling. Man, I love AC/DC.

It might seem odd that, after thirty years of devotion, I should suddenly find myself pondering the changing values and generational shifts that have occurred since I first heard them. Odder still, perhaps, is that my love for this wilfully unreconstructed rock band has led me to think about my relationship with my daughter, specifically the influence that a parent can have over a child's cultural life and the ideological quandaries that it can raise. And yet here I am.

I've adored AC/DC since I was twelve and it's not just nostalgia that keeps me going back. It's the fact that their songs are packed with precision and power, as catchy as the finest throwaway pop music. The opening riff to "Back In Black" has the same effect on me as the lengthy synthesised intro on "I Feel Love" by Donna Summer, or the thunk-thunk-thunk of New Order's "Blue Monday". I get a similar adrenaline surge when I hear the slow "dong... dong..." at the start of AC/DC's "Hells Bells", a tribute to their first singer Bon Scott who died from alcohol poisoning in 1980, and a song in which ruination and death never sounded so thrilling.

Predictability is rarely a virtue in music — it usually points to a shortage of ideas. In the case of AC/DC, however, the inexorability of their songs, the visceral, if-it-ain't-broke-don't-fix-it familiarity of those riffs, is precisely the appeal. This is rock 'n' roll cut to the bone. Lyrically they may be puerile but their pithiness is second to none. In employing minimal words to capture the overwhelming madness of teenage lust, there's artfulness to their innuendo.

Now, though, I have cause to question whether they are really a band to be celebrated. This is because my daughter loves AC/DC too. She's ten years old and, because of me, she adores "Rock 'n' Roll Train", in which singer Brian Johnson sings: "Take it to the spot, you know she'll make it really hot".[1] She also loves "You Shook Me All Night Long" in which Johnson's lover is a "fast machine" who keeps "her motor clean"[2], and is positively electrified by "Thunderstruck" where the singer announces he's got his "gun at the ready, gonna fire at will"[3]. So far I've kept her away from "Go Down", "Big Balls" and "Let Me Put My Love Into You", none of which require explanation, but it's only a matter of time before she finds them for herself.

What the hell have I done?

I am a proud feminist, and a sizeable proportion of my work as a journalist is about combatting sexism. I try, where possible, to encourage my daughter to think about how women are represented in art, music, film and everyday life. Together we have looked quizzically at the acres of pink in children's clothes shops and at the miniature cookers and plastic cupcakes aimed at little girls in Toys R Us. We have talked, possibly a little too earnestly, about why so many of the female characters in classic kids' books are dismissed as bossy, or cry a lot, or play second fiddle to the boys. We have had tentative conversations about sex, physical autonomy and body image. I try to be frank with her at all times, but even I'm not quite ready to give her a full breakdown of the body shaming, objectification and dehumanising of women in the AC/DC oeuvre.

These matters came to a head when the band announced a new tour and my daughter asked if we could go to see them together. It would be her first stadium gig and I couldn't have been more delighted. I snapped up a pair of tickets and sorted out some transport. And then I started to panic.

I remembered "Whole Lotta Rosie" in which the eponymous heroine, who we are cacklingly informed "ain't exactly pretty, ain't exactly small"[4], is brought to life during shows in the form of a massive blow-up effigy, busting out of her bra and knickers and sitting astride a cannon. This is a woman who, just so we're completely clear, "ain't no fairy story, ain't no skin and bones", and is as mandatory a part of the AC/DC live experience as tolling bells and old men in short trousers. They've been doing it for thirty years, I've seen it twice and I did not want my child to see it. Not yet.

In the end, salvation arrived when it was announced that Brian Johnson wouldn't be performing on the tour because of a problem with his hearing, and that Axl Rose of Guns N' Roses would be singing in his place. Suddenly I had the excuse I needed to get a refund. Phew.

Since then I've thought more about my blithe tolerance of AC/DC and wondered why, when I have seen other artists reducing women to walking vaginas and cried foul, I appear to have given them a free pass. The fact that they are rock 'n' roll catnip to me surely isn't enough. I've long denounced assorted Seventies and Eighties musicians for their lyrical depictions of sexual violence, their reductive attitude to women and their offstage penchant for underage girls. These are things that can ruin a band for me. And yet still I listen to AC/DC.

In the realms of hard rock, dissolution on and off stage simply comes with the territory. That, at least, is how the thinking goes. Look at AC/DC's hard-rocking peers and you'll find scores of vainglorious men treating women with contempt in real life while simultaneously objectifying them in their music. Mötley Crüe, described as "savages" by their manager Doc McGhee, detailed their awful escapades in their best-selling autobiography *The Dirt*, which took in copious drug use, hospitalisation and death. But it was the band's treatment of women that proved most chilling, most notably the coercion, the frequent bouts of violence and, in one instance, rape. Meanwhile Kiss, a rock band who have enjoyed a similar longevity to AC/DC, are famed for their libidinous behaviour both on and off stage, with singer Gene Simmons claiming to have slept with well over five thousand women. I interviewed him once and I can confidently report that the man is a creep incapable of viewing women as anything more than walking orifices.

What makes AC/DC an anomaly is that rock 'n' roll dissolution seems to have existed mostly in their fantasies. This wasn't always the case: in their early years they had Bon Scott, a hard-partying ex-jailbird who once had two girlfriends giving birth at different maternity wards at the same time. When he died, the band thought of giving up entirely. But then they regrouped with Johnson, made *Back in Black*, which went on to sell forty million copies, and have since largely kept a low profile in terms of their private lives.

Johnson's hobbies are cars and West End musicals, the school uniform-clad Angus Young is a married teetotaller whose favourite tipples are chocolate milk and tea, while, until his dementia diagnosis in 2014, Angus's guitarist brother Malcolm lived a quiet life and was the band's business brains. Since the death of Bon Scott, any hell-raising behaviour within the band has been confined to drummer Phil Rudd, whose drug use led to his eight-month house arrest last year.

But Rudd aside, does the band's comparative clean-living status make their lyrical content more palatable? Or, at the very least, less sinister?

AC/DC's defenders will often point to the bawdy humour in their songs. The big-breasted, thunder-thighed women and hopelessly horny boys that inhabit them bring to mind saucy seaside postcards and *Carry On* films. In 2004, in an interview with Sylvie Simmons for *Mojo* magazine, Angus Young remarked, "We're pranksters more than anything else", while Malcolm noted, "We're not like some macho band. We take the music far more seriously than we take the lyrics, which are just throwaway lines. Once you've got the music, the titles sort of write themselves." But if the band members are merely pranksters, then women are their punchlines. They are the joke, and so is the sexism that they must endure.

And yet, look closely at the lyrics, and while AC/DC's woman are pitifully one-dimensional, they are also having a good time and are, more often than not, in the driving seat in sexual terms. In "Whole Lotta Rosie" ("When it comes to lovin', she steals the show") and "She Shook Me All Night Long" ("taking more than her share, had me fighting for air") it's the men who come over as passive and hopeless, awestruck in the presence of sexual partners more experienced and adept than them. If we're looking at the power balance in these scenarios, there are plenty of instances where it is stacked in the women's favour.

Plenty, but not all. There's an unpleasant sneering quality to Bon Scott's assertion on "Carry Me Home": "You ain't no lady but you sure got taste in men, that head of yours has got you by time and time again."[5] In "Let Me Put My Love Into You", Johnson wrote: "Don't you struggle, don't you fight. Don't worry cause it's your turn tonight", a grim rape fantasy with the payoff: "Let me cut your cake with my knife."[6]

On hearing this, the conscientious feminist would surely stop listening and build a bonfire out of the band's back catalogue. But, much as I feel bad about it, I just can't. While there are elements of AC/DC's work that make me uncomfortable, and one or two that are unequivocally vile, there are many more that simply, through force of undiluted, old-fashioned rock 'n' roll swagger, simply make me punch the air with joy. What can I say? I'm weak.

But it's not just about me anymore because my daughter listens to them too. What is the new generation of young women to think of a band that cautions women not to resist their advances and reduces them to a series of body parts?

AC/DC were one of the first bands I heard as a child coming from my older brother's bedroom. I instinctively loved them and failed to notice that when Bon Scott pronounced his desire for Rosie, he was saying it in spite of her not being a perfect size eight. I still hadn't clocked this when I first saw them live at the age of eighteen and was faced with the inflatable Rosie who was, quite literally, the size of a house. I realise now that the crucial difference between my own musical discoveries as a child and those of my daughter is context.

Where I simply absorbed such archetypes in my youth, my daughter is already learning to question them. Right now, the details of AC/DC's innuendo may go over her head, but as she gets older all will become clear. Whether she continues to listen, or decides they are a ghastly throwback to an era she's delighted to have missed, is up to her. What is important is that she already understands that their portrayal of women, their bodies and their function, is not an accurate one.

This is because, even at the age of ten, she is already observing the female vision of perfection peddled by advertisers and fashion experts — the well-groomed, smooth-skinned, sparkling size eight. Or, as Carrie Fisher's Marie put it in *When Harry Met Sally*: "Thin. Pretty. Big tits. Your basic nightmare."

A few years ago, while my daughter was playing with a group of girls at a friend's house, I overheard one of them prancing around in front of a mirror and wondering out loud if she looked fat. It was just role-play, an imitation of something seen on television or perhaps said by a parent, but it was chilling to hear; an unsettling fantasy of future anxiety.

It's because of moments like this that I've made a point of offering my child an alternative narrative — one in which women can be proud of their bodies, exist apart from the male gaze and not just reject but hoot with laughter at the moronic archetypes presented in advertising and the media, and in film, television and music. It's worth noting that none of this — at least so far — has come at the expense of her enjoyment. She will roll her eyes at the teeny-weeny waists and bulging eyes of Disney heroines but she will still happily watch the movies.

It's this context that gives her power and confidence, and, in the case of AC/DC, renders their lyrics daft as opposed to damaging. In seeing the band for what they really are — a bunch of archly sex-obsessed old idiots with sharp tunes and some seriously killer riffs — she might just grow up to love them critically, but love them all the same.

Notes

1 AC/DC, "Rock 'N' Roll Train", *Black Ice* (2008), Columbia Records. Copyright Angus McKinnon Young, Malcolm Mitchell Young and J Albert and Son Pty Ltd, Leidseplein Presse B.V. (2008)

2 AC/DC, "You Shook Me All Night Long", *Back in Black* (1980), Albert Productions / Atlantic Records. Copyright Brian Johnson, Angus McKinnon Young, Malcolm Mitchell Young and J Albert and Son Pty Ltd, Leidseplein Presse B.V. (1980)

3 AC/DC, "Thunderstruck", *The Razor's Edge* (1990), Columbia Records. Copyright Angus McKinnon Young, Malcolm Mitchell Young and J Albert and Son Pty Ltd, Leidseplein Presse B.V. (1990).

4 AC/DC, "Whole Lotta Rosie", *Let There Be Rock* (1977), Albert Productions / Atlantic Records. Copyright Ronald Belford Scott, Angus McKinnon Young, Malcolm Mitchell Young and J Albert and Son Pty Ltd, Leidseplein Presse B.V. (1977)

5 AC/DC, "Carry Me Home", *Dog Eat Dog* single (1977), Atlantic Records. Copyright Ronald Belford Scott, Angus McKinnon Young, Malcolm Mitchell Young and J Albert and Son Pty Ltd, Leidseplein Presse B.V. (1977)

6 AC/DC, "Let Me Put My Love Into You", *Back in Black* (1980), Albert Productions / Atlantic Records Copyright Brian Johnson, Angus McKinnon Young, Malcolm Mitchell Young and J Albert and Son Pty Ltd, Leidseplein Presse B.V. (1980)

Appetite for Dysfunction or Just a Good Time? Growing Up with *Van Halen I* and *Appetite for Destruction*

Beatrice M. Hogg

Many rock 'n' roll girls who came of age in the Seventies and Eighties will remember when they first heard two of the seminal (bad pun intended) debut albums of those decades — *Van Halen I* in 1978 and *Appetite for Destruction* by Guns N' Roses in 1987. The music of those two albums was a major influence on hard rock and changed the sound of the genre forever. Eddie Van Halen and Slash became two of the most admired and copied musicians of the era, in addition to their physical appeal. We loved both bands — but did they love us?

Van Halen I came out on 10 February, 1978. It was two seasons removed from the loss of my virginity in the back seat of an AMC Rambler, a month after my twenty-first birthday, and a few months before my college graduation. Sex was in the air and my hormones were in full eruption. With the first notes of that opening song, Van Halen let the world know that the game had changed.

Being a black, female rocker in the Seventies wasn't easy. I was teased and ridiculed by friends and family alike, but ostracism couldn't diminish my enthusiasm. I loved many of the bands that formed in the late Sixties and early Seventies, but those older men were not the stuff of fantasies. They were ancient guys in their thirties, at least a decade my senior. But the boys of Van Halen were MY age. Eddie was only twenty-two days older than me. Unlike the English rock gods that I admired, Van Halen were from California — a short TWA flight away.

When combined with the flawless musicianship of Eddie, his brother Alex and Michael Anthony, David Lee Roth's macho posturing seemed like a game, which he invited all of us to play. After I drooled at the photos on the album cover, I listened to the lyrics. When they weren't "Runnin' with the Devil", what kind of women did VH sing about? In "Ain't Talking About Love", they warned us that their love was "rotten to the core".[1] Van Halen women were supposed to "plead for it". But VH also wanted ladies to "Show Your Love". After reading about the band in *Creem*, *Circus* and other rock magazines, I discovered that there were certain ways that VH wanted women to demonstrate their affection. They also had a soft spot for women in trouble. In "Jamie's Crying", I imagined Diamond Dave lending a comforting shoulder to a damsel in distress. He even apologises for "taking it a little too far", when he can't wait to "Feel Your Love Tonight".[2] I identified with "Little Dreamer". Even though she was a crier, she was also a survivor, armed with all she needed. As an orphan venturing out to make my way in the world, I felt encouraged by the song. The old blues song, "Ice Cream Man", was filled with innuendos that were whimsically crooned by Dave. But in spite of the bravado of the lyrics on that first album, I felt that Van Halen was a party band. They were young guys looking for a good time, not out to hurt anyone. They may have been on fire, but that heat was for a barbeque, not a conflagration.

I wish that I could have seen them on that tour. I ventured to downtown Pittsburgh on the evening of their sold-out show at the Stanley Theater during the *Van Halen II* tour, but I wasn't brave enough to approach a scalper. I had never been to a rock show before and I didn't see any other black fans in the crowd, which increased my hesitation. I went back home and turned on my stereo, using my imagination to propel myself to the front row. The energy and sexuality of *Van Halen I* will always remind me of the beginnings of adulthood, of the first rock band that I thought of as peers, as hot, horny "Atomic Punks" who just wanted to have fun.

A lot can change in nine years. *Appetite for Destruction* was released on 21 July, 1987. I was thirty, and I had been working a professional job for almost seven years. I was ready to leave western Pennsylvania, planning to quit my job in August to move to California. It was a little more than ten years since my first furtive sexual encounter. I had loved and lost, travelled to England and seen many rock shows. I was familiar with the ladies of rock with big hair and short skirts, who followed the bands with erotic intentions. Even though I could appreciate a handsome face and tight jeans, the music was still what mattered.

Like "Eruption", the opening of "Welcome To The Jungle" was a beginning of something new and influential. Like Eddie before him, Slash knew how to make a sonic entrance. But the slightly menacing drone or whine of W. Axl Rose replaced Diamond Dave's sexy drawl. Instead of sexy poses, the boys of G N' R were depicted as skulls on the album cover. The back cover featured a robotic skeleton standing above a blond woman with her panties below her knees, one scratched breast exposed, with her head thrown back in either ecstasy or horror. Which was it?

The music was predominantly loud, fast and bold. If Guns N' Roses were a party band, Satan might have been the host. The music was good — like VH, it grabbed you in a primal, visceral way. The fun and games that Axl promised in the opening song did not sound like the good time that Dave crowed about years earlier. G N' R liked women who were easy. These women didn't cry — even when the band had a "use" for them. Axl expected women to make his motor run, or make his money tonight. The songs were infectious and in spite of the lyrics, I found myself singing along.

Before I bought my ticket to San Francisco, I thought about relocating to Los Angeles. But the dystopian, misogynistic LA that Guns N' Roses inhabited frightened me. Ecstasy or horror — the music slammed you against the wall and the lyrics penetrated your psyche. G N'R would not be drying your tears — they would be tearing into you. But the fire and anger of the lyrics were seductive. The sonic force created by Slash, Steven, Duff and Izzy, wasn't for the faint of heart in 1987, when hair metal ruled the airways of the radio stations that I listened to at the time. "My Michelle" was a survivor, but not for long. She was ordered to stop her crying. "Sweet Child O' Mine" was a romantic ballad, but it was a song of possession and submission. The women that populated this world were crazy, damaged and available. "You're Crazy", "Anything Goes" and "Rocket Queen" end the album with tales of debauchery. Before the chorus of "Rocket Queen", a woman is moaning. Years later, I read in Slash's autobiography that the band members were taking turns having sex with a woman in the studio, recording her sounds of arousal for all of the world to hear. It made me uncomfortable, but I still listened. The album ends with Axl's admonishment that, "All I ever wanted / Was for you / To know that I care".[3] Caring wasn't the adjective that I would use to describe the relationship between Guns N' Roses and their women.

After I moved to Northern California in 1988, I saw Guns N' Roses open for Aerosmith at Sacramento's Arco Arena. I even bought a sweatshirt, with the image of the robot/skeleton rape on the back. But the image offended me so much that I gave away the sweatshirt. I remember the roar that greeted G N' R when they hit the stage — this band was dangerous, as volatile as a lit firecracker. If Guns N' Roses were on fire, the flames would torch everything in their vicinity — which unfortunately happened a few times after they became headliners. Unlike a lot of bands, I never wanted to meet Guns N' Roses. Even though my friends and I drove around West Hollywood in April 2016 trying to catch a glimpse of the reformed band before they played a well-publicised "secret" show at the Troubadour, I didn't want to actually encounter the band, even after almost thirty years.

But both of these albums remain among my favorites. When I'm in a party mood, I put on Van Halen. In a pissed off mood, only Guns N' Roses will do. Even though their lyrics reduced women to commodities — both good and bad — I will always love them. Just like that asshole first boyfriend in the AMC Rambler that I'll always remember fondly, even though he broke my heart.

Notes

1 Val Halen, "Ain't Talking About Love", *Van Halen* (1978), Warner Bros. Copyright Michael Anthony, David Lee Roth, Alex Van Halen, Edward Van Halen and Diamond Dave Music, Mugambi Publishing, W B Music Corp. (1978)

2 Van Halen, "Feel Your Love Tonight", *Van Halen* (1978), Warner Bros. Copyright Michael Anthony, David Lee Roth, Alex Van Halen, Edward Van Halen and Diamond Dave Music, Mugambi Publishing, W B Music Corp. (1978)

3 Guns N' Roses, "Rocket Queen", *Appetite For Destruction* (1987), Geffen Records. Copyright Steven Adler, Saul Hudson, Duff Rose McKagan, W Axl Rose, Izzy Stradlin and Black Frog Music, Guns N' Roses Music (1987).

Nothing for Nothing

Rachel Trezise

My name is Rachel Trezise and I'm a Guns N' Roses fan. In fact, "fan" doesn't seem quite enough of a word. "Doctrinaire" perhaps; "apostle" maybe. I'm thirty-eight years old and I've got a collection of twelve Guns N' Roses T-shirts. I don't even mind when I see a thirteen-year-old girl in a glittery G N' R T-shirt from H&M or Primark in the freezer aisle at Lidl because that golden G N' R sphere with the pistols and flowers embraced within it is as mollifying to me as the sunrise in the morning. I claimed that logo for myself when I was a thirteen-year-old girl living in a pebble-dashed maisonette on Penrhys Council Estate; daughter to a single, alcoholic mother, surrounded by squealy-voiced school girls, their fringe hair-sprayed up into Table-Mountain-sized crests, Vanilla Ice CDs in their Discmans, Air Jordans and big rubbery BK Knights on their feet. My older brother was listening to Iron Maiden's eighth studio album, but Guns N' Roses sounded and looked like what I thought rock 'n' roll was meant to be: punk and blues, leather and denim. The music was decadent and momentous, the attitude full of sweat and devil-may-care. I fell in love with the sheer fucking hell-ness of it.

But I was as obsessed by the neon lights and sunshine of West Hollywood as I was by the band that it had created. In every photograph I saw of them the sun was blazing and I still call any temperature above 25°C "Guns N' Roses weather". For our honeymoon I dragged my husband to Sunset Boulevard where we spent a week drinking in the Rainbow Bar & Grill, (they were playing *Appetite for Destruction* the first, third and fourth time we went in). One night, after drinking too many tequila shots with Lemmy Kilmister (resident barfly at the time) and subsequently wheedling Duff McKagan's approximate LA address out of him, I literally kissed the ground Guns N' Roses had walked on. Recovery took a good eight hours at the poolside of our Best Western motel the following day. That's what had felt glamorous to me at thirteen: hot weather, outdoor swimming pools, sixty-foot palm trees and not the excessive lifestyle that the band had become famous for glamourising. Because I lived in one of the poorest areas in the UK, 1,100 ft. above sea level, and even at thirteen there was nothing necessarily surprising about sex and drugs.

Back then I'd missed the media furore over the original *Appetite for Destruction* album cover, (a cartoon painting by *Zap Comix* artist Robert Williams featuring a robotic rapist, his victim sprawled on the sidewalk, knickers pulled down to her knees). It had been banned for three years by then, replaced with the well-known skull-and-cross motif. And I didn't know the story about Slash and Axl getting charged for rape in 1988. ("It turned out our drummer had fucked one of their mothers so it was a complicated story", Izzy had said when the charges were dropped.) I did of course know the lyrics to the song often cited as the band's most offensive:

It's so easy, easy / When everyone's tryin' to please me baby

Yeah it's so easy, easy /When everyone's tryin' to please me

So easy / But nothin' seems to please me

It all fits so right / When I fade into the night / See me hit you / You fall down

I see you standin' there / You think you're so cool / Why don't you just / FUCK OFF

You get nothin' for nothin' / If that's what you do

Turn around bitch I got a use for you

Besides you ain't got nothin' better to do / And I'm bored.[1]

In the cold light of womanhood, the only way to interpret that scalding stew is as highly problematic and I can't even get close nowadays to the adoration I felt as a thirteen-year-old girl for that clattering "FUCK OFF" in the middle. At live shows, Axl barked it louder than the remainder of the song with backing from McKagan, deliberately antagonistic. I was thinking of all the authority figures who'd troubled me in some way that week when I shouted along, maybe even of my mother.

"You get nothing for nothing" was the line that really resonated though. From that I deduced that the lyricist's gripe was not with women in general, but with women who did nothing. I knew those women; I was surrounded by them. Girls from school with an aversion to every lesson on the timetable but who were possessed by the prospect of getting fingered by Christian Watkins on the summer camping trip to Llangranog. My mother, who I'd seen spraying furniture polish around her boyfriend's living room the way you or I would spray air freshener. "He likes the smell of polish when he comes in from work", she told me when I asked what she was doing. I suppose I imagined that when I *did* something — became a tattooist or an architect or whatever I intended for myself at that time — I could still reap respect from men like the one who wrote these lyrics. Having a use for myself would mean that nobody else would need to find one for me. The "Turn around bitch" line I just sort of disregarded.

Much of the criticism for misogyny aimed at Guns N' Roses came after *Appetite for Destruction* had sold over thirty million copies. When the band were writing it they were holed up in an apartment on La Cienega, living off a $38,000 contract payment from the record company. It seems like a lot of money for a small group of blue-collar teenagers in early-Eighties recession-blighted USA. They blew the majority of it partying for two weeks straight and then, as "It's So Easy" implies, they got bored. A steady diet of excess can get that way, I know. No quantity of fancy lyricism could convince me that alcoholism and drug addiction were exciting. The alcoholism I'd witnessed on the estate, my mother's included, was the most tiresome, humdrum experience of my life. I suppose that's why the hedonism celebrated in "It's So Easy" aroused such passive indifference in me, even then. I accepted that Guns N' Roses were jaded about every person and thing around them, not just the strippers and groupies, and in that way I accepted the song.

In 2011, having survived all of these excesses, McKagan published his *New York Times* bestselling autobiography, *It's So Easy (and other lies)*. To promote it he was interviewed on the BBC World News programme *HARDtalk* about his addiction and consequent burst pancreas. He seemed shocked when presenter Sarah Montague broached the subject of misogyny and asked him how he explains the lyrics to "It's So Easy" to his daughters. He tried to answer the question. He tried to answer it a few times. "Those lyrics were tongue in cheek". "The spirit of rock 'n' roll is bigger than misogyny or homophobia or whatever". "I give people more credit than to take my songs so literally". "Being honest about what was going on around me at the time seemed way more important than making some crappy sugar-coated pop-rock".

At thirteen I would readily have accepted any one of those explanations. But I know now how sexism works; how the patriarchy maintains power in part by keeping women quiet and divided from each other. The drip, drip effect, which rock music and its macho narrative only adds to. Even if McKagan's "tongue in cheek" lyrics were only ever meant to pillory the toxic masculinity observed on the strip in 1986/7, the satire has become lost in the band's overwhelming popularity so that misogyny is perpetuated and reiterated every time the song is played. Reality, mirror, reality, mirror, ad infinitum. It doesn't even need to be taken literally. It's out there in the ether. "Turn around bitch, I've got a use for you". For McKagan's sins he's conceived, as mentioned, two daughters. The eldest at seventeen is now frontwoman of a punk band, the Pink Slips. They play regular gigs in the same Sunset Boulevard venues as Guns N' Roses did back in the day. That's a small consolation, isn't it? Let's hope she writes some breathtakingly empowering lyrics for her first album about the things she sees going on around her there.

In early February 2016, in the run up to the beginning of the Six Nations Rugby Championship, my MP Chris Bryant suddenly urged Welsh sports fans to stop singing Tom Jones' "Delilah" (the unofficial anthem at the Millennium Stadium), because, he claimed, "it glorifies domestic violence". Sadly, police figures do illustrate that domestic violence tends to peak in Wales during rugby tournaments and I realised that Bryant was using a much-loved tradition to draw attention to the matter while rugby was in the spotlight. But I was surprised by how irritated I was by the targeting of popular music to make his point.

I don't like "Delilah". I've always found the sight of half-cut crowds swinging their plastic pint pots around while they cackle the *Ah-ha-ha*[2] line in unison a little disturbing. But Bryant's suggestion seemed to be a gross oversimplification of the issues. I also detected some class snobbery in his proposal. Has anyone suggested that the upper middle classes should be protected from the performance of operas such as *Don Giovanni* or *The Abduction from Seraglio*, in which sexual violence towards women is frequent? Evidence from domestic abuse services does indeed show that the number of women from professional households seeking help from domestic violence services has risen since 2011. Maybe it's just the unsophisticated ball-game loving classes who are at risk of interpreting art and literature so literally.

So, what if we banned everything that could be construed as offensive? Goodbye pop culture. Maybe we should remind ourselves here of one of Guns N' Roses' early country-music inspired acoustic songs, "Used To Love Her" and all-female grunge band L7's lampooning of it. The original from 1986 tells the story of a man who murders his lover:

> I used to love her / But I had to kill her
> I used to love her, yeah / But I had to kill her
> She bitched so much / She drove me nuts / And I can
>   still hear her complain.

In 1992 on *I Used to Love Him*, a little-known live EP released only in Japan, L7 presented a rare realisation of the test that music critic Ellen Willis devised in 1971 to unearth male bias in rock songs.[3] They reversed the sexes on a cover of the song and added a hilarious impersonation of Axl Rose's high tenor squeaking on the ooh's:

> I used to love him / But I had to kill him
> I used to love him, yeah / But I had to kill him
> He bitched so much / He drove me nuts / And now I'm
>   happier this way.[4]

Interestingly, the band portray Axl Rose as the "bitch", with a whiny voice, higher than that of frontwoman

Donita Sparks. Maybe it's just another small consolation, but when I was beginning to understand and embrace feminism aged seventeen it meant as much to me as "It's So Easy" had four years earlier. For every voice in every loudspeaker there is a dissenting voice elsewhere questioning the status in quo.

Of course, in order to truly enjoy Guns N' Roses I've learned to compartmentalise, to disengage with certain lines from certain songs and even certain members of the band — but I can be critical on a political level and appreciative on an aesthetic level. I know the process sounds unwieldy, even hypocritical, but we all have to do this continuously in order to live in relative harmony every day. With hindsight, I see that when I stumbled upon this band as a jaded thirteen-year-old, I was in a precarious situation, so introverted and self-contained I wanted to collapse my own bones like a fold-away tent, to disappear into myself. And there they were, so confrontational and effervescent, demanding my attention. And rather than quietening me further, their songs seemed to scoop a hungry insolence out of me. They made me want to be heard. They made me want to do something.

Notes

1 Guns N' Roses, "It's So Easy", *Appetite For Destruction* (1987), Geffen Records. Copyright Steven Adler, Aaron West Arkeen, Saul Hudson, Duff Rose McKagan, W Axl Rose, Izzy Stradlin and Black Frog Music, Guns N' Roses Music, West Arkeen Music (1987).

2 Tom Jones, "Delilah", *Delilah*, (1968), Decca. Copyright John Barry Mason, Leslie David Reed, Donna Music Ltd, Francis Day and Hunter Ltd (1968).

3 In Ellen Willis, "Now I'm Gonna Move", in *Out of the Vinyl Deeps*. (University of Minnesota Press, 2011).

4 L7, "Used to Love Him", *Monster* single (1992), Slash Records. Written by Guns N' Roses as "Used to Love Her", *G N' R Lies* (1988), Geffen Records. Copyright Steven Adler, Saul Hudson, Duff Rose McKagan, W Axl Rose, Izzy Stradlin and Black Frog Music, Guns N' Roses Music (1988).

Knowing Him Now After Only Guessing

Eli Davies

For Tom, Hannah and Huw, who taught me everything worth knowing about pop music

It was January 1994. I'd just moved back to my suburban London home after three years living away with my family. I was fourteen and had just started my new school mid-way through the academic year when there was little space for me to squeeze myself into the hardened friendship groups of my peers. It was cold and dark. I was readjusting to life in a Tory suburb in a Tory country, where everything seemed to be permanently cloaked in a damp mizzle. I was a big knot of misery, confusion and resentment and I needed somebody to give voice to all this.

I already had the Smiths — they were the bread and butter of my teen angst soundtrack — but their longing and misery was sometimes a little too gentle, with a kind of poetic resignation that could verge on the cosy. I needed something harsher, spikier, to give my angst some edges. I wanted to push the boundaries and to stretch the limits of what I knew. And as I had no social outlet for this, I needed something else, something more solitary. Onto this fertile ground landed my older brother's copy of Elvis Costello and the Attractions' 1986 album *Blood and Chocolate*.

It was a strange choice in many ways. I'd had no schooling in Costello's music generally, or the punky new wave milieu that he'd sprung from in the late Seventies. In 1994, there was no subculture or scene centred on this guy that I could attach myself to, and it's not hard to see why. Even allowing for all this, though, *Blood and Chocolate*, with its low, heavy sound, sparse and often repetitive songs, was not an obvious entry point. By this album, Costello had moved away from the jerky three-minute bursts of his first couple of albums, had been to Nashville and recorded a country album, worked with the backing bands of Dylan and Presley, recorded *King of America* sans Attractions and had developed his sound into something altogether more complex and grown-up. On *Blood and Chocolate*, he folded these new aspects into some of the visceral energy of his earlier albums, and produced something utterly ferocious.

But ferocity was what I was after. I did not have a lot of love for the world around me, so the sound appealed to me; I registered his spite (Costello uses this word in his autobiography to characterise the playing on *Blood and Chocolate*) — his hate, his fury, I think I may even have picked up on the maleness of it all, but I wasn't interested in thinking about who this was for and where I, as a girl, fit into it all. There it was in my life; I had no context for it other than my own, which comes back to me now in dark colours — the bottle-green of the living room carpet, the old black hi-fi I played music on, the grey pavements of my street, the wintry darkness that cloaked everything by five o'clock and the colours of that record sleeve, the navy, brown and red daubings done by Costello himself.

All this was the perfect aesthetic backdrop for "Uncomplicated", the album's opening song, with the stark one-note thrumming of guitar and organ in its verses. The tune in this song, or what there is of it, is provided by Costello's vocals, as he hisses out the kinds of weird, disembodied images — big blue diamonds and cheap white plastic shoes — which fascinated me. I had no idea what any of it meant, but it was exotic and adult-sounding and like I was overhearing the fragments of a conversation I wasn't supposed to be hearing. Elvis sounded angry, and it seemed pretty clear he was angry at a woman, but I didn't mind — in fact, I think I quite liked it.

But it was the song of crazed, violent longing "I Want You" that was the real draw to this album and which sums up for me what is most brilliant and also most unsettling about Costello as a songwriter. I'd heard the song once before at a party, on an older friend's compilation tape. Like a lot of the culture I was encountering for the first time, I didn't love it instantly, rather it was a curiosity, something I wanted to understand, and when I got my hands on *Blood and Chocolate* I listened to the song over and over.

In his book, Costello is fairly defensive about the charges of misogyny that have periodically been thrown at him throughout his career; when he writes about performing "I Want You"[1] on stage he refers to it as "like a play"[2], and there is something so intense about the song, so full-on that it can seem like a piece of overblown theatre. In it he addresses a woman who no longer wants him, who has left him and found love with someone else, and it is a dark and frightening journey through raw pain and rejection. There's a warning of this note of fear in the intro: "I want you so it scares me to death", he sings over a deceptively gentle acoustic strum. ("I'm afraid I won't know where to stop", he sings later on when the song reaches fever pitch.) The phrase "I want you" is spat out with increasing intensity as the song progresses amidst the questions, pleas, accusations, demands and fantasies with which he attacks his former lover.

This woman's body becomes an image he tortures himself with as he imagines her shoulders shaking or her being held down by her new lover. He insults her intelligence, asking "Since when you were so generous and inarticulate?". And there is wallowing male self-pity towards the end: "I might as well be useless for all it means to you". The whole thing is a deep, thick pool of jealousy and pain; desire is transformed into something sinister and violent, a woman is sneered at, dismissed, her body instrumentalised, but none of this is this hidden; it's all on plain, ugly show.

There was indeed a strain of theatricality to Costello back then, and he's dabbled in playacting and shape shifting over the years. On *Blood and Chocolate* he uses three different names in the songwriting credits, one of which, "Napoleon Dynamite", is the name of the alter ego he used on stage during the *Spinning Songbook* tour, when audience members were invited on stage to spin a wheel to determine which song would be played next. Costello provides a pretty unpleasant insight into this act on the liner notes for a 2002 reissue of the album, writing that this character enabled him "to leer at young women and insult their dates"[3] during concerts. Perhaps his tongue is in his cheek here, but it seems distasteful, especially given the amount of grief women have historically had at music concerts. The overblown violence of "I Want You" is also somehow present in that anecdote and reminds me that theatrical misogyny is still misogyny; just because it's been ramped up for effect it doesn't mean it's not real or that we shouldn't think about the way it operates in a work of art.

As a teenager, though, I didn't really recognise the disturbing gender politics of that song. I'd not experienced any painful, bitter breakups, had been happily sheltered from anything like the cruelty expressed and didn't fully understand the violence of what I was listening to. I responded to the song's mood and energy, rather than anything in particular about the words, which is a handy strategy when learning to love problematic music, but it leaves me wondering what happens to those words and whether they wormed their way into my consciousness somehow.

The vicious sneering of the song and of the album more broadly appealed to me, the alienated teen, and spoke to the part of me that wanted to just sit and snarl at the world. So I set about discovering more. Luckily, later that winter Costello released *Brutal Youth*, his first album with the Attractions since *Blood and Chocolate*, and a record that also had its fair share of anger and snarl. The other material that I got to know was based on what my older siblings owned; *Punch the Clock*, *King of America*, *Spike* and a greatest hits compilation from 1985. There was also, slightly incongruously, the heavily produced and orchestrated 1991 album *Mighty Like a Rose* which my sister had (an album not rated by many as a classic, but a huge favourite of hers — and, subsequently, mine).

I was sulky, self-pitying and infected with a snobbish adolescent superiority. I had convinced myself that I was cleverer and more complicated than my peers and I remember one day, to prove this to myself, I made a list in my diary of all the words I knew that I thought the people in my class wouldn't know. Off the top of my head it included words like "complacent" and "pretentious" (ha!) and as well as being an example of a hilariously misplaced teenage arrogance, this strikes me now as a perfect activity for a young fan of Elvis Costello, whose songs often display an almost show-offy verbal canvas. Words were something I aspired to and defined myself by. Later that year during the summer, alone and friendless, I made a tape of my favourite Costello songs. I sat in my bedroom listening to it over and over and amidst the soupy heat of that room his words — misogyny and all — became my words.

You can't talk about Costello's gender politics without talking about the incredible force and skill of his lyrics; these things are inextricably bound up with one other, which is one reason I find it so hard to step back and judge. There's a paradox here, as on the one hand I have never been entirely clear in a lot of the songs what exactly is going on — many of them are impressionistic, dense with references and metaphor. But on the other hand, there are images that, even when I didn't understand them, seemed — and still seem — so crisp and vivid. A lot of the songs that seduced me and became mine that summer are about women; some of them love songs, some of them stories, some of them happy, some sad, some angry, some ambivalent. In all of them, though, there was a kind of attention to the subjects on show that drew me in.

But these women are frequently infuriating, duplicitous, naive or stupid. In the sultry "Sulky Girl", from *Brutal Youth*, Costello tells a story of intrigue and disguise and his voice is rasping and angry as he sings to the girl of the title: "Suddenly, you're talking like a duchess but you're still a waitress".[4] "Brilliant Mistake" from *King of America* is a tuneful romp through one man's disappointments in the US, and in amongst the bits of Americana — the Coca-Cola bottles and boulevards of broken dreams — appears a woman: "She said that she was working for the ABC news / It was as much of the alphabet that she knew how to use".[5] A lot of the power of Costello's words derives from his voice, in which you can often hear the curl of a sneer and contempt for his subjects as he spits out his lyrics.

There were two album tracks that I put on that tape — "All Grown Up" from *Mighty Like a Rose*, and "You Tripped at Every Step" from *Brutal Youth* — which involve Elvis addressing young women, giving them a vaguely poetic talking to. These women are sad, overcome by tragedy and drama in some way and I imagined myself as these characters, imagined Costello wisely giving me his counsel, telling me where I was going wrong. Condescension towards women is a recurrent feature throughout Costello's work and it concerns me slightly to think of myself as a young, impressionable teenage girl internalising all that. None of this is even mentioning "Alison", of course, which, embarrassingly, I took for years to be a gently bittersweet love song but which I now see a more subtle precursor to "I Want You", featuring similar themes of rejection and jealousy, a vague threat of violence and the recurrent character of the silly woman.

Despite all of this, though, and often doing with battle with some extreme uneasiness, there's something about these songs that still gets me like no others. The stories and characters are vivid and singular; they are rarely generic or sentimentalised. It strikes me that, like Jarvis Cocker, another of my problematic faves, Costello observes women, pays attention to them; the problem lies in the fact that he often then uses them as a locus of whatever broader war against stupidity, complacency or selfishness he happens to be feeling the need to wage. And this is difficult as a woman listener because it can make it hard to shake off the feeling that this music isn't really intended for you, that you are just a bit player in some bigger, more important drama.

But, like Cocker, when Costello does righteous, political fury he can really come up with the goods, as in the extraordinary "Tramp The Dirt Down", in which he outlines with cold clear anger the reasons for his hatred of Margaret Thatcher, the injustices and cruelty committed at her hands and how much he longs for her death. And as much as I might want to, I feel like I can't separate the violent fury of Elvis in "I Want You" and that of "Tramp The Dirt Down". And I'm not sure I do want to. Do they come from the same place? I think they might. But I don't quite know what to do with this.

I had a gift when I was younger for overlooking the maleness of the pop stars I loved, appropriating the lyrics for my own purposes and putting myself in the place of these men. Rock 'n' roll as a genre has, from its inception, pretty much always hated women, or mistrusted them, or resented them, or fetishised and caricatured them. Undoubtedly woman listeners have always managed to somehow work around this, sometimes aware of the dodgy politics, sometimes not, but always finding ways to use the music for their own purposes. The fact is that Elvis Costello nailed himself onto my psyche at such a formative stage that I am never going to not love him. His back catalogue provides such an abundance of material, such seriousness, joy, pain, anger and power, and I have to admit to myself that I wouldn't change anything about it.

Notes

1 Elvis Costello, "I Want You", *Blood and Chocolate*, (1986), Demon. Copyright Elvis Costello, Universal Music Publishing MGB Limited (1986).

2 Elvis Costello, *Unfaithful Music and Disappearing Ink* (2016), pp. 56 and 448

3 *Blood and Chocolate* 2002 Liner notes http://www.elviscostello.info/wiki/index.php/Blood_%26_Chocolate_(2002)_liner_notes

4 Elvis Costello, "Sulky Girl", *Brutal Youth*, (1994), Warner Bros. Copyright Declan Patrick MacManus, Universal Music Publishing MGB Limited (1994).

5 Elvis Costello, "Brilliant Mistake", *King of America*, (1986), F-Beat. Copyright Declan Patrick MacManus, Universal Music Publishing MGB Limited (1986).

Where the Wild Roses Grow: The Strange Allure of Murder Ballads

Kelly Robinson

As a lover of weird, dark history as well as weird, dark music, I've always been drawn to murder ballads. One of the high points of my life was hearing my music idol, Elvis Costello, sing "Knoxville Girl" one night in a darkened historic theatre in my actual hometown of Knoxville:

> I took her by her golden curls and I drug her round and around
> Throwing her into the river that flows through Knoxville town
> Go down, go down, you Knoxville girl with the dark and rolling eyes
> Go down, go down, you Knoxville girl, you can never be my bride.

Elvis Costello no doubt became acquainted with the song in one of its older incarnations as "Wexford Girl" or "Oxford Girl", but having been raised in Southern

Appalachia, I was introduced to murder ballads as part of a long local folk music tradition. Before there was such a thing as true crime re-enactment TV, stories of Tom Dooley murdering a pregnant Laura Foster or the brutal killing and beheading of the young Pearl Bryan were passed around in song, and nearly any bluegrass group worth their salt has some version of a murder ballad in their repertoire. Later, as my interest in crime history grew, I learned more of the European tradition of broadside ballads, the cheap penny papers distributed in England with verses dishing the sordid details of a number of grisly real-life murders — usually with the suggestion of a popular tune to which one could set the lyrics. Typical of these broadside ballads is "Pretty Polly":

> Oh Polly, Pretty Polly, your guess is about right
> Polly, Pretty Polly, your guess is about right
> I dug on your grave the biggest part of last night
> Oh she knelt down before him a pleading for her life
> She knelt down before him a pleading for her life
> Let me be a single girl if I can't be your wife.

These songs aren't mouldy, forgotten relics of the nineteenth century. They continue to be done and re-done even today, interpreted by modern artists. Rock band Okkervil River recorded a version of "Omie Wise", the story of a woman choked to death and thrown in a river in 1808. Alt-folk band Vandaveer resurrected "Banks of the Ohio", another traditional tale of a woman drowned by a lover. You can hear the above-mentioned "Pretty Polly" on the TV soundtracks to both *Deadwood* and *House of Cards*. The appeal of the subject matter is timeless, and fictitious story-songs of tragic deaths have peppered the charts throughout the decades, from Bobbie Gentry's "Ode To Billie Joe" to Cher's "Bang Bang". Familiar murder ballad themes permeate songs like Richard Marx's "Hazard" ("I swear, I left her by that river / I swear, I left her safe and sound"[1]) and Neil Young's "Down By The River", where the singer shoots his lover because "this much madness is too much sorrow"[2].

It doesn't take long to notice some patterns in murder ballads. While the traditional songs cover all manner of crimes and all types of victims, so many of them are female that they've been given their own sub-genre name by historians, who refer to "murdered girl ballads". The songs referenced above — "Pretty Polly", "Knoxville Girl", "Omie Wise" and "Banks Of The Ohio" — and the many others like them, are grisly descriptions of fatal domestic violence. The perpetrators are not strangers, but boyfriends, fiancés and lovers. The women are never guilty of much more than a perceived slight, which is often that they don't return the affections of the narrator — though sometimes they are suspected of infidelity, or have become pregnant. In retaliation, they are beaten, beheaded, hacked to pieces or — most frequently — drowned.

It's gruesome stuff, especially when one considers that these ballads are rooted in true stories. And yet, they have an undeniable romanticism at their core that draws me in. While reading about murder ballads, I've seen the same words used by other women — that they are "drawn to" these stories and songs. In the introduction to her thesis ("*This Murder Done*": *Misogyny, Femicide, and*

Modernity in 19th-Century Appalachian Murder Ballads), Christina Ruth Hastie writes that "I found myself *drawn to* these ballads, with their haunting lyrics and often-graphically-violent themes". Molly Boyle, writing for *The Hairpin*, talks of being "drawn to the darkness" of murder ballads and their "delicious peril". The word "allure" crops up just as often (NPR titled an album review "The allure of the murder ballad").

It's a confusing feeling, as an enlightened woman, to feel romantic about songs that so vividly and unequivocally depict the murders of women. From where does this problematic romanticism stem? My first thought was that the historical distance plays a role in helping us forget the reality of the brutality. After all, in most cases, the victims have been dead for well over a hundred years. On the other hand, it's the timelessness of these stories that gives them so much appeal, and is likely why so many artists revisit them. One of the most haunting things about murder ballads is that while they're rooted in history, murder and rape aren't artefacts of the past. Change a few details, update the names, and these ballads could be stories from our own local papers, or even our own diaries.

The persistent appeal of murder ballads may be connected with the similarity of the songs' subject matter to our own lives. Is there are woman alive who hasn't had a love interest that was a little too obsessive, too controlling? A little scary, even? In a way, murder ballads serve as cautionary tales. Some scholars have suggested that women passed on the songs as an oral tradition intended to warn young girls about what can befall them if they are not cautious around men. "The

Ballad Of Pearl Bryan" doesn't hide this fact, addressing the intended audience in the first line ("Young girls, if you'll listen, a story I'll relate..."), before launching into the sordid details of the lover who lured her away and removed her head (which, by the way, was never found). Several lines stand out as warnings to young women who might be too easily duped by men:

> She thought it was her lover's hand she could trust both night and day
> Although it was her lover's hand that took her life away

While the instructional nature of murder ballads may partly explain why they were handed down, it does little to explain their allure. There's an element of *frisson* in these songs that becomes obvious when they're heard in their entirety. They have an undercurrent that, for those who pick up on it, can only be described as sexual. To understand how a song about cruel murder can seem romantically exciting, I think we have to look a little more closely at the lyrics and what they have in common besides the act of murder.

One of the most obvious elements in the seductive aspects of the murdered girl ballad is the fact that the victim is young and beautiful. "Tom Dooley" describes the murdered Laura Foster as a "beautiful woman", while "Pretty Polly" has charms worth mentioning in the song's title. Some of the women are deemed so stunning that the murderer/narrator remarks on her attributes even as the killing is taking place. In "Knoxville Girl", the lover says he "picked a stick up off the ground and knocked *that fair girl* down", while in "Banks Of The

Ohio", he takes her by "her lily-white hands" before pushing her down into the water.

The water is worth noting, too. In fact, in the murder ballads where the woman is not explicitly drowned, she is usually tossed into a river after the fact. The picture painted of the women's corpses is one of loveliness, their hair streaming in the water like Millais' painting of Ophelia: eyes opened, lips parted and arms reaching as if ready to enfold a lover. This idea of a beautiful drowning victim is one frequently foisted on us in art, from George Frederick Watts' *Found Drowned*, in which the subject could easily be sleeping, to the washed-up body of Laura Palmer of *Twin Peaks*, who made blue seem like an appealing lip colour. While the reality of drowning is much different (bloating, discoloration), in film, art and music it's a method of preservation. The women in murder ballads may as well have been dipped in amber.

Also confusing the issue is the fact that the murders are the result of love rather than hate. The men perpetrating these acts describe the women as "my true love" and often claim at the end of the song to have murdered the woman they love. The killing is seen as an extension of love itself, an inevitable result of loving too much, and it's not uncommon for the loving and the murder to be treated lyrically as one thing. While most murder ballads have intimations of sexual relations (in "Lula Viers", he "ruined her reputation"), it's never explicitly described. With the details of the murder being the only detailed accounting of physical contact, it stands in for the more romantic interactions and becomes the sex act itself. Nowhere is this more explicit than in the various versions of "Omie Wise", where the words "kicked" and "kissed" as well as "choked" and "hugged" are used interchangeably, depending on the recording:

> But he kicked her and choked her and turned her
>   around:
> Held her under deep water where he knew that she
>   would drown.

Or:

> He hugged her and he kissed her and turned her
>   around
> And threw her in deep water where he knew that she
>   would drown.

In 1995, Nick Cave released an album called *Murder Ballads*, which included a track inspired lyrically by "Down By The Willow Garden". The song, "Where The Wild Roses Grow", features Cave in a duet with Kylie Minogue as they take turns with the killer and victim perspectives. The video to the song includes all of the tropes that have been prevalent in murdered girl ballads since the nineteenth century, laying them out visually so that their allure cannot possibly be misinterpreted. The video opens with the camera slowly crawling up the body of the drowned woman (Minogue), starting with her feet and up the length of her almost-shimmering, pale body. She is nearly naked, with a shred of gauzy fabric clinging to her wet flesh. She is an object of beauty and envy, and she is dead. The camera notably stops at her neck, leaving her faceless for the moment, so that she could be any woman — even you. Nick Cave is positioned as a lover more than a murderer, looking sensuous even as he washes her blood off of his hands in a ritualistic manner. Like the other narrators of murder ballads, he has killed because of love. Every move is seductive, and sometimes overtly, as when he caresses the corpse's breast. As the lyrics describe the moment of murder, "with a rock in his fist"[3], the video shows a water snake coiling on her body, a decidedly unsubtle way of linking the murder with sex.

"Where The Wild Roses Grow" takes the subtleties of traditional murder ballads and lays them bare. The allure of the songs, while still problematic from a feminist perspective, is easier to understand. The fantasy of being loved to the point of obsession is a frequent one. Studies of women who have erotic fantasies of being raped are quick to point out that the women who have them don't desire to be raped in reality — no more than my attraction to murder ballads means I desire to be murdered. What some of the rape fantasy studies have concluded, though, and what I think lies at the heart of the allure of the murder ballads, is that the fantasy is linked with the desire to *be* desired — to incite love and lust in a lover to the point that he can no longer control his actions. The resulting action of rape or murder is a fictional outcome of the fantasy of being wanted.

Being drawn to the seductiveness of murder ballads means being drawn to the idea of passion, and to a desire, however fantastic, to not only be thought of as beautiful enough to be chosen, but to *stay* beautiful and have that beauty preserved forever. The songs may be a macabre package for an expression of such basic human desires, but some of us are attracted to darker things. What seems like a true crime story to some can be a love song to others, and can even function as both simultaneously, if you're willing enough to look deeply.

Notes

1 Richard Marx, "Hazard", *Rush Street*, (1991), Capitol Records. Copyright Richard N Marx, BMG Monarch (1991).

2 Neil Young, "Down By The River", *Everybody Knows This Is Nowhere*, (1969), Reprise. Copyright Neil Young, Broken Arrow Music Corporation (1969).

3 Nick Cave and the Bad Seeds, "Where the Wild Roses Grow", *Murder Ballads*, (1996), Mute Records. Copyright Nicholas Edward Cave, Embassy Music CQRP (1996).

Bibliography

Cohen, Daniel A. "The Beautiful Female Murder Victim: Literary Genres and Courtship Practices in the Origins of a Cultural Motif, 1590-1850". *Journal of Social History* 31:2, Winter 1997. pp. 277–306.

Critelli, Joseph W. and Bivona, Jenny M. "Women's Erotic Rape Fantasies: An Evaluation of Theory and Research". *The Journal of Sex Research* 45.1, 2008. pp. 57–70.

Field, Arthur. "Why Is the 'Murdered Girl' so Popular". *Midwest Folklore* 1.2, 1951. Pp. 113–19.

Hastie, Christina Ruth. "'This Murder Done'": Misogyny, Femicide, and Modernity in 19th-Century Appalachian Murder Ballads". (Master's Thesis, University of Tennessee, 2011).

She's a Bitch:
Feminism and Hip Hop

Johanna Spiers

I am a hip hop DJ. When I'm listening to rappers, the sound replaces the blood that courses through my veins. Good hip hop invigorates me; it makes me feel whole, excited, connected.

Playing hip hop tunes to a room full of people makes me glow. I dance, I shout, I rap, and the adrenalin fills me fit to bursting as the crowd dance and shout and rap back at me. Hip hop's blend of big, bold beats and pure, powerful poetry is ecstatic and arresting. I often play hip hop for people who think they don't like it, and it is a blissful sensation to see them realising that they were wrong.

I have felt this way about hip hop since I was eleven years old and first heard Eric B and Rakim's "I Know You Got Soul". That tune mesmerised me — I sat on my bed listening to it over and over again, reading the lyrics that I had cut out of *Smash Hits* magazine and being unable to comprehend how something so fresh and thrilling was in existence.

I am a fierce collector of words, and so my love of hip hop seems natural. Your average rap tune contains so many more lyrics than your average pop song. Lyrics are my greatest weakness. I mine them for meaning and see myself in their nuances. I pride myself on knowing every song lyric I have ever heard, and a few I've only heard about.

Thus emerges a problem. While one doesn't have to look very far or very hard to find plenty of hip hop artists who rap about politics, equality or love, there is an undeniable chunk of the genre which delights in denigrating women. And so I often find myself asking: can a feminist who pays close attention to song lyrics really embrace these songs as well as the more savoury ones? Am I playing into the hands of the patriarchy by playing them to audiences, and potentially spreading the message of misogyny?

There are some tracks which could be mistaken to be women-bashing, and yet which I feel proud to play out:

> I like big butts and I cannot lie,
> You other brothers can't deny
> When a girl walks in with an itty bitty waist
> And a round thing in your face
> You get sprung, want to pull up tough
> 'Cause you notice that butt was stuffed.
> (Sir Mix-a-Lot, "Baby Got Back")

While that simple, staccato scratching and Knight Rider bassline are insistent and irresistible, it's clear that our good Sir is hardly rapsodising about his coy mistress's MA and parallel parking skills; he is entirely focused on the female form. However, I see this lyric as a lovable ode to women who eat properly ("Red beans and rice didn't miss her") and who should be proud of their round rears, a message that is not heard often enough in either or music or society:

> So Cosmo says you're fat
> Well I ain't down with that![1]

Being in a curvy, sexy, badass female body can be a lot of fun, and Sir Mix-a-Lot celebrates that notion in a fierce and funky fashion. It's the kind of tune that can make a woman feel proud of her body while she's dancing. The only problem I have with playing "Baby Got Back" is how the hell I follow it up.

While Sir Mix-a-Lot raps about his own love of sex, a recurring theme in a lot of US, male-led, commercial hip hop is men projecting their own horniness onto the women they immortalise. Women are frequently positioned as being entirely intent on sex. One could be forgiven for thinking that our sole role is to pleasure men and obediently churn out orgasms, reaffirming the rapper's virility. Should I be more conflicted about playing these sorts of tunes than I am?

Let's look at the classic N*E*R*D track "She Wants To Move". It's a killer tune; booming jungle drum, edgy guitar, and building tension that makes it impossible not to shake your booty. But the lyrics are questionable:

> Mister! Look at your girl, she loves it!
> (I know you love it girl) I can see it in her eyes
> She — hopes this lasts forever (hey) Hey!![2]

Despite its daft projection of male sexuality onto a woman's body, I will happily play "She Wants To Move" in a DJ set. Yet I would never, ever play Robin Thicke's "Blurred Lines" (another song written by N*E*R*D's Pharrell Williams), not for all the ponies in Peru.

Pharrell's bottom-based fantasies have escalated somewhat in the nine years between these two songs; there's nothing quite as stomach-turning in "She Wants To Move" as "I'll give you something big enough to tear your ass in two"[3] from "Blurred Lines", but the songs make similar points. I know you want it, I can tell by looking at you, let's get the obstacles (your boyfriend or your uncertainty) out of the way and then let's get to rammin'.

However, "Blurred Lines" is definitely perceived as being more sinister by both the public and myself; playing it to an audience would feel far too taboo, too violent. But, really, should I be condoning either track? You shouldn't be able to write about the "blurred lines" about whether women "want it" or not and expect to get away with it, and that is the take home message of both tracks.

And while we're on the topic of tracks I would never play for an audience:

Don't you get it, bitch, no one can hear you?
Now shut the fuck up and get what's coming to you
You were supposed to love me
[Choking sounds]
NOW BLEED! BITCH, BLEED![4]

This, from Eminem's "Kim", is next level shit; an extremely detailed song in which he describes killing his estranged wife. The slightly dubious party line is that these are the desires of Em's rap character Slim Shady, and are nothing that Marshall himself would actually want to do.

If he truly is just in "character" as Slim Shady, Eminem's vocal performance on "Kim" is astonishing. The anguish and madness in his voice combine with the simple dramatic piano loop to feel real and raw (particularly in the "you loved him, didn't you?" line). The emotion makes me start excusing him: we've all been in pain, we've all wished bad things on exes, of course it's not cool, but isn't it better to write a song than to actually do it?

This is nonsense. The song "Kim" is not OK, not on any level, not in a world where two women are killed every week by partners or ex-partners in England and Wales alone. It's an intensely uncomfortable listen, not least because the guy is such an expert lyricist that even when he's tackling the most reprehensible of topics, I am still desperately, guiltily enthralled.

Conversely, there are tracks which I would never play but which contain messages of feminist power that I really should be sharing. "Love Again (Akinyele Back)" by Run the Jewels sets up a typical sexist scenario and then turns it on its head. This is a tune which has a filthy bass noise unlike anything you've ever heard before, which demands that you wind and groove to its sleazy sound. As is often the way with hip hop, it's hard to pick out the words of the verses initially, but the crude, repeated edict of the chorus — "she got that dick in her mouth all day" — is loud and proud. People will hear that, they will believe the line reduces women to sexual vessels, and they will be offended. It would be intensely awkward to be behind the decks while that line booms out of the Funktion Ones again and again. However, a focus on the verses reveals a different story:

> The world won't let you be yourself
> I won't accept nothing else
> I be having none of that
> You be takin' all of this
> Pleasure come from punishment
> Your threshold astonishin'
> I think I'm in love again.

This is a love song about an S&M relationship. Killer Mike is giving Gangsta Boo the space to be herself, something the world, with its heels stuck firmly in the narrative of the Madonna/Whore, will not allow. How could a woman enjoy sadomasochistic sex and still be a good person? In this kitchenette, however, that is not only allowed, but applauded. And there's more, as Gangster Boo's final verse and chorus show:

> Keep it ratchet so sweet
> All these boys kiss my feet
> I be on that queen shit
> You better bless my realness.
> He want this clit in his mouth all day
> I've got this fool in love again.[5]

It is so refreshing to hear a man and a woman rapping about a sexual relationship in this way; one that represents two viewpoints. Run the Jewels, I applaud you. Yet I am far too inhibited to ever play the tune to a room full of people. Perhaps I should give the crowd more credit?

There are tensions between my feminism and my love for some of these songs; I am conflicted about listening to and enjoying them and playing them to rooms full of people. I can come to no real conclusion about these feelings and find that I have to let them exist inside me. I laugh them off, I analyse them, but a lot of it can't be excused. Yet hip hop will be my heroin forever. At its worst, it is sexist, homophobic and hateful. Yet at its best, hip hop is political, empowering, complex, infectious, joyful. And those beats are just too damn good to ignore.

Notes

1 Sir Mix-a-Lot, "Baby Got Back", *Mack Daddy* (1992), Def American. Copyright Anthony L Ray and Mix A Lot Publishing (1992).

2 N*E*R*D, "She Wants to Move", *Fly or Die* (2004), Virgin. Copyright Hugo Chad, Pharrell L Williams, EMI Blackwood Music Inc and Universal Music Careers (2004).

3 Robin Thicke feat. Pharrell, "Blurred Lines", *Blurred Lines*, (2013), Strak Track/Interscope. Copyright Pharrell Williams, Robin Thicke, T.I., More Water From Nazareth Publishing Inc., EMI April Music Inc., I Like Em Thicke Music, Sony ATV Allegro, Universal MCA Music Publishing (2013).

4 Eminem, "Kim", *The Marshall Mathers LP* (2000), Aftermath Entertainment/Shady Records/Interscope Records. Copyright Jeffrey Irwin Bass, Mark Randy Bass, Marshall B Mathers III and Eight Mile Style Music (2000).

5 Run the Jewels, "Love Again (Akinyele Back)", *Run the Jewels 2* (2014), Mass Appeal/RED. Copyright Jaime Meline, Lola Mitchell, Michael Santigo Render, Aniyah's Music, Definitive Jux Music and Pulse Worldwide (2014).

Equality is in the Doing not the Saying: What Tupac Taught Me

Zahra Dalilah

As a gawky twelve-year-old with thick-rimmed glasses and chunky plaits, complemented by the afro frizz which fluffed between them, my deepest passions consisted of the UK Maths Challenge and Sunday's *Home and Away* omnibus. Sandwiched somewhere between that was an intense love for hip hop and all its trimmings, which has remained infallible right up until today.

In 2002, when I was twelve, Nas had just dropped his best album since the classic debut *Illmatic*, DMX's *The Great Depression* was still deafening my household by way of my sister's bedroom, and unheard Tupac tapes leaked onto the airwaves as listeners stayed stupefied at just how much unreleased material the twenty-five-year-old had left behind.

Tupac had always hovered over my growing indulgence in the genre, a seemingly untouchable relic of a golden era, a legend, certainly, and perhaps one I feared I would never truly understand. But that year, the album *Better Dayz* dropped and I found myself sat, pressing pause, rewind, play, on track after track, relentlessly. It then became clear that I really, really did understand.

Both on *Better Dayz* and the works that predated it, Tupac's gift was always to unleash his truest self, sharing without hesitation his darkest thoughts, compulsively exploding whether in love or rage whenever he blessed a beat. On "Thugz Mansion" he states plainly, "I cry at times, I once contemplated suicide / and woulda tried / But when I held that nine / all I could see was my mama's eyes."[1] His ability to be so vulnerable whilst manifesting such conviction in his strength and survival drew me in swiftly and deeply. To be so unapologetically in oneself was something that was unconceivable to me. I was awestruck. To express hate for yourself, love for your people, to own wanting to die, demonstrated to me a courage that I had never known. Not long after we were introduced, Tupac fast ascended to God-like status in my life.

Tupac was a prophet. Tupac was a visionary. Tupac was a legend, a revolutionary. Tupac was a martyr who died for our sins. Tupac was basically Jesus. My views on my new-found hero were well-endorsed. To argue that Tupac was not one of the greatest artists and thinkers of our time was futile; if he didn't appear in your top five you simply didn't get hip hop. His death truly immortalised him. As he went on to release more material posthumously than in his lifetime, rumours that he was still alive refused to be silenced. We, hip hop fans, believers in the revolution, ordinary poor black folk, could not accept that we had lost someone so great, someone so important.

The core of Tupac's allure was his moral standing. He was not a moralist in the trite upper-class sense of the word, whereby judgment is cast upon those who don't dress properly for church and so-called promiscuous women are forced to wear their shame around their necks. Fundamentally, he believed in equality. He had come from poverty, had seen riches and deduced that that did not add up. He had seen girls birth babies when they were still children themselves and empathised with anyone who fell into the typical clutches of ghetto life. He knew every individual to be a product of their environment, himself included, and each and every one of us were therefore worthy of forgiveness, of redemption. Raised by a Black Panther, his pride in his blackness, and the injustices that his community faced, were at the centre of much of his work. It was through Tupac that I first learned of the LA riots, Malcolm X, of looting, of resisting, of oppression.

Tupac spoke at great length and emotional depth about women who had influenced his life like no other rapper I had been exposed to. "Dear Mama"[2] transcended my idea of what rap or rappers could do and of what hip hop was capable of as genre. Dedicated to the woman who raised him, he praises his "queen" in the same breath as he acknowledges her addiction to crack cocaine, which destroyed their relationship for some time. Despite everything that they went through, his love is unconditional and he considers himself forever indebted to this gracious and resilient woman.

Never had I seen such a three-dimensional female character painted in song. Prior to the discovery of Lauryn Hill, Lil' Kim and Foxy Brown weren't really painting those pictures any more than Eminem or Jay-Z were, at least not on my playlists. Pac went on to tell his sisters on welfare in no uncertain terms, "Tupac cares, if don't nobody else care / I know they like to beat you down a lot / But please don't cry, dry your eyes, never let up / Girl keep ya head up".[3] Knowing that women were beaten and torn down by society, he took it upon himself to offer the love, empathy and appreciation that we need.

Further still, Tupac was the first — and quite possibly only — man who ever told me that no one has the right to my body except me unless I decree otherwise. "If a man can't make one", he said, "he has no right to tell a woman when and where to create one."

In this lyric sex was described, as it often is when considered by from a woman's perspective, as the act of procreation. Often, respect bestowed upon women often comes in the form of bowing down to the ability to give life, as men realise that women must be preserved for the human race to continue to exist. Images of Mother Earth and African queens are often a "hotep" go-to, when a pseudo-conscious black man tries to break down why he won't stop calling you empress.

Of course, aged twelve, this analysis was well beyond me and of course, fundamentally, Tupac had done a beautiful and important thing in that song. So I bopped along to his wise words feeling vindicated, indeed blessed, that there existed a man who vocalised that rape was wrong. To be made visible was more than I could have ever wished for, but to be given the power of choice was pure freedom.

As an adult, I look back with disappointment at the framing of this anti-rape narrative. But far worse than this was the separation of the multi-dimensional women of "Dear Mama" and "Keep Ya Head Up", from the one dimensional, nameless, faceless women of the "harmless" party tracks. I remember songs like "2 of Amerikaz Most Wanted" and "California Love". Songs about young men who lived well, where words like "hoochie" "pimp" and "booty" scurried between the celebrations of success. Outside of those songs that centred women's struggles, women were decoration, a means to an end. Uncredited female vocals so often laced classics with a vibrancy and passion that defined Tupac's style, but they were in the background, quietly greenlighting what shone in the forefront.

"Wonda Why They Call U Bitch"[4] represented Tupac at his most intricately problematic. Composed of a blow-by-blow account of what made a woman bad enough of a human being to merit being called a bitch, it spoke volumes to how the perfect image I had of Tupac was so flawed. Masking itself as a "Mama's Just a Little Girl" or "Brenda's Got a Baby" type track, telling the story of a naïve young woman from the ghetto that fell into one of its many trappings, it appeared to care so deeply about a woman he "loved like a sister". The track expresses empathy for a woman from the hood whose decisions leave her in a tragic position (catching HIV and dying young). Whilst it had the potential to be a moving look at this woman's life, this track essentially exists to put forward a defence on why it's sometimes okay to call a woman a bitch. Not long after describing holding back tears as he watches this woman jump from man to man in her pursuit of riches, he explains in the close "why we call these ho's bitches".

When I first heard the lyric, "keep your head up, legs closed, eyes open" from this track, I embraced each and every word, believing that this was advice to live and die by. Again, grateful, above all, that someone cared enough to tell me what to do, to consider me. The fundamental purpose of the song aside, the hypocrisy of a man who describes "getting pussy" as the "sweetest joy" telling me to keep my legs closed did not land for years to come.

Women, not just in hip hop but anywhere in the world, are consistently referred to as hoes, bitches, sluts, hoochies, as whatever the popular word of the locality or era may be. I experienced, as did many women I know, a stubborn disassociation from women who fit into these categories. I believed that having a lot of sex made you a bad person. I believed that spending your state benefits on your haircut was morally corrupt. I understood that you would be liked, and get mentioned in a song, if you were great in bed — but I also got the impression that I shouldn't enjoy sex too much, lest I start having it all the time with multiple people and therefore warrant the title of bitch. Trapped by definitions of what a woman should be and hence what disqualifies you from the title of woman, Tupac the hero and saviour suddenly slipped onto the side of Tupac the problem.

His mother was in the minority, to be given the space in his music to exist as both woman and complex human being. Most women Tupac mentioned were paper-thin characters, just an ass, just a vagina, just some vocals, sometimes a love interest but usually absent altogether. Sure, Tupac cared enough to tell me how he thought I should best navigate the world. But he didn't care enough to address the double standard of sexual exploration. Instead, he dedicated an entire song in defence of a word used to silence and shame women daily. He didn't care enough to consider giving women the freedom to determine for themselves what they wanted to be and never, ever, did he demonstrate caring enough to actually interrogate his own role in a system of patriarchy.

Tupac's overtly political messages, his visceral frustration about the injustices he witnessed on a daily basis, were undoubtedly his greatest appeal to me. I got Tupac. I felt his anguish and rage at a system set up to see him and his peers fail. I still feel it today.

I respected and loved Tupac with no caveats for over a decade on these grounds. It took years of interrogation and analysis to accept that both mythical men who are artists and real life men who claim to be down for the cause will merrily sit upon the pedestal you give them, and not knowing or asking how not to, they will continue to hold in place every facet of the system that oppresses you.

Believing in equality and liberation — in theory — is not synonymous with actively removing the structures of oppression that govern your relationships with others with a different level of privilege from you. Saying that you respect women doesn't mean you'll stop staring when she asks you too, that you'll take your hand off her thigh when you can tell she feels uncomfortable, that you'll judge her less for her sexual history, or that you'll pull out when she asks you to stop.

Loving Tupac taught me that caring about women in theory was not enough. He told me that it was a harsh world for a young girl growing up in a rough part of town. That young girls get pregnant, promiscuous women get AIDS and that these were terrible things. He told me that women should take action to stop that from happening and that the troubles women get themselves into had nothing to do with how he behaved on tracks about young men who live well. And that simply isn't true.

To this day, I struggle to sit through Tupac interviews without welling up. The death of a great artist who was just twenty-five and who embodied the spirit of resistance and of change remains one of the greatest tragedies that hip hop has ever seen. But as I grow older I find less and less patience and forgiveness for men who uplift with words and oppress with actions. It just isn't good enough.

Yet there is a certain hope I carry as I watch old clips of Tupac, fresh out of jail, saying "I just want them to look back and be like, oh remember when he was bad." Or younger, aged seventeen, watching him express surprise and distress at being rejected by girls "for being too nice! And then they end up with these guys who use the b word!". The innocence of this younger Tupac, the exasperation of a post-incarceration Tupac, who knew he was so much more than the thug life tatted on his stomach, it reinforces this hope. There is a hope that it all starts with a theoretical respect for women. That given the years to grow and learn we begin to translate this theoretical respect through education from others around us or through seeing the reactions of the women scorned along the way, into a consistent behavioural shift that sees a transformation in the daily lived experiences of women — not just in the songs they can bop along to.

Notes

1 2Pac, "Thugz Mansion", *Better Dayz* (2002), Amaru. Copyright Seven Marcus Aurelius, Anthony Cornelius Hamilton, Johnny Lee Jackson, Tupac Amaru Shakur, Black Hispanic Music, EMI April Music Inc, Justin Combs Publishing, Marcus Aurelius Music, Songs of Universal Inc, Sony ATV Harmony and Tappy Whyte S Music (2002).

2 2Pac, "Dear Mama", *Me Against the World* (1995), Interscope. Copyright Bruce Hawes, Joseph B Jefferson, Tony D Pizarro, Joe Sample, Tupac Amaru Shakur, Charles B Simpson, Terence Thomas, BMG Blue, Master Lab Publishing, The Underground Connection, Universal Music Corporation and Warner-Tamerlane Publishing Corp (1995).

3 2Pac, "Keep Ya Head Up", *Strictly 4 My N.I.G.G.A.Z* (1993), Interscope. Copyright Daryl L Anderson, Tupac Amaru Shakur, Roger Troutman, Stan Vincent, Kama Sutra Music Inc, R2M Music, Rubber Band Music, Songs of Lastrada, Stan Vincent Music and Universal Music Corporation (1993).

4 2Pac, "Wonda Why They Call U Bitch", *All Eyez On Me*, (1996), Death Row/Interscope. Copyright Tupac Amaru Shakur, Universal Music Publishing (1996).

Till the Vocal Cords ~~Don't~~ Work: Redirecting Vehemence, Reimagining Power and Reclaiming Voice through the Lyrical Content of Marshall Mathers

K. E. Carver

I was twelve. Straight As, student council, class news–paper editor, jumping from one sport practice to another in order to make it to karate on time, doing homework days in advance because it was easy — *that* kid. Report cards were invisible, innocuous in my house: where my friends would get rewarded with a video game or grounded for a week, we barely looked at the things.

But if those grades didn't get me a new PS2 game every quarter, they *were* what convinced my mom to go into that HMV in the mall and buy the CDs.

Because as a young white girl in rural Ohio, it was my mother I convinced to make the purchase for me, given that I couldn't even *pretend* that I looked old enough to beat the Parental Advisory sticker. *You're not a troublemaker*, she reasoned as I stood outside; *you're a Straight-A kid*, she said as I reminded her: two albums.

Dark colours. They'll have big black-and-white stickers warning about content and stuff but it's just, like, a technicality. Do you remember what they're called? Are you sure?

Are you *sure* you're sure?

I opened them as soon as we got in the car and put the first one in. My mother narrowed her eyes at the art on the disc — *Is that a pill?*

(Yes.)

I pushed the disc in, let it latch and feed into the player.

Because I was twelve. Straight A student. I was frustrated, I was misunderstood, I grew up as the third member of my parents' dysfunctional marriage, an adult before my time and yet still a teenager, in the middle of nowhere with just the cows and the cornfields for company. Big fish, small pond; nothing special, not *really*, but unfed, unchallenged and stagnant for it. Stewing. Withering. Crawling inside my own skin.

And that made me *angry*.

And the first time I heard Eminem craft a rhyme, it felt like I was hearing someone who was angry, too, and angry because it felt like the world was failing them. And owning the two major-label albums that were out at the time — *The Slim Shady LP* and *The Marshall Mathers LP* — somehow validated the idea that I wasn't alone.

By the first day of school, however, in the kind of environment that held an annual "Drive Your Tractor to School" day, my t-shirt with the album art from the recently-dropped *The Eminem Show* proved immediately noteworthy. Intriguing: people I'd never talked to before came up and asked in apparent shocked, *I* liked *Eminem*?

Off-putting: vague frowns from teachers who couldn't *really* say anything, particularly not to the "good student" who helped clean up the lab stations at the end of class. And perhaps the thing that stuck with me most, divisive: *how*, a friend I'd known since the beginning of elementary school asked, *can you like his music? How can you like the things he says?*

It was that question — which was asked innocently, and was, I later learned, a parroting of the kid's mother's reasons for not buying *him* the new album — which introduced me in my early teens to the quandary of whether, how, and to what extent the media you enjoy and consume reflects upon you as a person. Because I was a good person, or I thought I was. I helped run tutoring sessions and mentoring groups, I volunteered for equal rights for minority and marginalised communities. I cared about people. The only goal I had in mind for any of the possible "things I wanted to be when I grew up" centred on the aim of helping others. So how *could* I like the music of an artist whose lyrics brutalise communities that I was and am a part of, that I value and that I'd been fighting and continue to fight for the rights and liberties of?

I was little more than twelve, though. And I was a straight-A student, sure. But at the time, I had other things to worry about. Like how to convince my dad to take me to Hot Topic over the weekend, given that my mom refused to go there because of the dark lighting, gated entrance and loud music that made my baby sister cry.

***

Yet everybody just feels like they can relate,
I guess words are a motherfucker they can be great
Or they can degrade, or even worse they can teach hate...
It's all political, if my music is literal, and I'm a criminal
    how the fuck can I raise a little girl
I couldn't, I wouldn't be fit to
— Eminem, "Sing For The Moment", 2002[1]

The fact is, we often don't know what ails us — or likewise, what drives us — when it first starts to burn. Frequently it takes time to recognise the cause. And the question that stuck with me, begging the examination of the entanglement of content, quality and morality in one's media preferences, that question never went away — in part because it was poignant, but also in part because I grew up. I went to college. I studied religion and philosophy, psychology and neuroscience, and literature and cultural theory, and you don't *get* to stop asking those sorts of questions when you pick those kinds of fields. And I picked those kinds of fields because I didn't *want* to stop asking those sorts of questions.

So, sure: clinical research has been generally inconclusive on whether, how, and to what degree media violence — music being just one of its presentations — influences one's actions, perceptions, biases, prejudices or inclinations toward violence, or shapes our sense of self. The history of literature, of writing and putting words together with or without music to match, has been coloured with authors' candid exemplifications of how words are pure reflections, pure *expressions*, of the human condition: whether Hemingway is telling you to "sit down at a typewriter and bleed", or Nin observing that written words contain the "taste" of life itself, or Vonnegut imagining the process of finding and telling story as

> [reaching] in with a thumb and forefinger to a point directly beneath his or her epiglottis. There is the free end of a spool of tape there. I pinched it, then pulled it out gradually, gently, so as not to make the student gag. When I got several feet of it out where we could see it, the student and I read what was written there.

Each of these making clear that story is reflective of, at its least, or constitutive of, at most, the deepest parts of the self.

Feuerbach's ever-quotable *"Der Mensch ist was er isst"*, perhaps, spoke best to my persistent question: man is what he eats; you *are* what you consume, but I'd argue this is true only in so far as it reflects a need inside. And sometimes: you consume what you need so that the hunger, the *need*, doesn't consume *you*.

Look at theories in perception, for instance, in the ways attention is drawn from art to advertising: we tend to turn toward things that shock, that trigger an immediate, unconscious response — but as humans, we tend to *resonate* with the things that are already in us, and we tend to gloss over the things that don't feed us, or that are incompatible — even to the point of being absolutely antithetical to our own beliefs and desires, so long as that *one nugget of resonance* is strong enough: feeds our need enough, in just the right one. Fills just the right void.

So for me: the thing that ailed took a long time to reveal itself, and it revealed itself like a flower, unfolding; like an onion, by layers and with tears you can't hold back. As a teenager, I was "depressed" like all teenagers and I was told I'd grow out of it — I didn't. As a woman, I was smart, I could do anything, I was convinced that the times were changing and sexism was dying — it didn't. As an activist, I stood up for the rights of those who faced prejudice and hate because, while I wasn't one of them, I was myself in a darker corner, more quiet and unnoticed but still on the outside, still different and "other" — maybe more so, in some ways, than the communities I could *see* being pushed to the sidelines.

And as a scholar, I finally gained the courage to own the one fundamental truth about myself that I'd always held, the deepest of all the hungers: I am a writer. I am in love with words. So as a poet at heart and an author in my bones, I hear words themselves like music. I savour words like fine wine and appreciate the symphonic resonations of their pairings. I believe in and thrive off the challenge of stringing words together in ways that tell a story — that speak to that neurological imperative of how we largely see and know the world — that sing preternatural to the unspeakable and unnameable Reality of Being; that is visceral and resonant and gives shape and form and can be felt in the marrow.

And language, prose, poetry, lyric: *language* is for wrangling, for confessing, for creating and renewing and sharing as communion and offering in the kind of grace that Mary Oliver speaks to: *I don't know what it is exactly, but I'll take it.*

I don't know what it is, either. But I *can* speak to what it can evoke, and perhaps also to what we miss in it, by thinking it too pure, too beyond our mortal coil; by allowing it to reside in cathedrals and doctrines higher than a human reach. Because well-wrangled words are like well-wrangled anything (and I speak to that as a farm girl when I was only small): they deal in truths, even when they're ugly, and they don't mask those truths, no — they let those truths shape beauty sometimes made of hurt, or wrath, or hate or despair. Because even "good" people are human. And humans have a vast breadth of experience, of feeling, and songs of joy and praise and giddy wonder speak only to one pole of that glorious, heartbreaking spectrum.

And we, as humans, need feeding, need filling. We crave the *whole*.

Music, perhaps most earnestly the kind that deals in the shadows of human feeling, often seeks to fill the voids that sting worst, often speaks to the neglected spaces.

That filling, that speaking, that resonance: that *must* be some kind of grace.

***

The first song I resonated with like this in Eminem's oeuvre was the ominously titled "Kill You", rife with violence and misogyny, murder and rape, abuse and incest and all sorts of horrible reflections of the human spectrum, none of which I agreed with, all of which appalled me in practice:

Slut, you think I won't choke no whore
'Til the vocal cords don't work in her throat no more?
   [...]
Shut up, slut! You're causing too much chaos
Just bend over and take it like a slut; okay, Ma?
"Oh, now he's raping his own mother
Abusing a whore, snorting coke
And we gave him the Rolling Stone cover?"
You're goddamn right, bitch, and now it's too late
I'm triple platinum and tragedies happened in two
    states
I invented violence, you vile venomous volatile
    vicious
Vain Vicodin, vrin vrin vrin!
Texas Chainsaw, left his brains all
Dangling from his neck, while his head barely hangs
    on
Blood, guts, guns, cuts
Knives, lives, wives, nuns, sluts;
Bitch, I'mma kill you

But its vehemence sounded more like passion, its threats never striking home so much as its desperation, its need to be heard. And the chorus:

You don't wanna fuck with Shady (Why?)
'Cause Shady will fucking kill you.[2]

That chorus wasn't about *killing*, not for me, and not for Mathers himself. It was not about taking life, but about redirecting anger at the status quo and the hypocrisies of the social order, of accepted mores and what "acceptable" means in itself, particularly after opening the song itself with a brief recap of the abuse he suffered by his own mother; his own victimisation. By re-envisioning where *power* was to be found, and what it looked like, the message wasn't about violence against women — the cheeky coda of "Ha ha, I'm just playing ladies / You know I love you" aside. Rather, it was about violence as appalling, and society as warping, as damaging in its perverse, degrading and dehumanising mores, fantasies and expectations.

For me, precocious until *I* was a challenge, an inconvenience, a threat to ascendency and the established order, I latched onto this idea that "fucking" with *me* was a thing unthinkable because I would retaliate, dismantle something cherished, held dear if pushed too far: that thing being a structure that held me at bay, that clipped my wings. *That* was a sudden and fierce reclamation, where the words were the metaphors they were meant to be, speaking to the complexity of emotions that don't fit literalisms, and that aren't made to: it was a reimagining of power, a communion between myself and the author, the rapper, the idea where I could sink into its truth, the core of its feeling, spat with personal hate and a vendetta that itself sounded violent, and yet: the song was not about choking bitches and screwing whores.

It was a discourse on power: the vocal cords choked until they "don't work" in the "throat no more" was desperate, was lashing out as any animal caged: it was a call to arms, perhaps in language more morally grey than necessary, but *powerful* because it spoke about the *powerless*, from one side or another. One topic's treatise inside another, twisted and violent and cyclical as violence too often is, Simone Weil's *Poem of Force* reenacted for a new millennium: the perpetrator a victim, over and again. And perhaps, if one is pushed too far, the cycle dies, breaks. Maybe that's the *only* way. In the words of Margaret Atwood: "A word after a word after a word is power." *This* was *power*.

Similarly, tracks like "'Till I Collapse" and "Lose Yourself" became anthems of power, of seizing opportunity and preparing for the battle of daily life against the weight of the world:

> 'Cause sometimes you just feel tired,
> Feel weak, and when you feel weak, you feel like you
> wanna just give up.
> But you gotta search within you, you gotta find that
> inner strength
> And just pull that shit out of you and get that
> motivation to not give up
> And not be a quitter, no matter how bad you wanna
> just fall flat on your face and collapse.[3]

"Lose Yourself", on the other hand, became a national anthem of sorts. Guinness Record Holder for "Longest Running Single at Number One for a Rap Song" that it is, it not only reclaims power but also voice. It speaks, again, to taking one's circumstances in hand and rising to the challenge: the very thing I was so angry about as a teenager being the *lack* of challenge. From athletic teams to the President of the United States, the message of this song has been used to "psych-up" some of the most talented and respected members of modern society, all while explicitly encouraging its precise impact in practice: *lose yourself in the music, the moment, you own it.*

*You better **never let it go**.*[4]

Beyond all of these redefinitions of what it meant to take anger and transmute it into drive, to use it as power, to claim it with voice, it wasn't under I got older — until the depression wasn't a phase and my womanhood proved a hindrance and my "otherness" was an oddity that made me all the more strange and wrong and broken-in-need-of-fixing — it wasn't until I was old enough to connect the dots and listen deeper, to see the petals of the blossom and the layers of the onion not only in myself, but in the music, that it became all the more clear.

The struggle, and the hate, and the violence to the Other: it was there in the lyrics — more prominent, more inclusive in recent years, but present in the past nevertheless. The shock took precedence, drew attention: overpowered and overshadowed — but beneath was the feeling. The resonance. That necessary human "hook" that supersedes and draws in.

In "Kill You", the lyrical bombardment of violence against women is followed in the last verse with revelation, vulnerability, and a sense of loathing for circumstance and arguably, to some extent, for self:

Know why I say these things?
Cause ladies' screams keep creeping in Shady's dreams
And the way things seem, I shouldn't have to pay these shrinks

this eighty G's a week to say the same things tweece

—

Twice? Whatever, I hate these things[5]

And again on the track "The Way I Am":

And since birth I've been cursed with this curse to
    just curse
And just blurt this berserk and bizarre shit that works
And it sells and it helps in itself to relieve
All this tension dispensing these sentences
Getting this stress that's been eating me recently off
    of this chest[6]

These resonances speak to the layers, to the imbalances, to the dark parts we *don't* speak of and the thoughts we cannot control for reasons of societal messages, stray neuronal firings and everything in between — these resonances, these moments of honesty amidst the flash and bombast, all guns and knives and shootouts and sexual deviance: the *real* message, the vulnerabilities confessed made me feel heard, feel seen. It was liberating; empowering. There was some unconventional *communitas*, a leveling. Equal ground. Close your eyes and let the music wash over and forget the boundaries, and find the spirit of the thing at the core.

More recent songs speak to the now. "The Monster", specifically, touches on the existential issues of depression, overthinking and anxiety ("Yeah, pondering'll do you wonders / No wonder you're losing your mind the way it wanders") and the whole potential host of one's personal demons with the chorus:

I'm friends with the monster that's under my bed
Get along with the voices inside of my head
You're trying to save me, stop holding your breath
And you think I'm crazy, yeah, you think I'm crazy
Well that's not fair.

And while I'm not a child anymore, that strikes truer than any other message in the music of Marshall Mathers, because for all the violence against women, against minorities; for all the hate and vitriol, all the shock-value train wrecks that ensnare the eyes (or ears, in this case) but not the soul: one of the last messages of this particular song rings out the true value, the true meaning — it resonates:

I ain't here to save the fucking children
But if one kid out of a hundred million
Who are going through a struggle feels it and then
relates that's great[7]

And it is: great, that is. Because I'm a woman, and there is violence, but I have a voice. I struggle with mental illness, but I "feel" it, and if you think I'm crazy? Well, that's just not fair. And for every moment I'm too tired, where I feel too weak to endure: there is a message, and it broke records and sold millions — not the violence. Not the shock-and-awe and blood-and-guts. No.

According to Carl Sagan, "Writing is perhaps the greatest of human invention, binding people together, citizens of distant epochs, who never knew one another. Books break the shackles of time — proof that humans can work magic."

And *that* is what sells: the magic in the words, in the meaning beneath the smokescreen: the idea that we're not alone, and that for all the monsters we fight and befriend, we reclaim a voice that is heard, we perform alchemy on our rage and make it fuel to overcome and we see power in the process — and in ourselves, somehow; resonant.

Some act of unspeakable grace.

Notes

1 Eminem, "Sing For the Moment," *The Eminem Show* (2002), Aftermath Entertainment/Shady Records/ Interscope Records. Copyright Jeff Bass, Marshall B Mathers III, Steven Tyler, Eight Mile Style Music, Music of Stage Three Aerosmith Account (2002)

2 Eminem, "Kill You", *The Marshall Mathers LP* (2000), Aftermath Entertainment/Shady Records/Interscope Records. Copyright Melvin Charles Bradford, Marshall Mathers, Andre Romell Young, Eight Mile Style Music, Ain't Nothin But Funkin' Music, Hard Working Black Folk Inc, Kobalt Music Publishing Limited, Societe P E C F, W B Music Corp (2000)

3 Eminem, "Till I Collapse", *The Eminem Show* (2002), Aftermath Entertainment/Shady Records/Interscope Records. Copyright Nathan D Hale, Marshall Mathers, Brian Harold May, Luis Edgardo Resto, Beechwood Music Corporation, Eight Mile Style Music, Nate Dogg Music, Reach Global Songs, Resto World Music and Universal Music Operations Ltd (2002)

4 Eminem, "Lose Yourself", *8 Mile* (2002), Aftermath Entertainment/Shady Records/Interscope Records. Copyright Jeffrey Irwin Bass, Marshall B Mathers III, Luis Edgardo Resto, Eight Mile Style Music, Kobalt Music Publishing Limited, Resto World Music and Universal Music Operations Ltd (2002)

5 Eminem, "Kill You", *The Marshall Mathers LP* (2000), Aftermath Entertainment/Shady Records/Interscope Records. Copyright Melvin Charles Bradford, Marshall Mathers, Andre Romell Young, Eight Mile Style Music, Ain't Nothin But Funkin' Music, Hard Working Black

Folk Inc, Kobalt Music Publishing Limited, Societe P E C F, W B Music Corp (2000)

6 Eminem, "The Way I Am", *The Marshall Mathers LP* (2000), Aftermath Entertainment/Shady Records/ Interscope Records. Copyright Marshall Mathers and Eight Mile Style Music (2000)

7 Eminem feat. Rihanna, "The Monster", *The Marshall Mathers LP* 2 (2013), Aftermath Entertainment/ Shady Records/Interscope Records. Copyright Maki Athanasiou, Jonathan David Bellion, Robyn R Fenty, Bryan G Fryzel, Aaron L Kleinstub, Marshall B Mathers III, Annarhi Music LLC, Art in the Fodder Music, BMG Bumblebee, BMG Platinum Songs US, Cashonlee Trax, EMI Blackwood Music Inc, Freq Show Music, Kiss Me If You Can Music, Primary Wave Beats, Reach Music Songs, Shroom Shady Music, Songs of a Beautiful Mind and Songs of Universal (2013)

From Enslavement to Obliteration: Extreme Metal's Problem with Women

Jasmine Hazel Shadrack

What happens when you love a form of music that doesn't love you back?[1] As a fan and performer of extreme metal for the last twenty years I, like many other women who love metal, have observed a problematic paradigm concerning extreme metal and women — more specifically, the obliterated female body, which exists as artwork, lyrical content and in band names. Even though the musical structure, technical and virtuosic playing and production qualities of these songs are undeniably brilliant, the content and ideological packaging can be deeply sexist. From Cannibal Corpse' "Fucked with a Knife" (*The Bleeding*, 1994) to Prostitute Disfigurement's "On Her Guts I Cum" (*Embalmed Madness*, 2001), it is important to analyse why violence against women exists as aesthetic and lyrical content when this form of "extremity" is a reality for too many women. There is no denying that extreme metal offers its listeners a lot

— solidarity, escape, a sense of empowerment — but there has to come a point when we must examine the content to demonstrate what exactly is being said given the socio-cultural reality of violence against women. When reality reflects art, a response is necessary.

I love extreme metal. I have been a fan and performer of this music form for the best part of the last twenty years, and it has not escaped my notice that there are some artists that seem to have a problem with women. Extreme metal includes, but is not limited to, death metal, grindcore and black metal, and it is within these categories that I have found some problematic engagements. I could approach this as a musicologist, as a cultural theorist or as a psychoanalyst, but for the sake of presenting the analysis in the most open way possible, I am approaching it first and foremost as a woman who appreciates extreme music as well as composing and performing it. As such, identifying how the category of "woman" is hailed, referenced and represented, and how extreme metal demonstrates and manifests hegemonic responses to women, is important to me.

Patriarchy as Structure: Frame and Performance

Metal's overarching metanarrative is a patriarchal one. If popular music as an overarching frame foregrounds the access and success of the masculine, then guitar-based music is perhaps the worst offender. Marion Leonard suggests that "rock has variously been described as a male form, male-run, masculine and misogynist".[2]

Metal, as a heavier extension of rock, performs that masculinity more overtly. Robert Walser suggests:

> Male bonding itself becomes crucial to the reception of metal that depends on masculine display, for it helps [to] produce and sustain consensus about meaning. Excripting texts do occasionally refer to sexuality, but typically as just another arena for enactment of male power. Mutual erotic pleasure rarely appears in the lyrics of heavy metal, just as it is seldom discussed by men in any other context. Metal shields men from the dangers of pleasure — loss of control — but also enables display, sometimes evoking images of armoured, metalised male bodies.[3]

Metal can be understood as male fantasies of empowerment that operate through the excription of women.[4] Representations of brotherhood, male bonding and images of metalised, male bodies performing masculine music forms are prevalent in the work of bands from Venom to Burzum. Deena Weinstein suggests that "the anti-female posturing of heavy metal stars relates less to misogyny than to a rejection of the cultural values associated with femininity",[5] but forcing a rupture between misogynist responses to women because of the cultural values associated with femininity is still sexist.

The "overtly macho subgenre[s]"[6] of rock, metal and extreme metal operate inside an already masculinist popular music frame. In their analysis of "cock rock", Simon Frith and Angela McRobbie suggest that "cock rock performers are defined as aggressive, dominating and boastful... Women, in their eyes, are either sexually aggressive and therefore doomed and unhappy, or else sexually repressed and therefore in need of male servicing".[7] The further into metal subgenres one travels, the more aggravated this framework becomes. Metal can be understood as a masculinist closed network, with male musicians performing to a predominantly male demographic that seems to function through the excription of women in musical form and as performers, yet appears happy to retain the use of women as aesthetic content.

The cultural values associated with womanhood and being female that are produced and developed by wholly masculinist hegemonic production enshrines and perpetuates its essentialist gender binary through its power differentials. Loving a popular music form that exists on the periphery of the social mainstream, it is easy to assume that with a rejection of the hegemony, there would also be a rejection of that gender binary — but this is not the case. Extreme metal is constructed, articulated and replicated as a masculine genre; the virtuosity and dexterity required to compose and perform it has its legacy in patriarchal cultural practices such as lead guitar solos and traditional band formations which are occupied in the main by men. These notions are set against the back drop of an assumption of female passivity.

Examining the Evidence:
The Misogynist Noise Makers

One of extreme metal's subgenres is death metal, a valuable example of which is the band Cannibal Corpse. Their back catalogue, whilst with singer Chris Barnes (1988–1995), was lyrically focussed around violence against women and abuse; their 1994 album *The Bleeding* showcased song titles including "Fucked with a Knife", "Stripped, Raped and Strangled" and "She was Asking for It". In his text *Choosing Death: The Improbable History of Death Metal and Grindcore*, Albert Mudrian quotes an interview with Arch Enemy's then-vocalist Angela Gossow, who states:

> I loved Cannibal Corpse's *Eaten Back to Life*, because it was so extreme at the time when I was a kid, but I didn't sing along with those lyrics... It's somehow just a bit intimidating. It's so much about violence against women. It's not a guy who's being totally shredded — it's always women... I just don't know how they can justify that.[8]

Certainly during the Chris Barnes era, Cannibal Corpse's shock value may have seemed more significant, but it pales in comparison with more contemporary examples such as the band Prostitute Disfigurement, whose misogynist position also extends to homosexual and LGBTQ communities. Their 2001 debut *Embalmed Madness* (re-released in 2003 through Unmatched Brutality Records) features songs called "Chainsaw Abortion", "On Her Guts I Cum", "Cadaver Blowjob" and

"Rotting Away Is Better Than Being Gay". Other examples such as "Deformed Slut", "Postmortal Devirginized", "She's Not Coming Home Tonight" and "Cum Covered Stab Wounds" (taken from *Deeds of Derangement*, 2003) also clearly detail their ideological position. Their 2005 and 2007 releases through Neurotic Records, *Left In Grisly Fashion* and *Descendants of Depravity*, seem to retract back into a more expected death metal lyrical format by not foregrounding gender in the song titles. Their 2014 release *From Crotch To Crown*, however, sees a return to the misogyny and anti-LGBT position of previous records with examples such as "Dismember The Transgender". Other song titles — "Battered To The Grave", "Under The Patio" and "Reduced To Stumps" — infer intimate partner violence without immediately identifying the gender of the victim, but given the context, history and name of the band, only serve to add to the existent problematic assumption that the victim is always a woman and deserving of brutality.

There is a possibility that they are using their band name, artwork and lyrics to foreground these issues, like the vegan band Cattle Decapitation. However, if that were the case, I'd have hoped for band members to be active in preventative measures and local charities that support victims of domestic violence.

Additionally, the caveat is also on the decoding of their total artworks by fans; namely if their ideological response is not clear, then one can assume they see no problem with what they are doing.

What's in a Word: Extremity as *Carte Blanche*

These examples tell us something. They speak of *extremity* as a fundamental part of what extreme metal is. Extremity as a concept that is inherently bound in violence and horror exists sonically and aesthetically; the distortion of the guitars and vocals and jackhammer drumming gives the timbral assault that exceeds its boundaries and exists as the haptic void, the "hypothetical total or maximal level of intensity. It is the horizon of the history of metal".[9] With this sonic brutality comes an equally brutal aesthetic representation, so that no one part of a band's artistic output can be accused of not being extreme and by extension weaker than its contemporaries. If it is to be considered weaker, then it is perceived as feminine, and in extreme metal terms, this is not acceptable.

Performed masculinity that manifests in sonically brutal music, aesthetically brutal lyrics, song names, band names and artwork, must all align for its artistic cohesion against the opposite of its core foundations to be authentic; it must represent the male as juridical system that enshrines and perpetuates itself and reproduces subjects in its own image. This representational discourse seeks to support existing essentialist gender binaries and their associated power differentials. Foucault notes that "juridical systems of power produce the subjects they subsequently come to represent".[10] The male as gatekeeper in metal is not only the default authority, but also the hegemonic juridical system that produces and reproduces its masculine frame: the male in metal discourse is the totality.

When I have pointed this out, I have been shut down as a Social Justice Warrior and told I am preventing freedom of speech. But calling out misogyny is not an attack on freedom of speech, it is necessary. Just because something exists in art, does not mean it is acceptable in reality. However, the idea of extremity seems to reduce the traction gained by arguments against it. Natalie Purcell states:

> Given the extreme nature of Death Metal, it is no surprise that the lyrical content is equally extreme and very often offensive, disturbing, and disgusting to the average outsider. [...] Often lyrics are poorly written (or even composed by foreign band members with little grasp of the language in which they write). For this reason, it is generally accepted that the lyrics in Death Metal (like album art and band photos) serve predominantly as a means for bands to promote an image that visually displays the aggression and extremity of their music.[11]

If ever there was a statement that read like an apologist *carte blanche*, this is it. I do not count myself as "the average outsider", given my involvement in extreme metal, and yet I still find Cuntscrape and Prostitute Disfigurement problematic. I am not easily shocked by the content and there is a reason for this: violence against women goes beyond being offended. The lived experience of most women can include domestic violence, rape, stalking, sexual harassment, rape in war, all of which happen within a culturally sexist framework that uses language to assert male dominance over us. Under patriarchal rule, we are fighting for our lives.

So this begs the question, who is this extremity for? How is this "extreme" when it becomes the normative modes of address and engagement that women are forced to deal with? In the UK alone, the figures are damning. Domestic violence affects one in four women in their lifetime and on average, two women are murdered each week by a current of former partner, with police data showing a rise in recorded sexual offences in the UK, the latest figures of which are up 29% on the previous year; equivalent to an additional 23,349 offences and bringing the total to over 100,000 in a single year for the first time (103,614). The numbers of reported rapes (34,741) and other sexual offences (68,873) were at the highest level recorded since the introduction of the National Crime Recording Standard in March 2003.[12] These are the reported statistics and the "real" figures are considerably higher.

Given the data, violence against women could be understood as an epidemic of very serious proportions, so forgive me if I don't cheer on extreme metal bands who think this is a source for artistic inspiration. Purcell's statement appears to confer a free pass onto death metal because it is supposed to be extreme, but there are a great many extreme problems in contemporary society — so many that artists are spoilt for choice. Would it not be incredible for a death metal band to compose a song on the light judicial treatment of rapists such as Brock Turner, or on police brutality against African-Americans? That is worthy of artistic competence, not penning lyrics called "On Her Guts I Cum". Really. Grow up.

There is a tipping point, and bands such as Prostitute Disfigurement are the axis. If I like their riffs for example, enough to buy their merchandise, can I in good conscience wear a t-shirt that promotes violence against women? No, I cannot. I refuse to walk around with the words "Prostitute Disfigurement" written across my breasts, because what does that say about me? That I am co-opting my own oppression? There a lot of amazing death metal bands (Decapitated are my favourite!) who do not need to use violence against women to manifest their representations of extremity. And if this really was an issue of free speech, then the consequences of that speech should mean these artists should be held to account.

Conclusion: Surviving the Game

I would like to write *#notallmetal*, but without it functioning as an exact parallel to *#notallmen*. I know, and am grateful, that there is a balance of sorts — that for every Prostitute Disfigurement there is a Napalm Death. Whilst not all death metal or black metal or grindcore is as explicitly misogynist as the bands featured here, they do all function within the sexist power differentials of a hegemony that tells women we are not welcome, we are too much, not enough, too loud, too opinionated, not good enough. But then, we get all of this misery anyway because we all live inside the frame that produces and enshrines it. So what do we do, where does this leave us?

I borrow a term here from post-colonial theory, that of "Writing Back to Empire". This term sees indigenous authors writing back to various modes of imperialism, but particularly the British Empire, as a form of reclamation and emancipation. What I take from this is the idea that art, writing, music and performance can be a mechanism to counter that imperialism. In this context, I call it "Performing Back to Patriarchy". Even though, as Gayatri Spivak notes, "when one takes a whack at shaking up the dominant structure, one sees how consolidated the opposition is",[13] we must continue to occupy space online, at gigs and on stages. We must continue to produce art — and if that involves calling out dearly loved musical forms, then so be it. We cannot and must not, stop. By using these formats to occupy space as women in extreme metal, whether as journalists, musicians, photographers or promoters, we must seek collectively to take up space that is otherwise demarcated as "not ours".

I am glad there are extreme metal bands such as Denigrata, Mortals and Castrator (who deserve articles in their own right!) who foreground women. Our ability to connect and perform extreme music is just as vital and brilliant as anyone else's. I will always love extreme metal and I will always be a feminist. And so we play...

Notes

1 See Dawes, Laina. *What Are You Doing Here?: A Black Woman's Life and Liberation in Heavy Metal*. (Bazillion Points Press, 2012).

2 Leonard, Marion. *Gender in the Music Industry*. (Ashgate, 2007) p. 19.

3 Walser, Robert. *Running with the Devil: Power, Gender, and Madness in Heavy Metal Music*. (Wesleyan University Press, 1993) p. 116.

4 The term "excription" is taken from Robert Walser's text *Running with the Devil: Power, Gender, and Madness in Heavy Metal Music* (Weslyan University Press, 1993). It is used expressly to identify the "writing out" and obfuscation of women's roles in heavy metal and has become a key signifier in metal academia when analysing gender, sexuality and representation.

5 Weinstein, Deena. *Heavy Metal: The Music and its Culture*. (Da Capo Press, 2000) p. 67.

6 Leonard, *Gender in the Music Industry* p. 19.

7 Frith, Simon and McRobbie, Angela. "Rock and Sexuality". In *On Record: Rock, Pop and the Written Word*. (Routledge, 1991) p. 373.

8 Quoted in Mudrian, Albert. *Choosing Death: The Improbable History of Death Metal and Grindcore*. (Feral House, 2004) p. 251.

9 Hunt-Hendrix, Hunter. "Transcendental Black Metal". In Masciandaro, N. (ed.) *Hideous Gnosis*. (Open Access Creative Commons, 2010) p. 55.

10 Quoted in Butler, Judith. *Gender Trouble: Feminism and the Subversion of Identity*. (Routledge, 1990) p. 2.

11 Purcell, Natalie. *Death Metal Music: The Passion and Politics of a Subculture*. (McFarland Press, 2003) p. 39.

12 Taken from http://www.ons.gov.uk.
13 Spivak, Gayatri. "Can the Subaltern Speak?". In *The Post-Colonial Studies Reader*. (Routledge, 1993) p. 16.

Bibliography

Barron, Lee. "Dworkin's Nightmare: Porngrind as the Sound of Feminist Fears". In *Heavy Metal: Controversies and Counterculture*. (Equinox Publishing, 2013).

Bayton, Mavis. *Frock Rock: Women Performing Popular Music*. (Oxford University Press, 2003).

Bourdage, Monique. *From Tinkerers to Gods: The Electric Guitar and the Social Construction of Gender*. (Auraria Digital Press, 2007).

Butler, Judith. *Gender Trouble: Feminism and the Subversion of Identity*. (Routledge, 1990).

Dawes, Laina. *What Are You Doing Here?: A Black Woman's Life and Liberation in Heavy Metal*. (Bazillion Points Press, 2012).

Hjelm, Titus et al. *Heavy Metal: Controversies and Countercultures*. (Equinox Publishing, 2013).

Hunt-Hendrix, Hunter. "Transcendental Black Metal". In Masciandaro, N. (ed.), *Hideous Gnosis*. (Open Access Creative Commons, 2010).

Jeffries, Sheila. *The Sexuality Debates*. (Routledge, 2010).

Kahn-Harris, Keith. *Extreme Metal: Music and Culture on the Edge*. (Berg Publishers, 2007).

Leonard, Marion. *Gender in the Music Industry*. (Ashgate, 2007).

Frith, Simon and McRobbie, Angela. "Rock and Sexuality". In *On Record: Rock, Pop and the Written Word*. (Routledge, 1991).

Massey, Doreen. *Space, Place and Gender*. (Polity Press, 2013).

McClary, Susan. *Feminine Endings: Music, Gender and Sexuality*. (University of Minnesota Press, 1991).

Mudrian, Albert. *Choosing Death: The Improbable History of Death Metal and Grindcore*. (Feral House, 2004).

Purcell, Natalie. *Death Metal Music: The Passion and Politics of a Subculture.* (McFarland Press, 2003).

Sarelin, Mikael. "Masculinities within Black Metal: Heteronormativity, Protest Masculinity or Queer". In *Reflections in the Metal Void.* (Interdisciplinary Press, 2016).

Shepherd, John. *Music as Social Text.* (Press, 1991).

Spivak, Gayatri. "Can the Subaltern Speak?". In *The Post-Colonial Studies Reader.* (Routledge, 1993).

Walser, Robert. *Running with the Devil: Power, Gender, and Madness in Heavy Metal Music.* (Wesleyan University Press, 1993).

Weinstein, Deena. *Heavy Metal: The Music and its Culture.* (Da Capo Press, 2000).

Bourdage, Monique. "A Young Girl's Dream: Examining the Barriers facing Female Electric Guitarists". *IASPM* 1:1, 2010. pp. 1–16.

Discography

Cannibal Corpse. *Eaten Back to Life.* (Metal Blade Records, 1990).

_____. *The Bleeding,* (Metal Blade Records, 1994).

Prostitute Disfigurement. *Embalmed Madness.* (Unmatched Brutality Records, 2003).

_____. *Deeds of Derangement.* (Morbid Records, 2003).

_____. *Left in Grisly Fashion.* (Neurotic Records, 2005).

_____. *Descendants of Depravity.* (Neurotic Records, 2007).

_____. *From Crotch to Crown.* (Willowtip Records, 2014).

I've Got Your Letter, You've Got My Song: On *Pinkerton*

Marissa Chen

Before the British and mass immigration, there were the nuns. The ones who made me were plucked from French villages like Surriauville and La Bouille two hundred years ago and promised to Christ like a crop of new peaches. While the tricolor was being hammered into the neck of neighbouring Indochina, the sisters of the Infant Jesus turned their eyes to less liquid commodities — little Oriental girls.

I fell in love with Weezer's *Pinkerton* in a place its narrator would have considered a veritable wet dream — a girls-only Catholic school located nearly 4,000 kilometres and a seven-hour plane ride from the westernmost tip of Japan. Rivers Cuomo was himself a boy when the songs were conceived in the frigid halls of Harvard University, synchronous with a Puccini obsession and an inelegant recovery from corrective foot surgery. Lonely, angry and implacably horny, he sought kinship in the fantasy of *Madame Butterfly*, the cautionary opera depicting the perils of interracial romance and nineteenth-century *Japonisme*, a movement encompassing van Gogh, Gauguin and Frank Lloyd Wright — but also men whose thinly disguised obsession with geishas would prevail as unequivocal authorities on Western art. Our countries didn't have the same languages. We weren't even technically East Asian. The British saw to it that Singapore's multiculturalism ran deep in the congenital, and reciting the Lord's Prayer when a quarter of the class happened to be Muslim had always seemed to me a fact of basic statistics. The nuns must have realised they stood no real chance against an immigrant nation devoted to the cult of the free market, but they decided, as history did, that we would have to do.

School sessions ran from Primary (Year) 1 through to the GCSEs, meaning two-thirds of our lives would have been spent in the company of 2,400 girls by the time we were sixteen. Our transition to secondary school was marked by the disappearance of baby fat and the corresponding trend of hiking our pinafores five inches past regulation length. It was a maths teacher who gently broached the "problem" of our developing bodies and the importance of sitting like ladies. Now that we were teenagers, the sight of bare thighs in the classroom was no longer matter-of-fact, but a sign of impending threat.

"What if we had a guest?" she said. "A male guest."

We never had guests. We had glimpses that warranted the faintest of visions, backlit magazine pages containing names like JC and AJ which we then Sellotaped to textbooks and circulated under our desks. For the most part though, we were obsessed with each other in the only way girls could've been, since for so long our orbits were comprised of nothing else.

***

It was a tradition of my father's to listen to BBC World Service in the morning, cranking the volume up between broadcasts to intercept Julian Marshall's blustery "This is London". I've known that musical passage[1] my entire life, but it would take twenty years and a phlegmatic bagpiper at Seven Dials to inform me I'd been marching off to Catholic school with Protestant dissent ringing in my ears. My father's music collection was painfully uncool, even for a dad — nothing that predated "Smoke Gets in Your Eyes" and nothing after the Bee Gees — but he let my sister and I play whatever we wanted as long as it was on his beloved home stereo system, a KGB-styled relic comprising a mammoth cassette deck and four studio monitors rigged to curtain rods for maximum surround.

In *The Importance of Music to Girls*, Lavinia Greenlaw calls the gift of a mix tape "the greatest act of love... It was the only way we could share music and it was also a way of advertising yourself." My friends and I turned thirteen at the start of the millennium, the last generation for whom radio was not a last resort.

Say It With Music was a legendary request show on which teenage reputations were made or broken. Between the hours of 9pm to 11pm on Mondays to Fridays, a perky DJ named Jean would read song dedications from listeners. Jean was no John Peel, so working knowledge of the Top 40 was essential if our letters stood any shot at appearing on *Say It With Music*. Never ever ever ever felt so alone. New Kids on the Block had a bunch of hits. We hedged our bets on

Britpop, Britney, the rise and thankful fall of nu-metal. My friends in particular took to R&B, waggling their unflared hips to Lauryn Hill, TLC, Aaliyah and 112's "Peaches and Cream":

> So sweet, so very wet
> So good, girl you make me sweat
> Girl I'm talkin' 'bout
> Peaches and cream
> I need it 'cause you know that I'm a fiend
> Gettin' freaky in my Bentley limousine
> It's even better when it's with ice cream
> Know what I mean?[2]

None of us did. But it wasn't enough just to hear your favourite song. *Say It With Music* was really about declaring allegiance to your tribe — "To my SEXY BABES from Class One-Seven! Jess, Ping, Daphne, Jules etc". As far as we were concerned, any song could be a love song, as long as it was given to somebody you love. We were at a loss to consider, as Tom Waits had, any possibility of beautiful melodies telling us terrible things.

***

My relationship with Weezer came down to guitar, and my relationship with guitar began when I was five and wanted nothing more in the world than piano lessons. I'd seen a girl playing "Für Elise" on TV in a fluffy pink dress with a bow. My mother knew the problem would be solved by buying me a pink dress. She also knew that if she played her cards right I would never back out of a deal for as long as I lived. Five months passed before she consented to paying for lessons — on the condition that I completed all eight grades of the ABRSM and not be allowed to quit. "Think about it", she warned. I said yes on the spot.

It took me nine years to complete eight years of the ABRSM (flubbing one exam in a thinly veiled attempt to undermine my mother), by which point I'd missed out on countless outings, parties and dates, and begged to quit over forty times. I wasn't simply lazy — I was bored. The sophistication and complexity of classical music theory might run rings around "I'm Goin' Down", but nobody would be caught dead requesting a Bartok concerto on *Say It With Music*. I was a competent player — years of acquired muscle memory will do that to anyone — but not nearly good enough to make music I wanted to hear.

Ignoring my mother's complaints about history repeating itself, I bought the cheapest guitar I could find — a Yamaha that had the timbre of a matchbox and rattled like an angry wasp whenever I grazed the lower E string — and set about teaching myself. By the end of the day my fingertips had swollen to the size of flank steaks, and my body burned with humiliation. Music theory might have taught me to compose for instruments like the clarinet and cello without having to learn how to play them, but the fretboard's alien terrain rendered this singularly useless. Years of pitch training made bum notes ten times more jarring to the ears. The sight of other people's fingers hurtling up and down the necks of guitars was like a sea of tongues in a congregation — supremely assured in their fluency and unintelligible to me.

My mother's plan worked. For too long I could only mime the shapes of songs I loved, turning incoherent frequencies over and over in my hands until, like joined-up writing, a new muscle memory bore its first lines.

***

The most famous chord progression of our time — I-V-vi-IV[3] — is so omnipresent that anyone who has heard a lick of pop music is likely to guess what chords come next in a verse from "Auld Lang Syne", or Springsteen's "I'm Goin' Down", even when hearing it for the first time. Worship songs also rely on pop progressions and repetitive verses to hammer home the message that God's love was not only awesome, it was catchy. I was nine before I realised that the "Hail" that preceded Mary was not a title (as in "Hail Doubtfire" or *Hey there wait a minute Hail Postman*).

During improvisation, jazz musicians are known to actively utilise both the brain's language centres — Broca's area in the frontal lobe for speech production and Wernicke's in the temporal for comprehension.[4] The recreational listener, on the other hand, tends to experience music as pure sound, the way we do when confronting an unfamiliar tongue for the first time. In this instance, the auditory systems are engaged, but the Broca's and Wernicke's areas remain dormant. A condition known as Wernicke's aphasia demonstrates how damage to the language centres can still lead to patients reproducing the grammar and syntax of normal speech fluently, though without corresponding awareness of what any of the words meant.

Tower Records was one of the only places in Singapore that bothered with English-language music outside of mainstream pop. Like everyone else who collected music as a teenager, this was where I finally ventured, alone, from the communal comforts of billboard radio and the Bee Gees into a great, very white yonder.

College rock, second-wave, "alt-rock", skate punk, emo-core — Weezer happened to fall into a long line of guitar bands I tried on for size, wagering time and patience until something fit. Many were boybanders dressed in Dickies, pumping sugary riffs out of distortion pedals and power chords, but it was precisely their pop *lingua franca* that made them instantly accessible. What fascinated me were the prodigal songs — those that answer reluctantly to I-V-vi-V, but with more obtuse lyrics, open tunings, and nine-minute run times — marking my infinite descent into back catalogues, defunct side projects and B-sides. *Pinkerton* was one of the first albums I bought after picking up guitar and the last Weezer album I would listen to from start to finish.

It opened with the nervous whine of a square wave synthesizer, and a bass line that became the sciatic nerve of:

I'm tired, so tired
I'm tired of having sex (so tired)
Arms spread so thin
I don't know who I am
Monday night I'm making Jen
Tuesday night I'm making Lynn
Wednesday night I'm making Catherine

Oh, why can't I be making love come true?
Help! Help![5]

I didn't recognise the names. What I remember best about "Tired Of Sex" is that indelible bass line — the moody descent that split like a thousand whips by the time the chorus rolled around. I would have followed it anywhere.

***

As an unspoken rule, any present-day defence of *Pinkerton* has to be exactly that — defensive. Released in 1996 on the heels of Weezer's multi-platinum self-titled debut, also known as *The Blue Album*, *Pinkerton* was a commercial flop and savaged by music magazines everywhere. Far from happy-go-lucky and certainly far from radio-friendly, the album was confounded by weird chromatics, abrupt key changes and tempo shifts. Songs were sliced up like arias, but strained under bales of fuzz so distorted my dad insisted I switched to headphones for fear they might destroy his precious monitors. Not only did *Pinkerton* straddle musical strata with the greatest of ease, it was loud.

But to even register these eccentricities, one had to wait out the words. Rivers Cuomo's voice howls incessantly over the rest of the band, entreating, lusting, then flat-out ranting against all the girls who had the audacity to not love him back — Denise, Therese, Louise, cello players, unattainable Asian teenagers ("God Damn You Half-Japanese Girls"), older women ("Mama It's All Your Fault"), even lesbians. "If everyone's a little queer", he rationalises self-righteously in "Pink Triangle", "Why can't she be a little straight?".[6]

Critics (most of them men) rightly took issue with *Pinkerton*'s problematic themes at first, calling them "juvenile" and "self-indulgent". *Melody Maker* conceded that "Weezer might write thumpingly irresistible choruses... [but] my advice is to ignore the lyrics entirely". *Magnet* simply wrote, "Sounds like the smell that shit makes". It was Cuomo who procured the final nail, denouncing his creation in an interview with *Rolling Stone* — "It's just a sick album, sick in a diseased sort of way... I never want to play those songs again; I never want to hear them again".

Pinkerton's bizarre transition from pariah to cult classic remains one of pop culture writing's biggest mysteries. The band went on release six more albums between 1996 and 2000, with *Pinkerton* written off as a blip on an otherwise illustrious career. Shortly after, it resurfaced unexpectedly on several best-of-the-decade lists, soared through the grapevine, and by 2009 was certified gold. A 2010 reissue of *Pinkerton* was met with universally glowing reviews (most of them from men) of the very tracks that drew such vitriol years ago. "Out of all the mainstream releases at the time, *Pinkerton* comes off looking like a rarity. It's the one album that didn't pander to its fans with soggy lyrics and polished sounds!"[7] Another *Consequence of Sound* feature declared "Across the Sea"[8], in which Cuomo describes "sniffing and licking" the "fragile and refined" stationery sent to him by a Japanese teenaged fan, as being "romantic... one of *Pinkerton*'s sweetest, most earnest songs". *Pitchfork*'s Ian Curtis gave the reissue a 10/10 rating, going so far as to call *Pinkerton* the "victim of a generation gap". Cuomo, too, would backtrack on his own criticism of *Pinkerton* multiple times, finally calling the album "great... super-deep, brave, and authentic... I can tell that I was really going for it when I wrote and recorded a lot of those songs".

The apologist chatter surrounding *Pinkerton* from conception soon devolved into the whitewashing of music history. Having just awarded full marks to an album containing the lines "If I'm a dog then you're a bitch", it seemed easier to erase the fact of its fetishising narrative than to be accountable for it. *NME*'s Emily Mackay questioned the legitimacy of the *Pitchfork* review, pointing out "there is never a line that hits home about the reality of human interaction. *Pinkerton* was not a masterpiece. It's creepy." In a heartbreaking essay about growing up in a predominantly white community in Long Island, Taiwanese-American poet Jenny Zhang says, "It embarrasses me to admit it now, but I used to worship the Weezer song, "Across The Sea" [...] I thought I should have been so lucky to be the girl in the song... There have been times when being described [as "fragile and refined"] has made me flush with pleasure, other times flush with disgust". British-Chinese songwriter Emma Lee-Moss (Emmy the Great) gravitated similarly towards the line while growing up in Hong Kong — "Unless you have lived in East Asia, you will not understand the sheer, particular delicacy of its stationary sets... Personally, I almost died when I found out "Across The Sea" was not about me".

I came to hear of *Pinkerton*'s odd history only after my own obsession with the album had peaked and waned. By the time I left university, YouTube was in full swing and Tower Records was no more. My tastes had predictably clambered backwards into the era of Dinosaur Jr. and Karp, leaving Weezer and its ilk a visible but fading point on the horizon. I was also starting to notice that guitar effects often had names like Camel Toe and Big Muff and Aqua Puss. Women were not a visible community in music forums, but nevertheless facilitated hours of heated debate — "DO HOT CHICKS LIKE GUYS WHO SHRED?!", "Name Girls Who Pwn at Guitar and Who Are Not Ugly" and "Girls playing guitar in an acceptional [sic] manner". I realised I'd been pledging membership to a club I didn't even have permission to be part of.

When asked about the preoccupation with Japanese culture in *Pinkerton*, Cuomo admits to being "fascinated by Asian girls. For some reason, they're particularly beautiful to me to me. I don't know why." While living in London, a creative writing tutor mentioned how disappointed he was that I hadn't chosen a "more Asian" setting for one of my stories. He later berated a female classmate for writing from the perspective of a male character, saying there couldn't possibly have been a way for her to know. "Why wouldn't you have anything to say about the feminine experience?" he asked, as though that were the only reason to write about anything else at all.

"Female", "foreigner", "Muslim", "swarms" became the scraps that determined there was nothing more that needed to be said. At some point, I don't know why turns into complete omniscience. What we didn't know could fill a book, so it seemed easier to assign a lack of value instead — a refugee has no right to remain; a person of colour is not white. A half is not whole. A girl is not a boy.

"Across The Sea" had been about me. In fact, it was about every girl whom Cuomo thought could look the slightest bit like me. It didn't matter if we'd worn our hair differently, or been born in different decades, or dreamt from different rooms in vastly different cities around the world. It wouldn't even matter if none of us were Japanese. "Stationery so fragile" was the flimsy scrap we converged on despite knowing who we were, because up that point there had been no scraps at all. "For girls of colour", Zhang says, "internalizing the message that we are inherently inferior... can happen just by repeated exclusion".

Defending *Pinkerton* as a man meant you were a tastemaker, a visionary who has finally received due credit. It preaches authenticity, while rewriting history. It is "really going for it". Defending *Pinkerton* as a woman was unthinkable. It is recognising that while our histories cannot be erased, they really should have been — we feel "disgust" and "embarrassment" for not having known better. Puccini concludes *Madame Butterfly* by having Cio Cio-san (the woman who was seduced, impregnated and abandoned by her American lover) go off and kill herself in an act of self-punishment. It is as though we had to apologise for attempting to comprehend the noises the men were making at us through bullhorns, through holes in the wall, in lewd babble scrawled onto bricks and hurled through a bedroom window.

***

But I couldn't quit *Pinkerton*. Its history betrays itself whenever I pick up a guitar, or in the thousands of songs written by anyone who has come across a Weezer album in their youth. The French sisters would be apoplectic to hear "As The Deer" shares the same chords as "Across The Sea".

Music is all kinds of identification. If it comes to life in the crevice between comprehension and expression, it follows that no two songs can be heard the same way. My experience could never have been Zhang's or Moss's, or any other monolith. So much of music is other people's songs, but they are also entirely mine — to choose, to put on a tape, to learn to play (however badly). As lucky as it may feel to be "that girl in the song" and have somebody love me, what mattered more was that I loved them back.

***

Fiction's greatest girl gangs — Thelma and Louise, the Baby-Sitters Club, the belles of St. Trinian's — tend to live forever. Even as villains, their strength in numbers was something fearful to behold. If being a girl meant you were powerful, as a group you were downright invincible.

In the real world though, girls don't live forever. In fact, too many will die before their time, often at the hands of someone else. Real life is 80 cents for every dollar and places like Yarl's Wood detention centre. It is uninvited male guests. It's realising, like Cassandra, that you can tell the truth and still not be believed, or learning that you "asked for it" without having actually been asked.

In a world that fails women, the myth that you cannot be touched is transposed to muscle memory. Proof of invincibility feels far away, yet permanent as suns. "Perhaps your favourite film isn't the one that you like best but the one that likes you best. Often, you first see it when you're young, but not too young, and on each subsequent viewing it is a home to which you return."[9]

If we tell ourselves these stories in order to live[10] — with music, with words, in film — we are also responsible for them. *Pinkerton* was always Cuomo's story. It was never mine. His voice monopolises, reverberates, howls its perpetual victimhood, but even Humbert Humbert realises the lie will not hold if there is nobody around to listen — "I need you, the reader, to imagine us, for we don't really exist if you don't".

Until then, it is pure sound. In November 2015, word arrived about a "bizarre" new Weezer video starring Rivers Cuomo, now forty-five, as a depraved evangelist preacher. The song was titled "Thank God For Girls". I won't be listening to it. I like to think, going by the words alone, I'd have written the same thing myself.

Notes

1 The Lilliburlero had been a hallmark of the BBC World Service since 1955, and was finally recalled from use in 2012.

2 112, "Peaches & Cream", *Part III* (2001), Bad Boy. Copyright Jason P D Boyd, Sean Puffy Combs, Aljamaal C Jones, Michael Marcel Keith, Quinnes Daymond Parker, Marvin E Scandrick, Courtney Douglas Sills, Mario Mendell Winans, C Sills Publishing, Da 12 Music, EMI April Music Inc, EMI Blackwood Music Inc, Janice Combs Music and Justin Combs Publishing (2001).

3 Permutations of I-V-vi-IV are equally favoured in popular culture. I-vi-IV-V, the doo-wop progression, was widespread in the Fifties and Sixties ("Blue Moon", "Stand By Me") but also appears in "Oliver's Army" by Elvis Costello and the Smiths' "There Is A Light That Never Goes Out". vi-IV-I-V, the so-called Sensitive Female Chord Progression, was named by writer Marc Hirst for its prominence among Lilith Fair artists, even though it was widely appropriated by the likes of Iggy Pop, the Doors and Alice Cooper.

4 Berkowitz A. L., Ansari, D. "Generation of Novel Motor Sequences: The Neural Correlates of Musical Improvisation", *Neuroimage* 41:2, 2008. pp. 535–543.

5 Weezer, "Tired of Sex", *Pinkerton*, (1996), DGC Records. Copyright Rivers Cuomo, E O Smith Music (1996).

6 Weezer, "Pink Triangle", *Pinkerton*, (1996), DGC Records. Copyright Rivers Cuomo, E O Smith Music (1996).

7 A three-page discourse written jointly by four men in which the words "women", "sexism" or "race" appear 0 times. "What if Weezer's *Pinkerton* was a major success in 1996?", *Consequence of Sound*, 7 February 2014. https://

consequenceofsound.net/2014/02/what-if-weezers-pinkerton-was-a-major-success-in-1996/

8   Weezer, "Across the Sea", *Pinkerton*, (1996), DGC Records. Copyright Rivers Cuomo, E O Smith Music (1996).

9   Cole, Teju. "Home". *New Yorker*, 29 December 2014.

10 Didion, Joan. "The White Album". In *The White Album*. (Farrar Straus Giroux, 2009).

The Casanova in Your Dreams: The Divine Comedy

Emily McQuade

Teenagers will often try on personas for size, and for some time in the mid-Nineties, my teenage inner life was taken over by the Divine Comedy's 1996 album *Casanova*. For me, its quirky chamber pop was magic. It was smart, it was witty and the melodies took me on pleasant journeys. It was a world away from the uber-blokey likes of Oasis. Or was it?

Casanova deals with romance and seductions and their aftermath. It was a peek into a world of naughtiness. I lapped it up, though at eighteen my life was distinctly lacking in anything remotely naughty.

The album was a bit cheeky, a bit literary. If the album had been a person, it would have been impeccably dressed and given to hooting at the ridiculousness of the world over a glass of vintage Claret. It might have had a Terry Thomas moustache. It would have been both a cad and a card, swanning into bars, snogging all the pretty people and sleeping with the prettiest before buggering off at the first light of day. All play. No hard feelings. It was occasionally a bit melancholy, but it was mostly a gentle, sighing, end of a party kind of melancholy. I'm sometimes unclear as to why this imaginary figure I'd constructed from Neil Hannon's songs appealed to me so much. I could never be that cartoon Casanova. I was a girl.

And I wasn't the kind of worldly, glamourous girl who might be the subject of these songs: a girl who might look a bit like Audrey Hepburn, who might wear a shift dress without fear of looking lumpen. I was an awkward, slightly scruffy and under-confident teenage girl. A lot of my favourite songs were about love. And some of them were about sex. But I had little — okay, no — experience of either. But still it drew me. Perhaps it appealed to my sense of longing.

When I first contemplated going away to university, I imagined a well-appointed library, sparkling conversation and dreaming spires. It was to be a place of transformation, away from the suburbs. Looking back, I can say that at least the library bit was true. For the most part university was a continuation of my teenage social awkwardness in a different setting, on a campus which used to be a biscuit factory. Romance seemed to be the kind of thing that happened to other people. And so I stayed in my dorm room, read books and drank a lot of black coffee. I brought about twenty CDs with me. It was difficult, almost painful, to choose the right ones for the trip. But *Casanova* was one of them.

As a girl I often had to overlook the sexism in my choices of what to watch or listen to or read; the TV shows that made me laugh but also made me feel slightly excluded, and those books I read because I'd heard they were good but disappointed me a little with their queasily retro gender politics. Re-reading or re-watching these things as an adult, I can see how problematic and annoying they are but can still manage to enjoy them. Post-university, though, I'd think about the books and these films and the TV shows and get very angry. How, I thought, could I have gotten on so well with something which hated me?

There's many things going on in *Casanova* — some of it hate, some of it love, some of it good old-fashioned lusting. More than anything else, though, it seems to be to be an album about play-acting, the wearing of masks and the assumption of different roles. There's a certain amount of performing masculinity in this album, though there's an ambivalence about it: it flits between critiquing, condemning and celebrating. The phenomenon of the "New Lad" was all over the place when the album came out in the mid-Nineties. The media was fetishising the acts of boozing, watching football and looking at pictures of ladies with no vests on. The album reflects both this and a more old-fashioned form of masculinity, which some of the more "sensitive" indie types adopted at the time: foppishness, suits and striking poses — as much of a pose as a Liam-swagger or a loud, beery football chant. And this is all perfectly exemplified by track two of *Casanova*, "Becoming More Like Alfie".[1]

One summer holiday, I watched *Alfie* on TV and was a little appalled. I'd assumed, from what I'd heard, that Alfie was going to be a cheeky sitcom style jack-the-lad, but in fact he was a charming monster — mistreating and lying to his conquests and repeatedly referred to them as "it". I was puzzled why anyone would want to "become" more like him. I can see now that The Divine Comedy's song didn't say that to "become" him was a necessarily good thing; there is more of an air of narrator being "resigned" to his Alfie-like path. He doesn't identify himself as a "lad", but his unenlightened approach to sex keeps steering him that way. Is he happy with this? Or is he making it all up?

And so the tone is set for the album — play-acting and fantasy, but with a fair chunk of doubt and self-loathing thrown in. Listening to it now, I see that the attraction/ repulsion contradiction I felt myself as a teenager is present in the music. But it's a different thing for a girl to be attracted/repelled by the "bohemian life" than for a boy. And the voice is very clearly established as a male one in the charmingly ridiculous opening track "Something For The Weekend". Neil has his posh man's purr on. "I say... how about a little kiss... oh don't be unkind."[2] It's daft rather than sexy and the objects of his affection are chuckling at the start of the song, though there's a feeling of ickiness about it all that I can't shake off. It's a camp piss-take of the kind of entitled man who'd follow a young lady home demanding her phone number. A harmless creep, perhaps. But a creep all the same.

And so the album progresses with its double entendres over Sixties soundtrack-style music, Prince impressions and a fair amount of not-quite self-awareness through to "Songs of Love".[3] This became the theme tune for *Father Ted* and takes a different approach. The narrator composes in his bedroom whilst all around him people are falling in lust, falling in love and copping off with one another. I was like him, I thought. Except I wasn't composing anything. I was drawn to *Casanova*, not just because of the lovely tunes, not just because of the literary references or the silly schoolboyish humour (someone having "trousers on fire" would fit just as well into *Father Ted* as into a *Carry On* film) but because it hinted at romance and libertinism of the kind that I could only imagine. A world that I was drawn to and was probably a teeny bit fearful of too.

The double-edged playfulness, and swooning music, continues with "The Frog Princess"[4], which is partly a "fuck you" song to an ex. The woman in this song has apparently "wronged" the singer, but of course we don't hear her point of view. She's a sexy lady in a see-through dress. They have their affair, she upsets him in some unspecified way and the song finishes with the promise of violence and the image of this "princess" "beneath a shining guillotine". Is this all a revenge fantasy, in which love is nothing but "a waste of time"? Or is it just a game they're both playing together? Whichever it is, it's a beautiful piece of music. The melody is delicate, spooling out of a blast of the French national anthem and rising to that magical chorus. I felt that hurt as I sang along. But — then, as now, I find myself wishing that I wasn't singing about killing someone, even if I'm doing it in the politest sounding way imaginable.

"A Woman Of The World"[5] sounds like it's from a Broadway show, and appears to borrow heavily from the film of *Breakfast at Tiffany's*. It's about a man looking at a woman and being confounded: a familiar pop trope, "Maybe I need her", the narrator muses, "because I want to be her." This is less familiar: this envious of the fake persona the woman — our Holly Golightly character —

has adopted. And then comes that air of menace again — "Maybe I'll kill her, just trying to thrill her." The line delivered as a casual observation, as natural as rhyming "girl" with "world", and it's all the more disturbing for that. But the song tries to cover itself with its wonderfully over-the-top Broadway crescendo. "If she don't kill me first!" Hannon sings followed by a bouncy instrumental ideal for a tap dance. We could think of the darker things, it seems to say, but isn't this more fun? Once again, the threat of violence is introduced, but then whisked away with a flourish, leaving me with that slightly uneasy feeling again.

For a while, a lot of female gig-goers could be said to want to "be" that glamorous Holly Golightly figure. Some even seemed like the real thing. In the mid- to late-Nineties, my friends and I dressed up to go to gigs: glitter, feather boas, elbow length gloves. Perhaps, I was never going to be that Casanova, or those imagined lady Casanovas. But it was fun to try to play around with the idea.

And for all of the libidinous adventuring that is forever evoked when his name is mentioned, the real Giacomo Casanova (1725–1798) wasn't merely a serial shagger. He was a scholar, a wit, and if he was well into "wham, bam, thank you, Ma'am" his approach was more about mutual pleasure than selfish conquests. Or at least, that was the tale he told about himself in the multiple-volume history of his life. Casanova created his own myth. He did some of things he claimed and did others (some even more outrageous) that he didn't want to include in his autobiography. And some things were presumably just... made up.

Casanova was his own creation — as was Miss Golightly, who was also a construct of the men around her, possibly like the Frog Princess of the song. They were playing with masks, as we all do sometimes and as Neil Hannon seemed to be doing with *Casanova* — play-acting and having fun. And occasionally having his ironic cake and eating it too. And there is, let's be honest, a certain attraction of following "The Casanova in your dreams", an image Hannon conjures up in "Through A Long And Sleepless Night"[6] before tossing it hastily aside. But as I could never be that flawed, fascinating and very male adventurer, I still felt like I was on the outside looking in. Never the bride and never the bridegroom.

The Divine Comedy continue to put out records and some of them have moments of great beauty. The silliness is still there too — Mr Hannon is dressed as a bike-riding Napoleon in his most recent video. And these days, I revisit *Casanova* like an old friend. It still makes me laugh. It still makes me dream and (sometimes) it does things which irritate me. But I feel I our relationship can handle the odd wobble. I very much like the cut of its jib, even if I find myself occasionally asking it what the hell it thinks it's doing.

Notes

1 The Divine Comedy, "Becoming More Like Alfie", *Casanova*, (1997), Setanta Records. Copyright Edward Neil Anthony Hannon, Universal Music – MGB Songs (1997).

2 The Divine Comedy, "Something For The Weekend", *Casanova*, (1997), Setanta Records. Copyright Edward Neil Anthony Hannon, Universal Music – MGB Songs (1997).

3 The Divine Comedy, "Songs of Love", *Casanova*, (1997), Setanta Records. Copyright Edward Neil Anthony Hannon, Universal Music – MGB Songs (1997).

4 The Divine Comedy, "The Frog Princess", *Casanova*, (1997), Setanta Records. Copyright Edward Neil Anthony Hannon, Universal Music – MGB Songs (1997).

5 The Divine Comedy, "A Woman of the World", *Casanova*, (1997), Setanta Records. Copyright Edward Neil Anthony Hannon, Universal Music – MGB Songs (1997).

6 The Divine Comedy, "Through a Long and Sleepless Night", *Casanova*, (1997), Setanta Records. Copyright Edward Neil Anthony Hannon, Universal Music – MGB Songs (1997).

You Want Something To Play With, Baby: On Being a Teenage Girl and a Pulp Fan

Jude Rogers

When you're sixteen, excitable and desperately inexperienced in the ways of the world, you want someone to teach you properly about the lessons of sex. In my case, I wanted — how embarrassing it is to write this now, two-and-a-bit decades later — A Man. Not a boy across the schoolyard that you're not sure if you like or don't like, who's staring at you, his mouth aggressively wet. That boy's real. He's flesh. You can't turn him off. At sixteen, you want a guide you can control. A voice in your ear. A voice that only *you* can turn on.

Jarvis Cocker was older — he was thirty, i.e. a wise, noble sage of advanced years — so he was obviously A Man. He also Knew About Things. He was from Sheffield, which felt desperately modern and exotic to a teenager growing up in the suburbs of Swansea (despite it being a similar Luftwaffe-blitzed, de-industrialised delight). He looked a bit like the boys I wanted to like: a bit weird, a bit interesting, not the bland beauties I felt I should like growing up. He was clever, and had a bone to pick about class. His clothes looked like they were bought from second-hand shops, like mine were (like mine were).

He also had a twitch to his hips, which I liked. His long fingers (his long fingers) extended to his cheekbones as his eyes saucered to the heavens. I liked how he wanted to touch my shoulder so tonight this room would become the centre of the entire universe, lie under the table and hold me tight while children played outside, and on a pink-quilted eiderdown pull my knickers down. He took me from romance to lust to fucking as his songs roamed through all-night garages and modern shopping centres and sweaty messy encounters on settees, a world where bare feet poked from beneath floral sheets, flaking bits of varnish from my nails. These relatable references, this rowdy soundtrack of suburban scenes I already knew, told me, Jude, it's OK: here sex can still happen. In short, Jarvis Cocker was filthy on an ordinary teenager's terms.

As the long days, weeks and months of my mid-teens wound on, my experiences were no longer simple snogs with boys that gave me cold sores, or awkward fumbles at school discos. Around this time, I also realised Jarvis was also a Peeping Tom and a cheat and a pervert — and yes, I knew he wrote in character, but to me all these characters were very much him. In "Babies", he hid in places to experience the sounds of other people he knew having sex. In "I-Spy", he was the remorseless third party in an adultery, enjoying pissing off a man by shagging his woman. In "F.E.E.L.I.N.G.C.A.L.L.E.D.L. O.V.E." he was a shameless voyeur: "I see flashes of the shape of your breasts and the curve of your belly / And they make me have to sit down and catch my breath".[1] I'd listen again and again to that particular line, his vocal breathless and heated, and I was excited, but scared — someone saying that in real life would chill me to the bone.

But in this context, it was OK. I was replaying the tape. I was rewinding the tape. I was pausing it, stopping it. I was master of the reel.

When a pop star is a voice in your ear, you're the person giving it consent. When their mouth and his tongue is between your hammer and anvil, you're saying yes. You're taking the words that filter through, the words *you* choose to hear, and giving them your own narrative and images. You're taking them in the ways you want to them: you're heightening their lustfulness, or dampening down their deviations, according to your own imagination. I did this with Jarvis every time I played *Different Class*' "Pencil Skirt", imagining I was the woman in the song, the woman who was engaged to someone else but having him, telling him it was alright. I also loved it when I told him to stop. After all, I knew the rules of the game. I was defining them.

I also gave consent to the listening experience when Jarvis was kind. I noticed when he begged a woman not "to go round to see him tonight"[2] in "Have You Seen Her Lately" ("he's already made such a mess of your life"). I noticed his regret about the "aftermath of our affair lying all around" in "Happy Endings" ("I can't clear it away")[3].

But I also turned off when Jarvis was being actively unpleasant. I adored "Lipgloss" in my teens for its indie-disco fizz and the dazzling oh-yeahs in its chorus, but its lyrics are cruel and vengeful, depriving a woman of her worth. "Have you lost your lipgloss, honey?" it goes, brightly. "Oh yeah. Now nothing you do can turn him on / There's something wrong / You had it once but now it's gone." The verses are worse: "What are they gonna say when they run into you again? / That your stomach looks bigger and your hair is a mess / And your eyes are just holes in your face".[4] When I was sixteen, I ignored them.

A listener's consent to allow a pop voice into their world can be instructive, exciting and liberating, but it's also a self-driven experience. It can lead to ignorance of other people's fates, and in "Lipgloss" I simply ignored the woman who wasn't me. When my lust waned for Jarvis in my late teens, it was because, once again, he wasn't singing to me. *This Is Hardcore* was the point where our connection was broken: a beautiful pneumatic blonde lying dead-eyed on its cover, as if she was being unemotionally, clinically, capitalistically screwed. Jarvis had entered a very different world, in all senses, and even though he was questioning how he was no longer one of us, he was now one of them. Even though he was now singing of glamorous women "lowering yourself to my level", he was no longer using language directed at (people like) me. When he sang "I don't know where you got those clothes", he wasn't singing about the local charity shop. When he sang, "you can take them off if it makes you feel better", mine stayed on.

In other words, consent is at its best when both people really want each other.

As I've grown older, I still go back to Pulp's music often, and remember the things that it taught me. I've listened to those songs feeling less ownership of their singer, enjoying the subtler stories being told. But I still feel a quickening in the pulse when I hear "Acrylic Afternoons", when I remember the first time (I can't remember a worse time), and when "Sheffield: Sex City" arches its back and exhales.

I thought of this earlier this year, when I met a man in a lift in Oslo. We went to the third floor together. He opened his mouth twice, to say "hello" and "thanks". It was just him and me. For twenty seconds, my head filled with half-formed lyrics about pressing buttons and the mechanics of things moving up and down. But when the lift stopped, I let Jarvis go. We were better apart. At least he left his voice with me.

Notes

1 Pulp, "F.E.E.L.I.N.G. C.A.L.L.E.D L.O.V.E.", *Different Class*, (1995), Island Records. Copyright Nicholas David Banks, Jarvis Branson Cocker, Candida Mary Doyle, Stephen Patrick Mackey, Mark Andrew Webber, Universal Music Publishing Group (1998).

2 Pulp, "Have You Seen Her Lately", *His 'n' Hers*, (1994), Island Records. Copyright Nicholas David Banks, Jarvis Branson Cocker, Candida Mary Doyle, Stephen Patrick Mackey, Universal Music Publishing Group (1998).

3 Pulp, "Happy Ending", *His 'n' Hers*, (1994), Island Records. Copyright Nicholas David Banks, Jarvis Branson Cocker, Candida Mary Doyle, Stephen Patrick Mackey, Universal Music Publishing Group (1998).

4 Pulp, "Lipgloss", *His 'n' Hers*, (1994), Island Records. Copyright Nicholas David Banks, Jarvis Branson Cocker, Candida Mary Doyle, Stephen Patrick Mackey, Universal Music Publishing Group (1998).

I Will Not "Shut Up And Swallow": Combichrist and Misogyny in Goth Industrial Subculture

Alison L. Fraser

There is an argument I have had time and time again with my friends and people who self-identify as part of the goth/industrial subculture. It always starts the same way: someone will mention the self-described "industrial metal core" band Combichrist and how amazing they are. Then I come along and completely disagree with them, arguing that it's not all right to idolise a band that has a number of songs, and one music video, that are openly violent towards women. Without fail, someone else will then chime in with something along the lines of "But I've met the band and they're all the nicest guys". I will say this for Combichrist: their hard work in touring and making themselves available to their fans has clearly worked. People in the goth/industrial subculture love their music. This love, and the fact that people have met the individuals that make up the band, undermine my argument every time. And when I dare to suggest that Combichrist is at fault for the violent content of their music, I am the bad guy in the eyes of my fellow goths who see them as "the nicest guys". But I know there's something important happening here of which goths need to be more critical.

I was first introduced to Combichrist when I was about seventeen years old, in about 2006, by a now ex-boyfriend. He was older than me and more familiar with industrial music, which he preferred over goth music. I remember being so enthralled by the pulsating electronic beats, the rage, distorted vocals and offensive lyrics of songs like "Enjoy The Abuse", "Shut Up And Swallow", and "This S*it Will Fuck You Up". These were some of my favourite songs. I would listen to them when I was angry and upset over the awful things life loves to dish out. I was young and full of rage myself. I grew up in an unhappy home (to say the least) and I hated everyone. And, for some very complicated reasons stemming from my environment, I definitely hated women.

My dad raised me to be boy-like. So I didn't then, and I still don't now, see myself as feminine. I was taught that the feminine, and by extension woman, was weak, pathetic, lazy and other negative attributes that stem from rationalist eighteenth-century Enlightenment thinking. In my mind, being feminine was a bad thing. I related to the lyrics from songs like "Enjoy The Abuse":

Next time you open your mouth / I'll put my fist down your throat
So deep you cannot swallow / I'll make your body hollow
You will enjoy the abuse / 'Cause you got nothing to lose
I swear I'll fist fuck your brain / Until I'm smiling again.[1]

Or even from "Shut Up And Swallow":

Now you want it in your ass as I spit in your face
Face down on the floor, holding you by your neck
Do you feel like a wreck?
Well that is life, kiddo
Now shut up and swallow, shut up and swallow.[2]

I was happy to wallow in my own hatred of life and people, and Combichrist songs allowed me to do this. I will openly admit that I used to love their music. It allowed me to be as terrible and worthless as I felt, and it made it alright to feel this way. And that is what alternative goth/industrial music should do. The music of Combichrist never judged or lectured me; it gave me an outlet. At the beginning, this was a really uncomplicated relationship: I was a fan of Combichrist.

***

After the break-up of pioneering electronic band Icon of Coil, beloved by the goth/industrial subculture, Andy LaPlegua founded Combichrist in 2003. This band is primarily LaPlegua, who writes and composes most of the songs, is the lead vocalist, and comes up with the ideas for music videos. It is very much his creation and driven by his desires, although drummer Joe Letz has been a long-term band member. Over the past thirteen years, Combichrist has been hailed as an important band influencing other EBM, industrial, aggrotech and metal acts. They have risen to fame through their music achieving recognised positions on *Billboard*'s Top

Dance/Electronic Albums chart. In order to understand Combichrist and their motivations, I have included an exhaustive list of interviews with the band in this essay's Appendix.

Combichrist has lasted so long because they are undeniably good at what they do. It is impressive that LaPlegua can drastically change the sound of his band for each new album and seamlessly still appeal to fans in the goth/industrial, electronic and metal subcultures all at the same time. There is a stylistic appeal to the music of Combichrist that people enjoy. I personally no longer know what this is, since I stopped listening to Combichrist around 2010 because their music stopped appealing to me. It had just become too repetitive and the lyrics I once enjoyed started to make me feel uncomfortable — for reasons I didn't fully understand until recently. But I remember Combichrist's music being straightforward and uncomplicated. The songs didn't ask you to think, understand their meaning, or evoke a complex set of emotions. They were loud, rude, violent and had a catchy industrial beat.

In the Seventies, all the musical precursors came together and industrial music began.[3] It was brash, loud and made no apologies. To quote Stephen Malliner, a founding member of Cabaret Voltaire:

> We made music that was often sonically brutal, we challenged ideas of authority and control, we toyed with moody and often taboo imagery, we were simultaneously intellectual and anti-intellectual, we thought ourselves iconoclastic, and we wore raincoats sometimes.[4]

From its inception, bands and artists that were part of the industrial genre were fearless in their musical and artistic experimentation that sought to critique the world around them. Industrial music interacted with and against the beginnings of neoliberal economics, post-industrial urban decay, new technologies including music and video technology and the punk DIY mentality.

The UK industrial band Throbbing Gristle was infamous for their musical displays that would attempt to shock the audience by showing graphic images of horror and violence. Their lyrics from songs like "Zyklon-B Zombie" even went so far as to reference the holocaust:

I'm just a little Jewish girl / Ain't got no clothes on / And if I had a steel hammer / I'd smash your teeth in / And as I walk her to the gas chamber / I'm out there laughing / Zyklon Zyklon Zyklon B Zombie Zombie.[5]

There are even more examples of industrial bands that offer us extreme critiques, such as Laibach who have been accused both of parodying fascists and of being fascists. There are even bands that celebrate sexual fetishes through their erotic electronic sounds like Leæther Strip.

Industrial music has a long history of being subversive, from the band Skinny Puppy standing up for animal rights in 1988 and Coil's cover of "Tainted Love" that addressed the unspoken AIDS crisis in 1985.[6] However, as quickly as industrial music began its avant-garde rampage, it was reabsorbed and made safe(ish) for the mainstream capitalist machine through bands like Nine

Inch Nails (NIN) in the Nineties. Most notably, Trent Reznor, NIN's lead singer and songwriter, removed any political messages from his songs while still maintaining an edgy, outsider status as an industrial musician. While it must be acknowledged that NIN doesn't exist in a vacuum, it is fair to say that the personal lyrical content and pop melodies of NIN songs managed to repackage industrial music into a consumable form that played right into the melancholy of suburban youth.[7]

It is against this background that *The Joy of Gunz*, Combichrist's first album, was released in 2003. Having listened to this album, I remembered loving the sounds of songs like "This Is The Joy Of Gunz" and "You Will Be The Bitch Now". The songs were simple, dark, and angry. The next album, *Everybody Hates You*, released in 2005, contains more songs with lyrical content that was angrier and more violent towards women including "This S*it Will Fuck You Up" and "Enjoy The Abuse". And, of course, with the release of *What the Fuck is Wrong with you People?* in 2007, the rest of my old favourite and sexually violent songs were released: "Shut Up And Swallow", "Give Head If You Got it", and "Get Your Body Beat". As a side note, it is interesting that besides the music video for "Throat Full of Glass", released in 2010, LaPlegua has become more aware of the critiques against his music and makes fewer songs that are objectively violent towards women. He has stated in interviews as far back as 2011 that his music was becoming more personal.[8]

But that doesn't mean the controversy is by any means over. People in the goth/industrial subculture, including myself, had become very complacent in their acceptance of bands like Combichrist. That is until two bands, Ad·ver·sary and Antigen Shift, decided to speak up against Combichrist (and another, equally offensive band, Nachtmahr) at Kinetik 5.0, which was Canada's largest industrial and electronic music festival until its end in 2014. In 2012, Ad·ver·sary and Antigen Shift created and played an amazing video live to the crowd at Kinetik. People had come from all over Canada, the US and Europe to see the headliners playing right after Ad·ver·sary and Antigen Shift: Combichrist and Nachtmahr. They played the video right at the end of their set.

The video, *We Demand Better*, only used production images from both bands to clearly demonstrate their use of violent, racist, and misogynistic imagery. The video (available online to watch on Vimeo) was composed of white bold text on black backgrounds interspersed with album cover images, images and clips from music videos, and text of lyrics that all contained misogynistic and racist content. Aesthetically, it was simple but powerful. The thesis of the video was undeniable: we in the goth/industrial subculture must demand better from our famous bands, like Combichrist and Nachtmar, who repeatedly use problematic imagery.

Having talked to my friends who were at that show, there were mixed emotions from the crowd. Some people cheered the video while others thought it was completely inappropriate, but most people were just surprised. At the end of *We Deserve Better* on Vimeo, you can hear a portion of the crowd cheering. During the festival, goth/industrial music reviewers *I Die: You Die* did an interview with Jairus Khan of Ad·ver·sary and, in a later update, published further interviews with LaPlegua and Thomas Rainer of Nachtmahr. In the interview, Khan described his motivations in making the video, and, in a very telling manner, both LaPlegua and Rainer had very uncritical responses to *We Demand Better*.[9] Having seen that video at home, I can say that it changed my own perception completely. I was already tired of Combichrist by 2012, but this video made me realise that I couldn't just sit idly by. And thus began the saga of my argument against Combichrist.

***

From the beginnings of industrial music in the Seventies to the release of Combichrist's second and third albums in 2005 and 2007 respectively, there seems to have been a shift from artistic music meant to critique to music made for mindless consumption. And for this music to be such a popular choice in a subculture that claims to provide an alternative to mainstream cultural norms and values presents a dangerous hypocrisy. Whereas bands like Throbbing Gristle always claimed to be political, LaPlegua has adamantly claimed the opposite in a number of interviews. From 2014: "I'm not political by any means but I'm aware of what is going on around me, and that's the whole thing".[10] Again in 2012:

> [T]hey think everything people do is political... it was just like if you were doing a horror movie; that's all there is to it. Nobody screams at Rob Zombie when he's doing something with shooting and killing and raping in his movies, so why would you blame me? It's the same thing.[11]

Even earlier than that, LaPlegua was justifying the use of overtly violent and sexual imagery by claiming that Combichrist was a character he had created in the early Nineties punk scene. As far back as 2005, LaPlegua has been mentioning this character: "I am doing a Combichrist comic book, based on the lyrics of the album, so you know there is a lot of degra[ad]tion and violence".[12] And again in 2011:

> I wrote the lyrics and the music based on that character. Over the years it became less and less that character and more and more 'me' writing... I used to do a punk rock, hardcore fanzine in the early 90's and I had this character in there that was a kind of punk rock messiah. He was part bad and part good depending on how drunk he was! It was a just a comic strip — something that was light-hearted and funny... It was just a great character to write for because you could get away with writing about anything — I could make it as funny as I wanted or I could make it as serious as I wanted or as violent as I wanted, and it never had to be about me.[13]

This character has been the basis around which LaPlegua has allowed himself to be violent and sexual, and to create some of the most beloved songs in the goth/industrial subculture that promote violence against women — in effect both normalising and excusing the content of his music. To this day in interviews, LaPlegua will never take a critical stance and reflect on his music:

[B]ut I also think it's the era of being over sensitive so everybody's offended by everything. You're supposed to get offended. Some humour is supposed to offend people for example and if you can't take it, just leave it alone. Don't get so offended by it... People go "you're sexist", "it's violent", whatever they call it and I go, "this is just a character. This is written as a character." Obviously, a lot of the stuff I've done is written as a character. It's written like... nobody's calling out Wes Craven and saying "you're sexist", so as soon as you put it in a music context you're suddenly a bigot or it was just really funny because anyone who really knows us, knows that it's the complete opposite. We are very liberal. I hate to be political, but I would say opinionated because I don't want to do politics in my music. I will keep it like that.[14]

In classic form, he will shift the blame to people simply getting offended or compare his music to the work of other people that likely have also been criticised. Time and time again, LaPlegua demonstrates a purposeful ignorance of his own safe and secure position in life. He owns property, makes a living creating and performing music, has a heterosexual marriage and, of course, is a white male. Even while living a subcultural lifestyle, LaPlegua is unlikely to face the same kinds of systematic oppressions as his fans, who at the very least are likely not as financially stable as he is and cannot earn as good a living making their music. These people look up to him as a model for success living an alternative lifestyle.

LaPlegua continuously shirks any responsibility for his problematic messages in his music onto the people that believe them. Even after Kinetik 5.0, he admitted he knew that people were taking the character of Combichrist too seriously:

> It's kind of like, if you start doing something for art or or a storyline and suddenly people take this seriously, they actually think that's how they should behave, you know, they think "Oh, we gotta go drink and fight and fuck and get some sluts", you know, it's bullshit. It's turning into Scientology, you know, like "you really believe this shit, it's a fictional book".[15]

And yet, what kind of disclaimer was there? Frankly, nothing. Our Euro-American society has taught us that some people matter more than others based on ideological, abstract concepts associated with certain bodies, e.g., men have more value than women because they are more rational. LaPlegua is the creator of problematic music that stems from a society in which those problems are deeply ingrained. He failed to do what his industrial predecessors tried to do, and what Wes Craven tries to do with his movies, which is take our reality and show it to us in all its actual horror. Instead, LaPlegua took something already normal in mainstream society — violence against women — and made it goth. There is no critique in Combichrist's music because LaPlegua doesn't want there to be one; he doesn't want to be political. Thus, I can safely say, that Combichrist is just perpetuating the problem of violence against women. And this is misogynistic. This is the realisation I came to, slowly at first, which I now understand, with all its negative ramifications.

People like me take part in subcultures like goth and industrial because we don't feel like we want to belong to a deeply flawed mainstream culture. We want to embrace the fact that we are wonderful, dark, spooky and passionate people with a wide variety of interests that we can't tell people about for fear of being labelled "weird" or "disturbed". The goth/industrial subculture is a far from perfect space, but it is the one that we have created for ourselves to find acceptance in our differences. And here lies the most important part of my argument against Combichrist.

Goths become goth in order to escape the boundaries of mainstream, heteronormative lifestyles. We don't want the 2.5 kids, a car and a home in the suburbs. Most of us will never even be able to afford those things. We want to be queer, find a job that we love even if it doesn't pay a lot and live life to the best of our ability despite how overwhelmingly hard that is when you are different in any sense of the word. As a famous band in the goth/industrial subculture, Combichrist took mainstream, heteronormative values, wrapped them up in a package goths would like and injected them right back into the subculture that tried to escape those values. If LaPlegua is as "nice a guy", as I hear he is, I hope that one day he will do more than move away from the misogynist Combichrist character that he created. I hope that he will help to fix the problem of misogyny in our subculture by at the very least acknowledging that the songs and overtly violent imagery against women that he created are problematic. LaPlegua failed to be insightful or humorous and instead created a harmful message that still exists in the goth/industrial subculture. Of course, this is why I am no longer a fan.

Appendix

A large selection of Combichrist interviews found on Google in English, organised chronologically from newest to oldest (there are more interviews on YouTube not listed here):

16 August 2016 (with Eric13) https://www.mixcloud.com/
DJWILLKILLWIDRFM/the-splatterhouse-ep-25-
interview-with-eric13-from-combichrist-25th-episode-
spectacular/

25 July 2016 https://splizzmag.wordpress.com/2016/07/25/
combichrist-interview/

25 July 2016 http://www.soundscapemagazine.com/
combichristinterview/comment-page-1/

13 July 2016 http://loud-stuff.com/music/2016/07/interview
-andy-laplegua-combichrist/

3 July 2016 http://distortedsoundmag.com/interview-andy
-laplegua-combichrist/

30 June 2016 http://www.moshville.co.uk/interview/2016/07
/interview-andy-laplegua-of-combichrist-glasgow-02-
abc-30th-june-2016/

June 2016 http://allabouttherock.co.uk/interview-andy
-laplegua/

16 May 2016 http://www.peek-a-boo-magazine.be/en/
interviews/combichrist-2016/

26 April 2016 (with Joe Letz) http://www.4zzzfm.org.au/
podcasts/music/dark-essence-interview-combichrist

2 April 2016 http://www.theaquarian.com/2014/04/02/
interview-with-combichrist-no-restrictions/

23 March 2015 (with Eric13) http://www.faygoluvers.net/
v5/2015/03/eric13-of-combichrist-interview-32315/

15 January 2015 http://www.dailymotion.com/video/x2esw
    32_bmva-zoomed-in-interview-with-combichrist_tv

24 July 2014 (not an interview but a statement from the band
    about dropping Blood on the Dance Floor from their
    US tour) http://bloody-disgusting.com/news/3304533/
    combichrist-announce-fall-us-tour/

30 June 2014 http://screamermagazine.com/interviews/
    proofed-combichrists-andy-laplegua-still-whatever-
    hell- wants/

26 April 2014 http://ajournalofmusicalthings.com/interview
    -andy-laplegua-combichrist/

2 December 2013 http://www.cassetteculture.com/blog/2013
    /12/combichrist-the-mind-of-andy-laplegua/

25 October 2013 http://www.rogerphotographics.com/blog
    /2013/11/interview-combichrist-friday-25-october-
    mezz-breda -nl

28 February 2013 https://www.youtube.com/watch?v=8xa
    UzhFNaA4

1 August 2012 http://www.metalblast.net/interviews/
    combichrist-interview/

26 July 2012 http://www.lyricloungereview.co.uk/an
    -interview-with-combichrists-andy-laplegua-rock-city-
    gig-30th-june/

16 July 2012 Part 1: https://www.youtube.com/watch?v=
    XyA6EFWWGxI Part 2: https://www.youtube.com/
    watch?v=Rc_09lLRxHk Part3: https://www.youtube.
    com/watch?v=Ak4ezhDLDKQ

7 July 2012 http://www.theindependentvoice.org/2012/07/27/
    combichrist-interview-2012/

27 June 2012 https://www.youtube.com/watch?v=2LzJp4
    OsndU

26 June 2012 https://problemofleisure.wordpress.com/2012
/12/16/interview-with-andy-laplegua-combichristicon-
of-coil-26th-june-2012/

5 March 2012 (with Joe Letz): http://www.soundspheremag.
com/spotlight/band/spotlight-joe-letz-combichrist/

3 March 2012 (with Joe Letz) http://playdead-nation.blogspot
.ca/2012/03/interview-joe-letz-combichrist.html

15 October 2011 http://www.soundspheremag.com/features/
interview-combichrist/

8 October 2011 http://rushonrock.com/2011/10/08/exclusive
-interview-combichrist/

25 July 2011 http://graveconcernsezine.com/interviews/ebm-
electro-electronica/3108-combichrist-interview.html

19 July 2011 http://planetmosh.com/bedlam-speaks-to-
combichrists -andy-laplegua/

10 July 2011 http://www.roomthirteen.com/features/862/
Combichrists_Andy_LaPlegua_Interview.html

24 May 2011 http://www.reflectionsofdarkness.com/-artists
-a-e-interviews-85/9586-interview-combichrist-may
-2011.html

10 May 2011 http://www.terrorizer.com/dominion/dominion
features/interview-andy-laplegua-combichrist/

7 May 2011 https://www.youtube.com/watch?v=
CogNo5F3zuA

2 May 2011 http://www.mycitybuzz.com/interview-w-andy-
laplegua -of-combichrist/

15 February 2011 http://www.radiometal.com/en/article/
andy-laplegua-the-man-with-the-christ-like-
clarity,19336

5 February 2011 http://tempelores.com/?p=3867

18 January 2011 (with Joe Letz) http://lilt.rammstein.me
/2011/01/speak-to-me-joe.html

18 November 2010 http://speakpenguin.blogspot.ca/2010/11/
    unedited-interview-with-andy-laplegua.html

1 October 2010 http://www.purplerevolver.com/music/open-
    mic/121032-combichrist-interview.html

30 July 2010 https://www.youtube.com/watch?time_
    continue=1&v=BKT69NHozC8

2010 Part 1: http://www.electrowelt.com/index.php?Itemid
    =72&catid=1&id=653:exclusive-interview-with-andy
    -laplegua-combichristpanzer-ag-icon-of-coil
    -scandy&option=com_content&view=articlePart2
    :http://www.electrowelt.com/index.php?option=com
    _content&view=article&id=676:exclusive-interview-
    with-andy-laplegua-combichrist-and-more-interview-
    pt-2&catid=1&Itemid=72

3 July 2009 http://auxiliarymagazine.com/2009/07/03/
    interviews-combichrist/

27 June 2009 http://www.dailymotion.com/video/x9pdtz_
    combichrist-interview_music

5 February 2009: https://www.youtube.com/watch?v
    =41LUr5Koxz8

15 January 2009 Part 1: https://www.youtube.com/watch?
    v=NUYDtmIcRhU Part 2: https://www.youtube.com/
    watch?v=6EAWRP7jiNM

26 September 2008 (with Joe Letz) http://www.
    soundspheremag.com/features/five-minutes-withjoey
    -letz-combichrist -drummer/

2008 http://bands.goanddomichigan.com/reviews/review.
    asp?ID=1902

March 2005 http://revelry.free.fr/itw/combichrist/
    COMBICHRIST%20interview%20UK(mars.2005).htm

Notes

1 Combichrist, "Enjoy the Abuse", *Everybody Hates You* (2005), Metropolis. Copyright Ole Anders Olsen and BMG Platinum Songs US (2005)

2 Combichrist, "Shut Up and Swallow", *What the F**k is Wrong with You People?* (2007), Metropolis. Copyright Ole Anders Olsen and BMG Platinum Songs US (2007)

3 Thompson, Dave. *The Industrial Revolution: Twentieth Anniversary Edition*. (CreateSpace, 2013) pp. 13–19.

4 Quoted in the Introduction to Reed, S. Alexander. *Assimilate: A Critical History of Industrial Music*. (Oxford University Press, 2013).

5 Throbbing Gristle, "Zyklon-B Zombie", *At the Brighton Polytechnic* (1979), Industrial Records. Copyright Chris Carter, Peter Martin Christopherson, Genesis P. Orridge and Cosey Fanni Tutti, Industrial Records and Peermusic III Ltd (1979).

6 Lev, Nadya. "On Misogyny in Industrial Music". *Coilhouse: A Love Letter to Alternative Culture*, 20 November 2012. http://coilhouse.net/2012/11/on-miso gyny-in-industrial-music/

7 Carr, Daphne. *Pretty Hate Machine*. (Continuum, 2011) p. 21.

8 Blanc, Amaury. "Andy LaPlegua: The Man with the Christ-Like Clarity." *Radio Metal*, 15 February 2011.

9 "Kinetik Update 2012: Ad·ver·sary's Performance". *I Die: You Die*, 17 May 2012.

10 Ebeling, Amy. "Interview with Combichrist: No Restrictions". *The Aquarian Weekly*, 2 April 2014.

11 "Combichrist Interview". *Splizzmag*, 25 July 2016.

12 Camus, Olivier. "Interview: Combichrist". *Revelry Radio Show*, 2005.

13 Rushworth, Simon. "Exclusive Interview – Combichrist".
    Rush on Rock, 8 October 2011.
14 "Combichrist Interview". *Splizzmag*, 25 July 2016.
15 "Kinetik Update 2012: Ad·ver·sary's Performance". *I Die:
    You Die*, 17 May 2012.

Bibliography

Blanc, Amaury. "Andy LaPlegua: The Man with the Christ-Like Clarity". *Radio Metal*, 15 February 2011. www.radiometal.com/en/article/andy-laplegua-the-man-with-the-christ-like-clarity,19336

Carr, Daphne. *Pretty Hate Machine*. (Continuum, 2011).

Camus, Olivier. "Interview: Combichrist". *Revelry Radio Show*, 2005. revelry.free.fr/itw/combichrist/COMBICHRIST%20interview%20UK(mars.2005).htm.

"Combichrist Interview". *Splizzmag*, 25 July 2016. splizzmag.wordpress.com/2016/07/25/combichrist-interview/

"Combichrist Top Dance/Electronic Albums". *Billboard*, 2016. www.billboard.com/artist/299555/combichrist/chart?f=322

Ebeling, Amy. "Interview with Combichrist: No Restrictions". *The Aquarian Weekly*, 2 April 2014. www.theaquarian.com/2014/04/02/interview-with-combichrist-no-restrictions/

"Kinetik Update 2012: Ad·ver·sary's Performance." *I Die: You Die*, 17 May 2012. www.idieyoudie.com/2012/05/kinetik-update-2012-ad%C2%B7ver%C2%B7sarys-performance/

J. "Combichrist Interview." *Metal Blast*, 1 August 2012. www.metalblast.net/interviews/combichrist-interview/

Lev, Nadya. "On Misogyny in Industrial Music." *Coilhouse: A Love Letter to Alternative Culture*, 20 November 2012. coilhouse.net/2012/11/on-misogyny-in-industrial-music/

Mistress Nancy. "Combichrist @ in the Venue 10.18 with William Control, Davery Suicide, Darksiderz". *Slug Magazine*, 22 October 2014. http://www.slugmag.com/

show-reviews/combichrist-in-the-venue-1018-with-william-control-davey-suicide-darksiderz/

P-Orridge, Genesis. "Throbbing Gristle Words Lyrics." *Brainwashed*, www.brainwashed.com/tg/lyrics.html#zyklon.

Reed, S. Alexander. *Assimilate: A Critical History of Industrial Music*. (Oxford University Press, 2013).

Rushworth, Simon. "Exclusive Interview – Combichrist". *Rush on Rock*, 8 October 2011. rushonrock.com/2011/10/08/exclusive-interview-combichrist/

Thompson, Dave. *The Industrial Revolution: Twentieth Anniversary Edition*. (CreateSpace, 2013).

"Throbbing Gristle". userpages.umbc.edu/~vijay/TG/reviews/tg_live.html. Accessed 26 August 2016.

Wilson, Joanna. "Interview – Andy LaPlegua: Combichrist". *Loud Stuff*, 13 July 2016. www.loud-stuff.com/music/2016/07/interview-andy-laplegua-combichrist/.

How I Learned to Stop Worrying and Love "Big Pimpin'"

Amanda Barokh

In my glamorous job as an assistant hotel manager, I was once given the sexy task of stocktaking cleaning products. To pass the time, as I counted the bottles of Toilet Duck and the packets of sanitary disposal bags, I put some music on. A young male colleague came into the dingy basement room I was working in and caught me singing along enthusiastically to Jay-Z's "Big Pimpin'". He gave me a puzzled look of approval and walked out of the room before I had a chance to say, "Wait! It's possible to be a committed feminist and still appreciate the genius of this song!" I didn't get a chance to give my young colleague an explanation, but I do have an opportunity to do that now.

Let's be clear here: "Big Pimpin'" is, without a doubt, one of the most caustically misogynistic songs of recent times. Yet I find that I never tire of listening to it. How can I justify my love of this song? Surely every feminist worth her salt should say fifty *Hail de Beauvoirs* every time she dares to indulge in a listen?

By way of explanation, I have to take you way back in time to my childhood in the late Eighties. Picture a little brown child with frizzy hair, a faint moustache and a monobrow sitting in the back of her dad's (also brown) Ford Cortina, driving around the sterile streets of suburban north London. Her dad, an Arab, had a penchant for playing tunes from his homeland. The glove compartment of the Cortina was filled with tapes hand-labelled in a scrawly language the little brown child couldn't understand.

Her father would play the tapes loudly and sing along enthusiastically. The little brown child would cry, "Dad please turn that music off it sounds like a cat being strangled. I want to listen to Kylie."

If ever the little brown child had an esteemed Caucasian friend in the car, she would cower in shame and beg her father to play something more palatable. Back then, the little brown child didn't realise it, but she was ashamed of being brown. At the time, she didn't know the meaning of the word "assimilate", but that's what she desperately wanted to do. The music her father listened to was different. It somehow revealed that she too was different. She didn't want to be different; she wanted to fit in. She wished her dad would listen to Led Zeppelin and the Beatles.

Now let's fast-forward to the late Nineties. I was no longer a little brown child. I was now a young woman who had thankfully discovered tweezers, Veet and Frizz-Ease by John Freda. I was working in a bar called Norman in Leeds while studying English at the university. The bar was staffed almost exclusively by women of colour. By this time, I was over my itch to assimilate and was busy owning my otherness. The limes we sliced up and put into the mojitos and G&Ts would arrive with little stickers that said "exotic" on them. The other girls and I would peel off the stickers and stick them proudly to our chests. At the time, I didn't consider that there could be negative connotations to the word, but that's another story.

One night working in the bar, I heard the DJ play a song that grabbed me instantly. Something about it catapulted straight back to the backseat of my father's car. At the time I didn't know it, but the song was "Big Pimpin'" and the sound that took me back to my childhood was a sample of an Egyptian song from the 1960s called "Khosara" by Abdel Halim Hafez.

In the hands of Jay-Z, the emotive flutes of my father's faraway and mysterious culture no longer sounded foreign and shameful. Recontextualised, I was able finally to appreciate their magic. If Arabic music was cool enough for Jay-Z then maybe it was cool enough for me.

At the time, I believed I was educated, but I didn't know much about feminism and I certainly wouldn't have known intersectional socialist feminism if it bit me on the arse. I didn't give a minute's thought to the lyrics — I just knew, with a visceral gut reaction, that I loved the song.

I didn't understand it at the time but one of the reasons I loved the song so much was because it made Arabic culture feel less marginalised. Being brown no longer felt isolating. In fact, it felt like a USP.

And then 9/11 happened.

George Bush was on the TV banging on about the "Axis of Evil" almost 24/7. If I was from the Axis of Evil then did that make me evil by association? Men would chat me up in bars:

"Hey baby, where you from?"

"London."

"Nah, I mean where are you really from? You got them exotic looks."

"Guess."

"Brazil? Barbados?"

"Um, Iraq."

In those days, nothing killed sexy talk like having to explain that you hailed from the Axis of Evil. I began to hate my otherness again. I was back to being desperate to assimilate. I peeled off the "exotic" sticker and went to work in the whiteboy bar across the street. There I renounced all PoC music and began to listen almost exclusively to music made by various combinations of white men in tight denim like the Strokes and Kings of Leon. I genuinely loved indie music, but there was more to it. Subconsciously, I believed that embracing white culture would somehow mitigate my brownness. I put "Big Pimpin'" in a box and didn't listen to it again for many years.

Let's bring you almost up to the present day. I am now a (not so) young woman in my mid-thirties. I have thankfully discovered another Freda even better than John — Frida Kahlo — and I understand that I don't need to adhere to unattainable white beauty standards in order to be attractive. Occasionally, I don't mind rocking a monobrow and a faint 'tache.

With the benefit of a potent combo of expensive therapy and hindsight I understand that most of my life has been blighted by misogyny in its various forms.

I have educated myself and I have read all the feminist texts I could lay my hands on: everything from Germaine Greer to Roxanne Gay to Andrea Dworkin to bell hooks to Betty Frieden to Audre Lorde. Like the Gambler in the famous Kenny Rogers song, I finally believe that when it comes to feminism, I know what to throw away and what to keep.

I am conscious of my battle with my conflicting identity — being both Iraqi and British. I am finally more able to just be myself without apology. This means I don't try to assimilate or claim my otherness. I just try to be me. I am not like anyone else and for that I am grateful. I don't let the music I listen to define me. I listen to music that sounds good and that elicits a reaction in me.

One day, I am jogging down Talamanca promenade in Ibiza. I am by no means a natural runner and it's hot — we're talking 35 degrees. I'm desperate to stop and go paddle in the sea but suddenly "Big Pimpin'" comes up on shuffle. Although in the past I have claimed to dislike the song due to the sexist lyrics, it has somehow found its way back into my iTunes library. Hmm.

As the song plays I find myself running faster perhaps than I have ever have before. Feminist theory bounces around in my head. The lyrics are unflinchingly brutal. What makes a man write such a malevolent song about women? How could I ever have listened to this song without questioning the lyrics? Must I press the stop button immediately? Does the lyrical content invalidate the spell Jay-Z weaves with his deft rapping and his almost unparalleled ear for a unique sample?

As I run, instead of being a woman, I imagine myself to be the protagonist of the song. I feel instantly powerful. Slowly I begin to understand why a man might write these lines.

I recall the two power structures of capitalism and patriarchy. I wonder whether the issues brought forth by this song might somehow be created, not by individuals, but by the interplay between these two structures. I wonder also, if hypermasculinity is employed as a shield against the vulnerability men expose themselves to if they leave themselves open to love.

The song opens with the lines:

You know I thug 'em, fuck 'em, love 'em, leave 'em
Cause I don't fuckin' need 'em

If I approach the song from a woman's perspective it's unquestionably deplorable, but when I approach it from a man's perspective it is (grudgingly) understandable. There is power in not surrendering to love and in staying free from the shackles of emotional attachment. One way to do that is to objectify women and treat them purely as sex objects.

In the song, women are objectified to such a degree that they are reduced to animals:

Take 'em out the hood, keep 'em lookin' good
But I don't fuckin' feed 'em

There would be an outcry if someone sung about treating Pomeranians in such an abject manner, and yet in our capitalist and patriarchal society this mistreatment of women is lauded because the prevailing idea is that a woman's main objective is to trap a man and take all of his money:

> Many chicks want to put Jigga fist in cuffs
> Divorce him and split his bucks
> Just because you got good head, I'mma break bread
> So you can be livin' it up?

This is where the double bind of capitalism and patriarchy imprisons men too. It may be true that successful male artists fall prey to mercenary women, but that's where we have to question a system that makes women beholden to men's earning power. Women from deprived backgrounds who are not offered careers may find that their only way out of grinding poverty is to attach themselves to a successful man. The idea that women might be trying to take advantage of his wealth serves as a justification for their mistreatment. The protagonist cannot allow himself to get close to anyone and therefore he is also a victim of a patriarchal and capitalist system. The protagonist reminds me of King Midas — so obsessed with material wealth that he is unable to experience love.

If you really dig deeper, beyond the bravado there is something vulnerable about this man. The construct of hypermasculinity acts as a shield to deflect heartache:

> Shit I
> Parts with nothin', y'all be frontin'
> Me give my heart to a woman?
> Not for nothin', never happen
> I'll be forever mackin'

Heart cold as assassins, I got no passion
I got no patience
And I hate waitin'
Ho get yo' ass in[1]

When I cast myself in the role of the protagonist, those lines feel empowering. Love lowers our defences and one way to protect ourselves is to become impervious to it.

If you consider that Jay-Z is also one of the artists behind "Crazy in Love", it becomes apparent that people are mutable, everyone is capable of feeling love and to deny it is to deny our humanity. Men also pay the price for existing within a system that forces them to deny any tenderness or vulnerability.

As I reach the end of Talamanca promenade, I am finally able to reconcile my feminist values and my love for this song, because I recognise that we are all victims of power structures and the only way forward is to dismantle them. I also recognise a damn good hook when I hear one.

Notes

1 Jay Z, "Big Pimpin'", *Vol 3...Life and Times of S Carter* (1999), Roc-A –Fella/Def Jam. Copyright Shawn Carter, Kyambo R Joshua, Timothy Z Mosley, I Love K J Music, Lil Lu Lu Publishing and W B Music Corp (1999)

Cool Girls and Boys in Bands: Grappling with the Mid-2000s British Indie Scene

Abi Millar

In April 2016, the hashtag "#indieamnesty" hit Twitter, turning the spotlight on a genre that had last burned bright ten years earlier. Too far removed to feel relevant — and too luridly memorable to claw back any real *cachet* — mid-2000s British indie had become the source of a very specific kind of humblebrag. "An ex-girlfriend cheated on me with a Zuton" read one tweet. "Accidentally stood on Morrissey's hand once" read another. The tweets painted a picture of a long-gone world with Camden at its epicentre, when every band name began with "The" and stylish boys wore waistcoats and thin ties.

Listening to mid-2000s indie today, it's hard to remember exactly what all the fuss was about. For sure, the better acts have an energy and anarchy about them, a MySpace-era version of rock 'n' roll. But the style as a whole has aged badly. If today's more zeitgeist-friendly acts are marked by the absence of genre — pop blending into EDM blending into rap — then this music sounds very obviously of another time. For the most part, these are guitar bands, influenced by guitar bands, stemming from a purebred lineage of guitar bands. You don't get them referencing Jamaican dancehall or sampling psychedelic folk. What's more, from 2016's perspective, its demographic makeup is hard to overlook. Although there were, certainly, female indie acts, non-white indie acts and gay or bisexual indie acts (with Bloc Party's frontman, Kele Okereke, perhaps unique in covering the latter two bases), these were the minority. Straight white male was the default.

In one sense, indie culture was egalitarian. The scene had many strands and multiple influences, with Riot Grrrl looming just as large as rock revivalism. It also allowed some blurring of gender boundaries. Fans of all genders opted for the same androgynous aesthetic — eyeliner, band T-shirts, skinny jeans — while raw emotionality was key to many of the songs. Just think of Franz Ferdinand's breakup anthem, "Walk Away", or the yearning "Radio America" by the Libertines.

At the outermost edges of the scene, where indie blurred into emo, acts like Placebo sung about queer culture and toyed with gender expectations. (Whether or not Placebo was truly "mid-2000s indie" depends on where you draw the line.) Still, there was a shaggy-haired elephant in the room, in that the scene was overwhelmingly male.

When I look back this era now, I struggle to recall many of the names I once spent hours searching for on Napster. They have fused into a single, homogenous mass of male grandstanding, male heartbreak, male bonding and — worst — male cod-profundity. But I do remember the Long Blondes, precisely because they were different. And while the likes of the Automatic have long since faded from view, the Kills are still going strong. It is the bands that deviated most from the "four white boys and a scratchy guitar" template that sound the freshest to 2016 ears.

Youth culture is supposed to capture a spirit of rebellion. So why was this particular youth culture so in thrall to the status quo?

In 2005, the US writer Ariel Levy published *Female Chauvinist Pigs*, which discussed the rise of so-called "raunch culture". As she saw it, women were doing things that would have outraged their mothers — getting breast implants, going to strip clubs, wearing T-shirts emblazoned with the Playboy bunny logo — all the while framing it as a postfeminist act of rebellion. According to Levy, these women were adopting two strategies to "deal with [their] femaleness". Some were objectifying other women — reading Playboy, talking about porn stars — while others were objectifying themselves. In both cases, the "postfeminist" justification seemed tenuous. Why would they bother aligning themselves with men, or performing sexiness to men, if men had truly stopped being the dominant cultural force?

It was around this time that the "Cool Girl" trope began to gain traction. The Cool Girl was a young woman who, rather questionably, claimed to be different from all the other girls. Because she saw anything coded female as inferior, she took pride in distancing herself from her own gender and positioning herself as "one of the guys". In Gillian Flynn's 2012 thriller *Gone*

Girl, the narrator describes Cool Girl as the "defining compliment":

> Being the Cool Girl means I am a hot, brilliant, funny woman who adores football, poker, dirty jokes, and burping, who plays video games, drinks cheap beer, loves threesomes and anal sex, and jams hot dogs and hamburgers into her mouth like she's hosting the world's biggest culinary gang bang while somehow maintaining a size 2, because Cool Girls are above all hot. Hot and understanding. Cool Girls never get angry; they only smile in a chagrined, loving manner and let their men do whatever they want. Go ahead, shit on me, I don't mind, I'm the Cool Girl.[1]

The Cool Girl, then, is a perfect conflation of Ariel Levy's two categories of Female Chauvinist Pig. She distinguishes herself from girly girls, in a bid to attain the status of a guy. And she attempts to gain more social power on top of that by becoming an object of male desire.

To my thirty-year-old self in 2016, the Cool Girl sounds like a textbook case of internalised misogyny. But to my twenty-year-old self in 2006 — still trying to work out how to "deal with my femaleness" — she was a paradigm to follow. She was a way to show the world that you were a full human being, rather than a reductive feminine stereotype, and she enabled you to do that while remaining attractive to boys.

***

The Libertines' first album, *Up the Bracket*, came out when I was sixteen. It's still a great album. It's the distillation of being in a dive bar — jumping about and splashing lager everywhere while you eye up a guy with sleeve tattoos. To many commentators, it marked the return to the UK of credible guitar music, which had dwindled into dirge-like irrelevance by the turn of the century.

Pete Doherty and Carl Barat, the Libertines' frontmen, had swagger. They had many unsavoury qualities too, if you bought into their mythology, but the swagger was what carried the band. They were shambolic, they were wayward, they were exuberant; they owed more to post-punk than to Britpop. Nobody could have accused their music of being sanitised or watered down.

Of course, the very idea of being a rock 'n' roll star is laden with gendered baggage, much of it too obvious to need unpicking. At the most reductionist level, it's the men who are the creators and the sybarites; the women who are the muses and the groupies. This is not to say there has ever been a shortage of female-led or co-ed guitar bands. There's a long and illustrious line of them. But the rock that informed the Libertines' sound — and above all, the rock lore that informed their image crafting — overwhelmingly fits that basic template.

Take the song "Boys In The Band", which many have taken to be about groupies ("And they all get them out / For the boys in the band").[2] At the very least, the song points to the magnetism of the male musician and the supposed servility of fandom. In the Libertines' narrative, women were always somewhat beside the point, with Pete and Carl's own homosocial bond forming the band's emotional core.

Between 2003 and 2007, wave upon wave of British indie acts came to prominence — Franz Ferdinand, Editors, Razorlight, Kaiser Chiefs, Bloc Party, the Fratellis, the Kooks — some of which aspired to punk rock or art rock, some of which skewed middle-of-the-road. By the end of this period, the genre was beginning its fatal slide into so-called "Landfill Indie" — the result of lazy record labels throwing money at winning formulas. "The airwaves just became a dump that needed to be filled with product that looked a bit like other product that had done okay", said Johnny Borrell, Razorlight's frontman, in 2016. After that point, only the acts with a particularly distinctive sound, or scope to evolve, like the Arctic Monkeys, were able to survive. Indie mutated into nu-rave, which gave way to a synthpop revival. For a few years, however, indie music was *the* scene to be a part of if you were a disillusioned kid in an average British town.

A question I would now ask my twenty-year-old self is this: what do you do when the music you like consistently places women as remote, inaccessible objects of yearning? Or as resented girlfriends who are holding the narrator back? Or as sexual conduits to self-realisation? Perhaps you go along with it, aware that you don't need to place yourself in an artist's shoes in order to be a fan. Maybe you don't see the subject matter as gendered at all, but view desire and claustrophobia and nihilism as universal themes. Or perhaps you see the songs as storytelling, pure and simple. More likely, however, you go into Cool Girl mode — deferring to a male world view, while secretly unsure where to place yourself.

I can't speak for anybody but myself, but it's clear that my Cool Girl phase — a rite of passage for many young women at that time — found a natural corollary in mid-2000s indie. The hallmark of a Cool Girl was that you "got it". You didn't moan about trivial things, like the fact that every single musician at your local indie night was a bloke, or that the lineup at every festival was 90% male, or that female artists within the scene could expect music journalists to focus predominantly on their looks. Your fandom was always going to be more complex than mere identification, but what could you do but perfect your eyeliner, debate the bassist's shaggability, and try not to splash too much lager as you swayed about near the stage?

***

Over the last decade, a lot has changed. In broad-brush terms, as indie died, a wave of female solo artists swept in. And rather than being dismissed as "just pop", they were taken somewhat seriously — the watershed moment arriving in 2011 when Beyoncé headlined Glastonbury.

Without wanting to be too starry-eyed about it, I think the boom of "internet feminism" has given young women more and better templates for how to see themselves. You can say what you like about Instagram, but at least the girls posting #bodypos selfies or vlogging their diaries are defining their self-image on their own terms. I've not heard anyone claim to be "postfeminist" in a while.

The internet has also, according to some schools of thought, negated the need for clearly defined youth subcultures. If you can tweak your identity to your heart's content online, then why would you need an IRL means to signal your preferences? Today's twenty-year-olds are image-crafting individualists, rather than a lumpen mass of scenesters. As Alexis Petridis argued in 2014:

> As with virtually every area of popular culture, [youth subcultures have] been radically altered by the advent of the internet... we now live in a world where teenagers are more interested in constructing an identity online than they are in making an outward show of their allegiances and interests.[3]

Then there are all the ways that the music industry itself has mutated. If you can stream any artist you like, from any era or genre, within a few swipes of your phone, you're probably not going to end up listening to exactly the same bands as everyone else in your halls at university. I don't know what people *are* listening to in uni halls these days, but I'd wager their tastes have grown more fragmented and more sophisticated, with the wormhole of "related artists" on Spotify just as salient as whatever's getting airplay on Radio 1.

Guitar music is bound to make a comeback. The music wheel always turns full circle, and #indieamnesty did point to a real depth of nostalgia for our ripped T-shirts and ridiculous haircuts. That said, there's no going back to the more homogeneous, narrowly focused parts of that scene. By the time the kids start forming nu-indie bands, I am hopeful they will take the energy and the romance without the whitewashed, male-centric tedium that ultimately contributed to its demise.

Notes

1 Flynn, Gillian. *Gone Girl*. (Crown Publishing, 2012).

2 The Libertines, "Boys in the Band", *Up The Bracket*, (2002), Rough Trade. Copyright Peter Doherty, Carl Barat, EMI Publishing (2002).

3 Petridis, Alexis. "Youth subcultures: what are they now?". *The Guardian*, 20 March 2014. https://www.theguardian.com/culture/2014/mar/20/youth-subcultures-where-have-they-gone

Invisible Girls: Emo, Gender Trouble and the Problem of Femininity

Judith May Fathallah

The road outside my house is paved with good intentions
Hired a construction crew, 'cause it's hell on the engine
You are the dreamer and we are the dream.
I could write it better than you ever felt it.
— Fall Out Boy, "Hum Hallelujah"[1]

When I was thirteen, I was institutionalised for anorexia nervosa. That's not what this chapter is about. This chapter is about emo, fandom, being a mixed race middle-class girl whose chief interests were writing and unhappiness, and finding my genre affiliation almost more in spite of my embodied gender than because of it.

We should probably note from the outset, however, that despite my aspirations to rescript my mental illness along the lines of Romantic artistry, I have never been comfortable in a feminine-coded body. Oppressed groups often split themselves along the lines of their stereotypes,[2] a psychological adaptation that Amber

Ault names "split subjectivity".[3] Accordingly, I was a girl, I supposed, if I must be — but never *that* kind of girl, not the stupid kind, the giggly made-up kind who wouldn't know an authentic thought if it hit her between the ears.

At the time, my brother was listening to Eminem. He had problems — girl problems, school problems, the kinds all teenagers have, the problems kids have when their siblings are crazy. Fancying myself as a connoisseur of language, I supposed it was rather good in places. Rather emotionally one-note, though, and being a girl, it was only a matter of time before Eminem's stated intentions to "put anthrax on a Tampax and slap you till you can't stand"[4] started to crawl under my skin in uncomfortable ways — it was, after all, *that* sort of boy who belonged to the groups that would bully me, who looked at me in disgusting ways, who advised me to suck on ice before blowing them, whose girlfriends called my Arab hair "pubes" because, you know, coloured girls are whores but also unsexable, or something, unless we're on our knees. That was the kind of school it was.

I'm not sure how I discovered emo, precisely. Whether loose association with the goth kids, after institutionalisation made me interesting, led to the music, or whether I picked up My Chem off the radio and we found each other that way around. Before that there had been pop-punk — Sum 41, Blink 182 — but I only really liked the sad songs and not the funny ones. Anyway, my sort-of boyfriend and I made a sort-of band, and I considered myself the creative type, so the first time I heard *Welcome to the Black Parade* its combination of musical sophistication, instruments I knew, lyrics about all the horrible things that comprised my primary interests, and sensitive painted boys with their makeup and exhibitionist suffering made me realise I was home.

***

Musically speaking, *Black Parade* is an album that gets funnier the older you get, but at sixteen I was thoroughly sincere. From My Chem to Fall Out Boy: it seemed that if MCR made songs about my *life*, Pete Wentz wrote the lyrics of what it was like to *live inside my mind*. This was the era of Livejournal: all the quiet kids had blogs, which we themed black and adorned with lyrics and wrote passionate, cryptic screeds on the intensity of being fifteen and smart. Emo bands had blogs too, interacting with their young fans on this weirdly levelled network, and having my new favourite writer share a platform and chat openly with kids like me brought a sense of community. It turned out there were other kids as smart and sensitive and self-important as I was (I couldn't really take anyone seriously who hadn't tried to kill themselves at least once. Clearly, they hadn't thought this life business through). Now, here was a genre smart enough for me, sounds ranging from the full orchestral bombast of mid-period My Chem to stripped-down acoustic and fast bare rhythms, lyrics rewarding my cultural capital and rapidly expanding knowledge of the English literary canon.

Emo has sometimes been hailed as the alternative to the misogyny and homophobia of the punk scene: Pete Wentz and FOB drummer Andy Hurley often cite these as reasons for quitting their earlier hardcore bands,

Racetraitor and Arma Angelus. And whilst it's true that, *Take This To Your Grave* possibly excepted, one does not encounter the naked misogyny of Dr Dre and Eminem in the catalogue of emo classics, there is frequently a subtler and more pervasive sexism at work — something that has been dubbed beta-male misogyny.[5] Hegemonic masculinity is a flexible concept, and much of its power comes from that very adaptability with the times.[6] If hegemonic masculinity is, as Raewyn Connell argues, the current cultural justification for patriarchy, that justification must change with every social, economic and cultural configuration that patriarchy survives, from the physical power of the tribal leader to the analytical intelligence attributed to male business leaders. The figure of the sensitive man, as Sam dé Boise demonstrated, the artist of refined sensibility, has as frequently been used to shore up patriarchal dominance as it has to challenge it.[7] If we consider the Romantic period which emo references both semiotically and lyrically (see: the entire stage wardrobes of Panic! At the Disco), we can observe that the dominant figure of the male artist-auteur depends on his exceptional sensitivity, his specialness in a painfully obtuse and mundane world.

Where does this leave women? In her scathing rant titled "Emo: Where the Girls Aren't", Jessica Hopper argues that in the post-2000 revival of emo, girls are denied personality and agency, relegated to the tired Romantic tropes of "Muses at best, cum-rags or invisible at worse" — a criticism equally applicable to the poems of Donne or Keats.[8] In emo's vulnerability, Hopper adds, there is no empathy, no peerage or parallelism.

Emo's yearning doesn't connect it with women — it omits them. "I could write it better than you ever felt it", Patrick Stump accuses the imagined addressee in Pete Wentz's words. Authenticity of feeling and experience is reserved for the male narrator.

The addressee of this song is a girl, naturally: he "loves [her] in the same way / There's a chapel in hospital / One foot in [her] bedroom / And one foot out the door". "Hum Hallelujah" is the only FOB song explicitly referencing Wentz's 2005 suicide attempt: the line "I sing the blues and swallow them too" is a pun referring to the Ativan pills on which he overdosed. The girl in question, as every fan knows, is Jeanae White: Wentz's on-off girlfriend throughout the early FOB years, explicitly named as a primary source of suffering and creativity. As he told reporter Brian Hiatt in a now-famous *Rolling Stone* spread:

> "She's irresistible, I guess. The best ones are crazy, for sure... There are parts of me that are like, 'Yeah, we could get married', but there are parts of me that couldn't spend tonight with her. [...] I don't know that she cares about the songs [he writes] as much as everybody else who listens to them does," he says. He seems half-asleep, his eyelids drifting down. "But I don't know if I could write them if she cared that much. If you could ever explain yourself to somebody, why would you keep explaining again and again?"[9]

Jeanae disappears from the scene around the turn of the decade, but it barely matters. Jeanae-as-addressee emblematises the invisible girl in emo culture: scene queen, inspiration, villainess, addressee; but never agent, person, narrator.

***

As a teenager, I couldn't have cared less about the lack of female subjects in emo, largely because I identified with the boys. I saw myself as a writer before I saw myself as a girl. Suffering from a fair degree of internalised misogyny, I did see default-girl as lesser: less intelligent, less creative, more preoccupied with trivial nonsense. I didn't identify with those people at all, but with the narrator as self-conscious suffering poet. Emo provided a narrative through which I could understand my pain, set to gorgeous complex soundscapes I could never dream of composing, with which I could block out my present surroundings and the monotonous thud-thump of my brother's rap.

Emo is a distinctly middle-class genre.[10] Its performers and audience are middle-class, and in order to understand the range of reference and quotation bands like My Chem make use of, one needs a basic degree of musical education and a more-than-basic literary one. Like all teenagers, I perceived myself as the exceptional one in my family, the misunderstood genius, a belief which was consolidated by my acceptance to the University of Cambridge. My mother told me off for spending all my time reading, on the computer, and/or with headphones in my ears, a reprimand I found excruciatingly painful, for wasn't it obvious I was too special, too sensitive for my immediate surroundings? Once I got past the initial appreciation of Eminem's wordplay, the stuff my brother was listening to began to horrify me:

> They said I can't rap about being broke no more
> They ain't say I can't rap about coke no more
> (AH!) Slut, you think I won't choke no whore
> 'Til the vocal cords don't work in her throat no more?![11]

My mother's comment on this was, "well he's an angry young man, Eminem's an angry young man". But I was angry too: angrier than all of them, in the quiet burning way girls are taught to be angry, the kind of anger that fuels seven-day fasts of nothing but diet hot chocolate (40 cals) and a couple of slimmer soups a day. Emo rewarded and confirmed my self-image, the good kid quietly burning up with rage, the writer, the artist, trapped in mundane mediocre surroundings, by crudity and philistinism, going to school with idiots. I was the one with legitimate pain, after all: I was the one who went crazy. Eminem used to pulse through our house, but I only listened to my music privately, possessive and enlightened and secret.

***

And then there was the "stage-gay". Emo bands are notorious for boy-on-boy kissing and make-outs onstage, nominally as a fuck-you to homophobic hecklers. Naturally, slash fiction inspired by this abounds; I'd been reading slash since I was fourteen or so, but emo bands provided the material themselves, enthusiastically, politically, performatively.

Academic responses to stage-gay are mixed. Emo marks a departure from the structural political critiques of Eighties hardcore bands, a turning inwards to address interpersonal and intra-personal politics, though not without reference to broader social categories. Unsurprisingly, then, often Butler and queer theory form the bases of some readings of emo;[12] on the one hand, if all gender is performative, such statements absolutely introduce catalysts for change into the often homophobic, sexist environment of the rock show and the mosh pit. Emo bands are explicit about the political dimensions of queer performance, opposing it in a Butlerian sense to essentialist gender and sexual identity. MCR's Gerard Way describes his on-stage make-outs with rhythm guitarist Frank Iero as designed "to challenge gender standards and homophobia".[13] Claiming to identify more with women than men, he describes his combination of leather jackets and feminine makeup as "pushing against homophobia and gender boundaries".[14] Fall Out Boy's Pete Wentz has appeared on the cover of *OUT* magazine (July 2008) with the headline, "Yeah, I am a fag", though he elaborates in the interview:

> There is a sense of self-empowerment or recapturing who you are by people calling you "fag", and being like, "Yeah, I am a fag". Even though you're not. What does somebody respond?[15]

He goes on to describe his sexual activities with men as involving "a slight sense of sexual rebellion", admitting that he "probably even made it a bigger deal than it was".

Ultimately, most emo band members are married or in long-term relationships with women, and some critics read stage-gay as an insulting and calculated masquerade, a profit-and-publicity orientated perform‑ ance available to straight men who don't run the real physical and financial risks of coming out. Perhaps this is a little harsh, seeing as both My Chem and Panic! have been bottled at festivals for appearing too queer, for feminine trespass on masculine-coded territory. Clearly, stage-gay carries some degree of risk, or did in the early 2000s. That risk is not on the level of actually coming out, though, and there is no doubt stage-gay was a profitable strategy and means of garnering attention. At fifteen, I knew none of this. I just knew it was hot. I just knew that it pleased my developing queer sexuality. I just knew I loved watching androgynous boys kiss, that it gratified and ratified me while a million heteronormative narratives left me cold.

So, while emo has its problems with gender dynamics and even misogyny, it also makes gender trouble.[16] Emo problematises the straight/gay masculine/feminine divides in ways that are absolutely part of a capitalist money-making machine, but which offer avenues and affordances to young queer intellectuals who are stigmatised and erased in other areas of their life. The *uses* (and gratifications) made of emo bands, the enjoyment and manipulation of these texts, particularly by girls but also by un-masculine boys, are interesting and valuable in an era of feminist backlash where, even as binaries are problematised in the public sphere, the conservative right seeks to reinstate boundaries and re-box women into passive femininity.

Notes

1   Fall Out Boy, "Hum Hallelujah", *Infinity on High*, (2007), Island Records. Copyright Leonard Cohen, Andrew John Hurley, Patrick Martin Stump, Joseph Mark Trohman, Peter L Wentz, Bad Monk Publishing, Chicago X Softcore Songs, Sony, ATV Songs LLC (2007).

2   Ault 1996; Collins 2000; Fanon 1994; Ferguson 2003; Stanfil 2013.

3   Ault, Amber. "The Dilemma of Identity: Bi Women's Negotiations". In Seidman, S. (ed.), *Queer Theory/ Sociology*. (Wiley-Blackwell, 1996) p. 314

4   Eminem, "Superman", *The Eminem Show* (2003). Copyright Eminem, Bass Jeffrey Irwin, King Steven Lee, Eight Mile Style Music, Kobalt Music Publishing Ltd (2003).

5   Kennedy, Joe. "Ariel Pink and Beta-Male Misogyny". *The Quietus*, 24 September 2012; de Boise, Sam. "Cheer Up Emo Kid: Rethinking the 'Crisis of Masculinity' in Emo". *Popular Music* 33, 2014.

6   Connell, Raewyn. *Masculinities*. (University of California Press, 2005).

7   de Boise 2014.

8   See e.g., DiPascale, Teresa. "Donne, Women and the Space of Misogyny". In Flynn, D.M., Hester, T. and Shami, J. (eds.) *The Oxford Handbook of John Donne*. (Oxford University Press, 2012); Alwes, Karla. *Imagination Transformed: The Evolution of the Female Character in Keats's Poetry*. (Southern Illinois University Press, 2013).

9   Quoted in Hiatt, Brian. "Fall Out Boy: The Fabulous Life and Secret Torment of America's Hottest Band". *Rolling Stone* 8, March 2007.

10 Greenwald, Andy. *Nothing Feels Good: Punk Rock, Teenagers and Emo.* (Macmillan, 2003) p. 55.

11 Eminem, "Kill You", *The Marshall Mathers LP* (2000), Aftermath Entertainment/Shady Records/Interscope Records. Copyright Melvin Charles Bradford, Marshall Mathers, Andre Romell Young, Eight Mile Style Music, Ain't Nothin But Funkin' Music, Hard Working Black Folk Inc, Kobalt Music Publishing Limited, Societe P E C F, W B Music Corp (2000)

12 Peters, Brian. "Emo Gay Boys and Subculture: Postpunk Queer Youth and (Re)Thinking Images of Masculinity". *Journal of LGBT Youth*, 7:2, 2010; de Boise 2014.

13 Via Twitter. Available at: https://twitter.com/gerardway/status/348534038497206272

14 Way, Gerard. "Fell to Earth, but He's Back on His Feet: Gerard Way Talks About His Comeback Album, 'Hesitant Alien'". *New York Times.* 18 October 2014.

15 Krochmal, Shana Naomi. "This Charming Man". *OUT*, 29 June 2008.

16 Butler, Judith. *Gender Trouble: Feminism and the Subversion of Identity.* (Routledge, 1990).

Bibliography

Alwes, Karla. *Imagination Transformed: The Evolution of the Female Character in Keats's Poetry*. (Southern Illinois University Press, 2013).

Ault, Amber. "The Dilemma of Identity: Bi Women's Negotiations". In Seidman, S. (ed.), *Queer Theory/Sociology*. (Wiley-Blackwell, 1996) pp. 311–330.

Butler, Judith. *Gender Trouble: Feminism and the Subversion of Identity*. (Routledge, 1990).

Collins, Patricia Hill. *Black Feminist Thought: Knowledge, Consciousness, and the Politics of Empowerment*. (Routledge, 2000).

Connell, Raewyn. *Masculinities*. (University of California Press, 2005).

de Boise, Sam. "Cheer Up Emo Kid: Rethinking the 'Crisis of Masculinity' in Emo". *Popular Music* 33, 2014, pp. 225–242.

DiPascale, Teresa. "Donne, Women and the Space of Misogyny". In *The Oxford Handbook of John Donne*. (Oxford University Press, 2012). http://www.oxfordhandbooks.com/view/10.1093/oxfordhb/9780199218608.001.0001/oxfordhb-9780199218608-e-56

Fanon, Franz. 1994. *Black Skin, White Masks*. (Grove Press, 1994).

Ferguson, Roderick. *Aberrations in Black: Toward a Queer of Color Critique*. (University of Minnesota Press, 2003).

Greenwald, Andy. *Nothing Feels Good: Punk Rock, Teenagers and Emo*. (Macmillan, 2003).

Hiatt, Brian. "Fall Out Boy: The Fabulous Life and Secret Torment of America's Hottest Band". *Rolling Stone*, 8 March 2007. http://www.rollingstone.com/music/

news/fall-out-boy-the-fabulous-life-and-secret-torment-of-americas-hottest-band-20070308

Hopper, Jessica. "Emo: Where the Girls Aren't". *Punk Planet* 56, 2003. http://www.rookiemag.com/2015/07/where-the-girls-arent

Kennedy, Joe. "Ariel Pink and Beta-Male Misogyny". *The Quietus*, 24 September 2012. http://thequietus.com/articles/10133-ariel-pink-beta-male-misogyny

Krochmal, Shana Naomi. "This Charming Man". *OUT*, 29 June 2008. http://www.out.com/entertainment/2008/06/29/charming-man

Peters, Brian. "Emo Gay Boys and Subculture: Postpunk Queer Youth and (Re)Thinking Images of Masculinity". *Journal of LGBT Youth*, 7:2, 2010. pp. 129–146.

Stanfill, Mel. "'They're losers, but I know better': Intra-Fandom Stereotyping and the Normalization of the Fan Subject". *Critical Studies in Media Communication* 30:2 2012. pp. 117–134.

Way, Gerard. "Fell to Earth, but He's Back on His Feet: Gerard Way Talks About His Comeback Album, 'Hesitant Alien'". *New York Times*, 18 October 2014. http://www.nytimes.com/2014/10/19/arts/music/gerard-way-talks-about-his-comeback-album-hesitant-alien.html?_r=0

We At War With Ourselves: On Being a Kanye Fan

Laura Friesen

I was eighteen when *The College Dropout* was released. It was a formative time. I was very near the beginning of my nascent music obsession, my emerging pop vocabulary, and Kanye West entered the public — and my own — pop consciousness in his then-current form: tweed-blazer'd and doubt-laden, airing his personal and academic misgivings in Chaka Khan- and Lauryn Hill-sampling hooks and self-deprecating verses that were tormented and hilarious in equal measure. Heads and ears were turned West-ward, and I was no exception.

Liking rap was new to me. I seemed to fulfill a stereotype back then, although I was less aware of it than I am now: I was a white woman who usually liked rock music but who also dabbled in Kanye West, because of course I did. West had a reputation, or at least his first three albums do, of being entry-level hip hop for white people. His tweed blazer wasn't intimidating; his preppy, respectable appearance signalled approachability before I even put the CD on. When I did, I heard him rap about feeling like an outsider, insecure and unsure. His skits had DeRay Davis saying ridiculous and identifiable things like, "No, I've never had sex, but my degree keeps me satisfied." I laughed along with him, and I listened. This was rap I could relate to.

To be fair, in 2004, a portion of this wide, mainstream acceptance had to do with how West positioned himself as a performer. He was marketed to the rock kids, those listeners who didn't know about his previous hip hop production credits, his now-so-familiar-they've-become-almost-dated soul samples. He was primed for huge success in all the pop markets. Regardless of my own naiveté when approaching West's music, it met me halfway. It took hardly any effort to be a Kanye fan in 2004.

It's been an uphill effort since then. His music has, in some cases, become less instantly head-boppable and more of an investment, but his antics have made him fully controversial. West started out famous and has only become more astronomically public — and publicly consumable — since then. Celebrities are always eaten up and spat out by the whims and prejudices of their time, and West is indeed maligned by the public; sometimes for the right reasons and sometimes for the wrong ones. Aligning himself with someone as egregiously racist, misogynist and terrifyingly powerful as Donald Trump is not going to be a lauded move: not only is this violently cognitively dissonant, but it underlines West's extreme privilege and wealth that Trump's damaging policies slide off him as they harm marginalised people, some of whom look up to him. It's a baffling manoeuvre, and he deserves the backlash he's getting. But people also hate his ego, his hubris, his hyperbolic approach to masculinity and life in the public eye, and these are the things I often find myself revelling in. I do, however, find fault in his constant onslaught of sexism.

The infamous "George Bush doesn't care about black people" line, unforgettably delivered on live TV in 2005, served as an indication of Kanye-isms to come, among the first in a long series of explosive statements. However, as we've seen, not all of the inflammatory things West has uttered — or tweeted — have been truthful or socially productive, but he's still bent on what seems like a compulsive need to share his thoughts with the world, using the cultural megaphone he wields.

As I became a fan and continued to devour his albums and observe his antics, I started to examine why I feel drawn to West's work and what that says about my own identity. Part of that means examining aspects of his music that make me uncomfortable and sometimes nauseous, like the fact that West has shown (and he has, irrefutably), over the course of seven albums and thirteen years, that he hates women. And that, as a mostly woman-identified person myself, I'm included in that.

I have an uneasy relationship with gender. I suppose I'm bad at being a woman — I feel alienated from many feminine, socially constructed signifiers of womanhood and am indifferent to my biological femaleness — but I always viewed it as someone else's problem. I didn't feel the need to change myself; more that if other people wanted to impose things on me and and blame it on gender or what girls were supposed to be like, then it wasn't my issue but theirs. I was perfectly content being the only kind of girl, or person, I knew how to be. In my personal pursuit of happiness, I'm continually inventing and defining myself. I'm perfectly fine with being a woman as long as I can be a big fucked-up mess of contradictions and mistakes, and most of the time, this feels possible.

Laurie Penny has written about how, after a long journey on the way to genderqueerness, she came to identify outside of the gender binary, yet she shifts back under its categorisation for political reasons: as long as women's reproductive freedom is under attack, she identifies as a woman.[1] I feel similarly, but at the same time I've never been comfortable joining groups or identifying as part of a community. To put it another way, I've always felt myself to be a spectator, outside of West's gender politics and his hierarchy of fuckability. I don't feel myself especially identified or named in his complaints about bitches and hos and exes who've double-crossed him. But this is, of course, dangerous territory to tread. This could assume that those identities outside of the ones in Kanye's order of women — those he deems fuckable and consequently fuck-with-able — aren't implicated in his misogyny and can engage with his work as fans from a safe, removed distance. For me, this is wrong. His words are about me and my community. The implications for the women in his songs are always terrible: women are seductive and sly and never to be trusted: at their most benign they'll come after his money and at their most wicked they'll steal his soul.

Listen to most of his songs and the misogyny is front and centre. It varies in vehemence, but it's always there. The earliest, perhaps most casual, offense was "The New Workout Plan"; the one even your mom sang along to was "Gold Digger"; the scariest, most menacing was "Monster" (both song and video); and the most recent was "Famous", again in both song and video. The thing about West and women is that they always want something from him; they're always using him for money or fame or both. He just can't seem to get these desperate women off his back. He paints them so rudimentarily, as mere outlines of people, and compared with the contradictions and complexities he allows himself, it feels threatening.

There's a small yet vital flame that disappears in me when the thread of connection I previously felt with a musician dies, and it came very close to happening with West early in 2016 with his inflammatory "Bill Cosby innocent" tweets. The connection between me and an artist can be tenuous at times, but instances like this force me to consider what it might take to remove myself from the fan roster, to disengage, to stop looking for the humanity in his work because he failed to find the humanity in the lives of women.

His misogyny does matter to me, and while I have no interest in defending it, I will defend his artistic freedom, his self-love and opportunism, and yes, his vulnerability — even his right — to ebbs in mental health, just like the rest of us. I like his scene-making urge — the urge that has him identify that "I'm not out of control / I'm just not in they control"[2] ("Saint Pablo"). The outsider in me sees the outsider in him. A lot of this identification lies in that need to push buttons and be contradictory, seen and acknowledged; defiant at any cost.

For better or worse, I identify with West's need to document his own contradictions. In "All Of The Lights" he invites listeners to look at everything in his life: the irresponsible and the criminal, with all of its ugliness magnified under the harsh glare of fame. In the verses of "Power", he's totally onboard with his own brilliance — his black genius — but falters at the hook and checks himself with surprisingly believable self-reproach: "No one man should have all that power".[3] He almost convinced himself that he deserves it.

There's more than a whiff of the perpetually haunted *artiste* about West that's endlessly compelling. Despite his middle-class origins and instant success, despite fame and fortune, despite notoriety and power, his art for me will always come from an outsider's perspective. Popularity and fame make it worse. Fans and critics alike make it worse. "FML" spells it out explicitly: "Even though I always fuck my life up, only I can mention me".[4] On "Lost in the World" he's "been down my whole life".[5] And he admits that freedom is the only thing that matters to him: "I just wanna feel liberated / If I ever instigated, I am sorry / Tell me who in here can relate"[6] ("Father Stretch My Hands Pts. 1 and 2"). Whether he goes with or against society's expectations of him, it doesn't look like he'll ever be free from his own self-contradictory, forever shifting expectations, and that speaks to me.

"Runaway" vamps an extended outro, and while much of *My Beautiful Dark Twisted Fantasy* uses the same plasticky synthesizers of *808s and Heartbreak*, I can't help but feel that its use here is purposeful, a return to the emotions-on-ice suppression of *808s*. The cold grip of these machines has taken him over and his words are barely decipherable through ragged cutaway gasps, irregular and raw. As I listen, I start to dwell on the pain of his imperfections and infidelities as much as he does. I hear him realise what's happening, unable to break the cycle, and feeling doomed to repeat his mistakes for his own foreseeable future. It's bleak, and it rings true to me. I relate to the feeling that I will never stop disappointing the people I care for.

Yeezy *has* taught me, but not with his myopic notions of sex and gender and reupholstery and performance ("The Blame Game"). His views are utterly, disappointingly average in that respect. But his insights about himself taught me valuable things about myself: about feeling alien for everything I am and everything I can never be, about that constant, niggling feeling of self-doubt that will not just never go away, but become louder and more persistent with each day. At the same time, his line on "Dark Fantasy" is true for me: there *is* bravery in bravado, and there's particular bravery in bravado when you're a person whose identity is marginalised, vilified and misrepresented. West's music trades on his struggle with being a flawed, changing person: the bare minimum of humanity we all, regardless of gender, deserve.

Notes

1 Penny, Laurie. "How To Be A Genderqueer Feminist." *BuzzFeed*, 31 October 2015. www.buzzfeed.com/ lauriepenny/how-to-be-a-genderqueer-feminist

2 Kanye West, "Saint Pablo", *The Life of Pablo* (2016), GOOD/Def Jam. Copyright Michael Deric Angelettie, Shawn Carter, Mike Dean, Ronald Anthony Lawrence, Sampha Sisay, Kanye West, Jesse Norman Whitfield, Ausar Music, Beggars Tunes, Deric Angelettie Music, Donda Music Publishing, EMI April Music Inc, EMI Blackwood Music Inc, Lil Lu Lu Publishing, Noah Goldstein Music, Papa George Music, Please Gimme My Publishing Inc, Stone Diamond Music Corporation, Universal Music Careers, Warner-Tamerlane Publishing Corp and W B Music Corp (2016).

3 Kanye West, "POWER", *My Beautiful Dark Twisted Fantasy* (2010), Roc-A-Fella/Def Jam. Copyright Boris Bergman, Francois Pierre Camille Bernheim, Jeffrey Bhasker, Mike Dean, Robert Fripp, Michael Rex Giles, Larry Darnell Griffin, Malik Yusef El Shabazz Jones, Greg Lake, Jean-Pierre Lang, Ian Richard McDonald, Nathan Perez, Peter John Sinfield, Kanye West, Amaya Sofia Publishing, E G Music Limited, EMI Blackwood Music Inc, EMI Music Publishing France, Jabriel Iz Myne, Please Gimme My Publishing Inc, Roc Nation Music, Sony/ATV Songs LLC, Universal Music Careers, Universal Music Corporation, Vohndee's Soul Music Publishing, Warner Chappell Music France and Way Above Music (2010).

4 Kanye West, "FML", *The Life of Pablo* (2016), GOOD/ Def Jam. Copyright Ross Matthew Birchard, Christian Keyon Boggs Jr, Ernest Eugene Brown III, Marcus

Darrell Byrd, Lawrence John Cassidy, Vincent Nicholas Cassidy, Andrew Dawson, Michael G Dean, Noah D Goldstein, Darius Jenkins, Grape Jelly Jams, Katherine Rachel Mills, Travis Scott, Abel Tesfaye, Leland Tyler Wayne, Kanye West, Paul Michael Wiggin, Cydel Charles Young, BMG Platinum Songs US, EMI Blackwood Music Inc, Irving Music, Mr Redan, Please Gimme My Publishing, Pluto Mars Music, Songs By Seventy 7 Music, Songs of Universal Inc, Travis Scott Music and Warp Music Limited (2016).

5 Kanye West, "Lost in the World", *My Beautiful Dark Twisted Fantasy* (2010), Roc-A-Fella/Def Jam. Copyright Jeffrey Bhasker, Edwin J Bocage, James Brown, Odilien Dibango, Gil Scott Heron, Alfred Scramuzza, Justin DeYarmond Edison Vernon, Kanye West, April Base Publishing, Brouhaha Music, Dynatone Publishing, EMI Blackwood Music Inc, EMI Music Publishing France, Please Gimme My Publishing Inc, Sony/ATV Songs LLC, Sony ATV Music Publishing France, Swing Beat Songs, Uzza Publishing Co and Way Above Music (2010).

6 Kanye West, "Father Stretch My Hands Pt 1", *The Life of Pablo* (2016), GOOD/Def Jam. Copyright T L Barrett Jr, Chancelor Johnathan Bennett, Mike Dean, Noah D Goldstein, Samuel Zadoc Griesemer, Malik Yusef El Shabazz Jones, Scott Ramon Seguro Mescudi, Jerome Christophe Potter, Allen Raphael Ritter, Rick Rubin, Leland Tyler Wayne, Kanye Omari West, Cydel Charles Young, All The Noise, American Def Tune, Big Wave More Fire, BMG Platinum Songs US, Boogiedown Music, Donda Music Publishing, Elsie's Baby Boy, EMI April Music Inc, EMI Blackwood Music Inc, Irving Music, Jabriel Iz Myne, JLOL ASCAP, Mr Redan, Noah Goldstein Music,

Ain't Nothing Like a Smart Bitch

Anna Fielding

I went dancing a lot that year. A long relationship had ended and I was running about town with more friends than I'd ever remembered having made. It was 2010 and we stayed up all night to watch the strange, inconclusive general election. There were house parties, art shows, fanzine launches, supposedly quiet evenings in the pub ("Three pints of Staropramen and a bottle of house white, please!"). And there was dancing. In a disused multi-storey car park where a friend met her future husband. In a warehouse, pre-Christmas, where it was so cold that parts of the floor were skiddy with ice. In various basement clubs, opening and shutting and changing names so frequently it felt they merged into one venue, and where the wiring never seemed to get finished, however often you went back.

That night we were in a tiny room above one of the longer-standing bars on London's Kingsland Road. The lights were red-orange and Romy from the electronic indie band the XX was playing a set of the RnB records she always spoke about in interviews. I was just happy to be out, because at that point I was happiest moving through the night.

L to the O. V to the E. K to the I. N to the G.

There's a feeling, on dancefloors, when a track you really love drops. A current zapping a circuit between every moving body. A collective exhale.

I don't know how they treat you / I don't know where you at / But all I'm trying to say is / You should know me like that.

It was The-Dream. It was "Love King"[1], from the album with the same title he'd released that year. The-Dream, real name Terius Nash, has had his most obvious successes as a songwriter and a producer. He's the man behind Justin Bieber's "Baby", Rihanna's "Umbrella" and Beyoncé's "Single Ladies (Put A Ring On It)". These are global mega hits: songs that can make swathes of the world move in sync. The music he creates for himself is less widely known (most music is less widely known), but it's sonically complex and often beautiful. Lyrically, he veers between shameless sex god posturing, clever turns of phrase, astute emotional intelligence and the downright daft. "Love King", at its most basic, is a list of all the women he's shagging and how he portions himself out amongst them ("half to my main girl, quarter to my side chick"). It's also a shimmering piece of synthesised magic. For my group, it was one of the songs of the summer.

Got girls in heels / Girls in Adidas / Tracey, Kim / Tameka, Fatima.

The-Dream was listing his girls. I was dancing with some of the lads, but I was looking for a girl too.

Got a girl that's shy / A girl that's a freak / A girl when I'm sick / She watch what I eat.

Where was Annabel? My lovely mate Annabel. I needed to find her before a particular line. Because she would get it, like no one else I was with.

Got a girl up in Target / A girl out of college

There she was.

Because, sorry ladies / There ain't nothing like a smart bitch

The high-five landed. We danced the rest of the song out together. Girls, women, several years out of college. The journalist and the search engine optimisation specialist. Smart bitches.

There is so much to go through here that it makes me groan. Unpacking The-Dream in relation to feminism prompts similar feelings of tiredness and confusion to looking at the boxes you have moved into a new house: there is no obvious place to start and you may still mislay some essentials.

I realise, listening to "Love King", that there are references that would strike a different chord if I were American and not British. I have never flown on Delta Air Lines, for example (but what would The-Dream — lucky man — know of easyJet?). There are certainly parts of the song which would carry a different resonance if I were black and not white. I interpret a lyric to do with claiming a weave as your own hair as being rather catty on The-Dream's part, but I'm aware there are complexities I will miss.

Throughout the song, women are set up as contrasting types: church service attendee or club goer? Shy kid or bedroom freak? The girl working in Target, the US chain of discount shops, suffers from the implication she isn't very bright, purely because she's placed next to the smart-bitch college girl. At no point does The-Dream say these girls fight over him — his tone is of a man cheerfully enjoying pick-and-mix variety — but the juxtaposition calls up all the horrible ideas of feminine competitiveness: all the mean girls and queen bees hustling for first place, pulling hair, turning backs and detonating psychological bombs in not-quite whispers.

And yet, despite everything that sense and thoughtfulness tell me, I still want to fit myself into The-Dream's taxonomy of girls.

Hold with me on this one, but I find there's something comforting in the confessions of serial womanisers. "Christ, what a way to carry on", you think, reading the confessions of an ageing advertising executive in the weekend papers. "Sounds exhausting. And lonely." You would never want to go out with them, have them date your friends or marry your mother. And yet there's something exuberant in the way these men talk about women. Wide hips or small tits, natural afro or poker straight ginger, a birthmark, a chipped tooth, a Sheffield accent, swimmer's shoulders: everything is food for their fantasy, all women have desirable attributes. Wider beauty standards lose their currency. This can be seductive reading. If everything listed is attractive, then, surely, your own distinctive characteristics can be attractive too.

The-Dream's kid-in-a-sweet-shop approach to the women in "Love King" is far from ideal, but it's also miles away from outright misogyny. He thinks these girls are great! He doesn't want to see them humiliated or to chip away at their confidence with endless negging. There's a lovely, shiny pedestal for each of these women to stand on. He's after a good time for everyone and he doesn't need games for you to sleep with him. He's the Love King, after all. Ladies, he sings, we should know him like *that*.

There's obviously an issue here with depending on others for your self-esteem. With being viewed as a type or an interchangeable object. But it's easy for vanity to override sense and who can't say they don't feel a small, flattered thrill when discovering someone fancies them? No one likes to be creeped on, but most of us enjoy being desired. When you can use art of some kind to imagine being desired, without any of the attendant real world issues, then you're into a happy place. Of sorts.

"Sexy" is an attribute bestowed by others: by the culture at large or by an individual who wants to take you to bed. For heterosexual women, sexiness, in its many forms, is defined by men. "Love King" is full of joy at the infinite, wonderful variety of women. It reminds me of John Updike lovingly describing the quirks, physical differences and sex appeal of each of the Witches of Eastwick, or of his character Piet in *Couples* eyeing up his neighbours, all of whom are different from his wife. There are the girls Jack Kerouac's Sal and Dean meet on the road. The Beach Boys' considering all the women of America before deciding to keep things local with the California girls. Bukowski. Hemingway. Roth. Men of the twentieth century. Horndogs one and all.

Film critic Laura Mulvey developed the concept of "the male gaze" in 1975, pointing out how women in film are often portrayed as objects, because the eyes behind the camera often belong to men. Her idea has been used to analyse many other aspects of culture, from novels to adverts. Loving a song like "Love King", wanting to make yourself part of it, is not so much colluding with the male gaze as gleefully prancing about in front of it, wearing a bikini.

In Junot Diaz's 2012 short story collection *This Is How You Lose Her*, the central character Yunior sleeps around with such a vast variety of women — with Latinas, black women, *blanquitas*, an Iranian graduate student, a nurse, a woman who later publishes an online poem calling him a whore — that his fiancé catches him cheating in a spectacular fashion. "Because you are a totally batshit *cuero* who never empties his e-mail trash can, she caught you with fifty! Sure, over a six-year period, but still. Fifty fucking girls! *God damn!*"

Yeah. God damn.

Diaz's creation of Yunior, and Yunior's view of women, was described by Joe Fassler, writing in *The Atlantic*, as "chauvinistic method acting": the character was sexist, not the book, and not the author. I wonder if The-Dream is also slightly fictional, a hyper-real persona distinct from Terius Nash. Nash may have played a part in the creation of some of the twenty-first century's most known and loved songs, but he's not intrinsically cool or traditionally handsome. "He is a man incapable of looking good in photographs", noted journalist Alex Macpherson in a piece for *The National*. In his 2009 track "Put It Down", he admits he can't "sing like Usher" or "dance like Chris [Brown]".[2] But even if Nash does feel less-than in some areas, he's still lyrically confident about being a great lover. When he says "I could make you sing like Mariah", he's not bragging about his skills as a producer in the recording studio, more the ability to produce an orgasm that spans a seven-octave vocal range.

So, The-Dream gets to be the Love King and, on the dancefloor with my mate, I claimed the role of "smart bitch". There are other parts of the song I could probably shoehorn myself into (right now I'm sitting at a desk with both a pair of heels and a pair of Adidas kicked off underneath), so why that one? I'll leave the use of the word bitch, because that's a whole other essay that's been written many times before. It's the appeal of smart that interests me.

Intelligence isn't often equated with sex appeal, not in pop culture's broadest sweep. The bookish girl is relegated to the role of quirky best friend or unrequited lover (at least until she has a make-over). Conversely, actresses who primarily trade on their sex appeal are mocked when they're cast as "intelligent" characters. Denise Roberts, playing nuclear physicist Doctor Christmas Jones in the 1999 Bond film *The World Is Not Enough*, is a classic example of the latter. She was damned by cheesy script writing ("I've always wanted to have Christmas in Turkey") and then by the media reaction: even in 007's hyper-glamorous universe, Denise isn't plausible as a scientist.

The-Dream, however, thinks his smart girl is sexy. It's the reason he lists for finding her attractive and including her in the song. It also suggests that, at some point, he's spoken and listened to her (possibly on one of the many mobile-phone networks he namechecks). Her presence on the list suggests that all of the women may be more than objects.

I'm far from being the cleverest person I know, but I was a teenager who passed exams and I'm an adult who plays with words for a living. Intelligence is what

I value, in myself and others. When I hear "there ain't nothing like a smart bitch", I hear The-Dream telling me that he appreciates what I value, too. If I placed a relationship with God at the centre of my life, or a career at The-Dream's record label or a private-jet lifestyle, then I would hear The-Dream telling me he values that too. Clever man. It's very seductive.

This is what we all want, to be valued and desired. To have our uniqueness appreciated and understood. It's a lot to ask of a four-minute-twelve-second pop song. But it works well enough to ignore some of the other aspects. Even if you're a smart bitch who tends to overthink things.

Notes

1 The-Dream, "Love King", *Love King* (2010), Radio Killa/ Def Jam. Copyright Carlos Alexander McKinney, Terius Youngdell Nash, 2082 Music Publishing, Sony ATV Melody and W B Music Corp (2010).

2 The-Dream, "Put It Down", *Love vs. Money* (2009), Radio Killa/Def Jam. Copyright Carlos Alexander McKinney, Terius Youngdell Nash and Sony ATV Melody (2010).

Breaking Binary Codes: On Being a Female Fan Who Prefers Music Produced by Men

Larissa Wodtke

Jehnny Beth, vocalist for the band Savages, has said that asking how it feels to be a woman in a band is comparable to asking how it feels to be a woman eating a sandwich. This comparison resonated with me and my own thoughts about being a female. As a heterosexual female who often doesn't identify with femaleness, I spent a large part of my life seeing gender as artificial and irrelevant, and not understanding why being any particular gender mattered at all. For most of my life, I didn't feel like an outsider or other because of my gender, and I didn't see the point in emphasising, or even acknowledging, it as an aspect of my identity. If anything made me feel other, it was social class, or my introverted personality. I realise now that my attitude toward gender is based on premises comparable to those in post-racial ideology; theoretically, gender and its artificial, assumed characteristics can't be the basis of defining and discriminating against human beings. But just as we're not living in a post-racial society, we're not living in a post-gender society either.

My gender-fluid, androgynous, or non-binary preferences permeated all of my artistic tastes — books, film, comedy and music — but particularly dominated music. Taking a hard look at my favourite bands and musicians over my adolescence and early adulthood, and even to some extent at this current moment, I find an overwhelming majority of males. Though this percentage is undoubtedly influenced by the entrenched inequalities in the music industry, in which male artists were/are signed and promoted by record labels to a much higher degree than females, I know that my predilections have favoured a disproportionate number of males. Am I complicit in unequal gender power structures? Are my preferences and identification with these male artists part of an indirect misogyny? In this essay I want to problematise my seemingly "natural" tastes and dissect the music fan part of my identity, and in doing so ask how gender failure and performance can speak to fandom and connoisseurship of an often misogynist art form and industry. When I speak of gender performance I draw on Judith Butler's theory of gender being a cultural construction that needs to be repeated, making it an unnatural and fluid concept rather than ontological. Gender failure springs from the idea of gender performance in that it highlights the assumptions and artificiality of gender binary norms in failing to adhere to them and the performances they would require.

Although I enjoy and favour music created and performed by males, they tend to be males who exist in a fraught relationship with gender and sexuality. In other words, I never liked grunge or gangsta rap because masculinity in these genres appears more conventional, and in some cases, stereotypical. In analysing my favourite artists over the past twenty years or so, I can trace three main categories: androgynous/gender-fluid male artists (ie. David Bowie, Prince, Lou Reed, the Smiths, the Associates, Manic Street Preachers, Sparks, Suede, Patrick Wolf, Of Montreal, Wild Beasts, Jonny Cola and the A-Grades, King of Luxembourg, Japan, New York Dolls), asexual or cerebral males (ie. the Clash, Gang of Four, McCarthy, Joy Division/New Order, the Sound, Kraftwerk, Sex Pistols, Pet Shop Boys, British Sea Power, Einstürzende Neubauten, Scritti Politti, Pere Ubu, the Auteurs, PiL, Artery, the Passage, Swans, Can, Earl Brutus/the Pre New, Brian Eno, Algiers, Magazine, Orange Juice, the The, Death, Ultravox/John Foxx, Swell Maps/Nikki Sudden, Art Brut, Devo) and males who use a hyperbolic male sexuality to the point of irony (Jarvis Cocker, Nick Cave, Momus, Iggy Pop). Some artists fall into overlapping categories — for example, the Smiths, Manic Street Preachers, Sparks, Japan, Jarvis Cocker and Momus could also be perceived as asexual/cerebral, whilst Pet Shop Boys and Orange Juice perform non-normative masculinities.

In the music of my favourite artists, females either don't figure at all, or are filtered through the artists' place of privilege, figures written through and circumscribed by a male gaze that is historically determined to be a position of advantage and dominance. Oddly enough, it never occurred to me that I wasn't represented in these songs, nor that I was being misrepresented. Because

I saw myself as apart from gender, I didn't look to the objects of these songs for identification; if anything, I looked to the subjects and aspired to their agency, their intelligence and their gender play, and if they were a band, their homosociality. The aspects that draw me to this music are narrative, aesthetic and atypical content, both lyrical and musical. My affection for the affectless and artificial points to a distance from sentiment and emotions altogether. If romantic love of any sort was expressed in my favourite songs, it was lost, unimportant, frustrated or ironic. Whilst not all of these artists are as explicitly disinterested in love as McCarthy's "Boy Meets Girl So What", emotions, such as romantic love, are so clichéd in these songs as to be rendered a ludicrous pose. I don't think anyone could believe in the Jesus and Mary Chain's cherry-candy-razorblade love; pastiche prevents emotional connection as much as the more incisive, intellectual critiques of bands like Scritti Politti and McCarthy.

I enjoy Sixties girl-group music, but in the same capacity that I enjoy it when it's transmogrified into the Jesus and Mary Chain. It's a genre haunted by a spectre/Spector with often sinister undertones and a knowing attitude, giving it a more intriguing depth for me. I certainly don't take the sentiments in this genre at face value. In my penchant for the emotional distance in this music, am I buying into the masculinity/rationality versus femininity/emotionality tropes? If I am, it's because *I* don't fit these tropes, but my favourite music does.

All the same, my love for androgynous and ironically masculine male artists complicates this position.

Gender performance, as Judith Butler defines it, is emphasised in these examples; authenticity is absent as both reality and concept, and the artificiality of gender binary tropes are emphasised and blurred. In popular music, the performative aspect of gender is often noted in the hyperbolic glam aesthetic of artists like David Bowie, Roxy Music, T. Rex, New York Dolls and Sparks, which, in work like Philip Auslander's, is associated with inauthenticity and ambiguity. In 1964, Susan Sontag may have only witnessed her theory of camp in the popular music of "post rock-'n'-roll, what the French call yé yé", but later writers, such as Simon Reynolds, could draw on her theory to describe glam. Like drag, the glam genre reveals the underlying falsity and performativity of gender that can be added and removed at will. However, the "feminine" characteristics assumed by these male artists often do not render them straightforwardly female, but something other and alien; their theatricality is read as escapism and an act of imagination.

In a similar way, the falsetto of Prince, Kevin Barnes from Of Montreal, Hayden Thorpe of Wild Beasts, Russell Mael of Sparks and Green Gartside of Scritti Politti produce an effect of otherness. According to the *Oxford English Dictionary*, falsetto is the diminutive of *falso*, the Italian for false. Like the coded feminine attributes adopted by glam artists, falsetto does not transform male artists into a straightforward performance of the opposite gender. The falsetto voices of my favourite artists are transcendent and supernatural, disembodied and alien. In the case of Green Gartside, the vocal even sounds eerily synthetic and hyperreal — much like the meticulous simulacrum of a soulful voice — bolstering his already deconstructionist pop music. Of course, the fact that males can use falsetto to achieve this otherness and use it artistically speaks to their inherent position of power and the corresponding opportunity to deviate from it; as Jeffrey Melnick describes falsetto, it "announces that the singer is male but has the ability to travel away from this established identity". In fact, for some of these artists, including Prince, Kevin Barnes, and Hayden Thorpe, falsetto is used to reinscribe their heterosexual male sexuality.

Genderqueerness need not be tied to queer sexuality, and when gender is untangled from sexuality, additional ways of being open up. For me, my occasional desire for these male artists co-exists with my desire to be like them; these simultaneous and interconnected desires complicate notions of heterosexuality and heteronormativity, especially since I don't experience this duality of desire for female artists. Furthermore, much of the music I love turns these desires in on themselves and reinforces the pleasures of the inner world that accompanies my introverted personality even when this music would seem to be outwardly encouraging the opposite.

If I turn to another of my favourite genres, northern soul, I see an example of a collective aloneness, using the upbeat melodies and rhythms with their emotional lyrics as a cathartic escape, especially from class conditions, but also from race and gender expectations — a care of self, set to a four-four beat. It's pure kinetic energy and adrenaline flushing out thought itself — the lyrics move beyond love and loss, and can stand in for other emotions and other situations, regret and survival can apply to everyday trials and setbacks. The obscurity of the music and opposition to the mainstream that defined the genre paradoxically created liberation through elitism. In other words, its reliance on subcultural capital endowed its fans with a sense of power otherwise missing from their lives.

This kind of empowerment relates to the kind of strength I found in mastering particular musical canons even though they were, like other cultural canons, dominated by males. Even though its founding resources largely exclude females, I find it difficult to dismiss my development of confidence about making connections between genres, artists, cultural contexts and time periods, and the sense of belonging and meaning that came with it. Becoming a music fan grew in tandem with my other interests in culture and its theories, and I view this growth as a positive, and often self-preserving, experience. Music became one of many access points to critical thought and an understanding of socioeconomic systems, especially in Marxist terms.

The artists I classify here as cerebral often use popular music to express leftist politics and an affinity with the working class. These are issues that govern my identity more closely and make themselves felt in my everyday existence. I haven't found this emphasis on social class and identity in the music of female artists (with the exception of mixed-gender bands like the Au Pairs, the Indelicates and Shopping). Perhaps this tendency exists because gender politics dominate the music of female artists as a primary concern — indeed it makes sense to represent gender politics when you belong to a group whose gendered existence is underrepresented in the music industry and society as a whole. Whether you like it or not, your existence as a female musician is already a political act. There's an implicit obligation to give a voice to this group because ignoring it seems morally wrong when gender inequality and misogyny continue to exist. It's this sense of obligation that is essentially driving this essay.

In their privileged position of default, male performers (and male fans) don't necessarily have to undergo the same scrutiny, and they don't have to be standard bearers on behalf of an entire group. They don't have obligations to respond to and constantly renegotiate their position within the art form they chose. They are allowed to exist as artfully, artificially or affectlessly as they want. They can engage with a wide range of material, with or without feeling, with free range over the gender spectrum. Conversely, in Simon Reynolds and Joy Press's *The Sex Revolts: Gender, Rebellion and Rock 'N ' Roll*, female musicians ultimately find themselves in a catch-22: if they're too conventionally feminine, they're reinforcing stereotypes about their gender, but if they're too masculine, they're denying their gender and mimicking the negative characteristics associated with male performance. Despite some heteronormative male pressures, male musicians are not encumbered to this extent; they are more likely to be seen as expanding the ways of being male, whereas females are more often seen as demonstrating the ways in which they are restricted by their gender. I myself wanted to be a less restrictive default and to be seen as essentially genderless or non-binary. I definitely don't hate female musicians and music (in fact, there are an increasing number of those whom I love), but I hate the ways in which societal norms prescribe and circumscribe them. Just as Jonathan Miller has only agreed to be identified as Jewish when faced with anti-Semitism, I'll stand as female if confronted with irrational gender assumptions or misogyny, veiled or otherwise.

I am repeatedly irritated and exasperated by assumptions made about females and music fandom in general. My first real confrontation with these assumptions was when I began a music blog in 2008. I wrote under a genderless pseudonym and thought nothing about it until I discovered several readers had assumed I was male. This wasn't a negative experience, just more of a surprise. However, in more recent years, these incidents have increased in absurdity. On several occasions, I've been told by older males that the record I'm currently buying from them is a good one; this exchange is not one expressing a mutual love of the album, but meant as an educational offering and a reassurance. My usual response is "I know. That's why I'm buying it."

This kind of patronising tone is also present in situations in which I occupy the male-dominated role of DJ. After successfully correcting a technical issue involving the balance of the tone arm mid-set, I've been confidently told by an older male that my turntable has a belt issue that I should get fixed. My turntable is direct-drive. I've also experienced a bit of what Madeleine Holden has eloquently described as fetishisation for being a "cute and rare anomal[y]" and an "Exceptional Cool Girl" because I know and enjoy music in a way that "other girls" don't. The most baffling experience was finding myself in the middle of what I thought was a discussion about the Stone Roses and whether they were acid house, and discovering that it was apparently perceived as an argument of the utmost importance to the male participant. Though I (and my fellow female music fan and friend) knew that the Stone Roses were definitely part of the Madchester/baggy scene and thus definitely contained elements of acid house, the male in question took our refusal to defer to his counter-argument (that the band had nothing to do with acid house and only fell under the Sixties jangle pop revival) as the deepest effrontery. The pathetic climax of this argument was his frustrated jabbing at the mod RAF target tattooed on his forearm, saying "Do you know who I am?" I honestly didn't know who he was, having only met him twenty minutes before this, and my blank stare sent him into a frothy exit from not just the room, but the apartment. When he finally returned, he didn't speak to me or my friend for the rest of the evening. This was one of the least important conversations I've had in my life, but at the same time, one of the most telling.

Whilst I agree that there shouldn't be prescribed ways of being a female fan, I also don't often find myself reflected in a lot of the descriptions of these other ways of being a female fan, and music nerdiness is one among many attributes that can alienate me from other females. I recognise that much of my self-education about music was achieved through reading the music press and music criticism, and watching documentaries, which were dominated by male voices, and these voices likely served as an indoctrination of sorts. At the same time, I found that, for the most part, these voices made sense to and of me in a period of figuring out what I was actually passionate about and interested in.

What happens when you recognise yourself and forge your identity in these supposed indoctrinations, and end up resembling the kind of fan feminists would identify as dominant and male? I *do* collect a ridiculous number of carefully alphabetised records. I *do* enjoy writing, reading and discussing music criticism. I *do* travel large distances just to see gigs, often at expense to my finances and health. I *do* correct people about music trivia (even if they storm out of the building as a result).

In "failing" at my gender, am I failing my gender? If I am, perhaps this failure could actually be productive and generative, as theorised by Jack (Judith) Halberstam in *The Queer Art of Failure*. Halberstam argues that the failure queer people already experience in existing outside of heteronormative logic that predicates "success" on reproductive maturity and futurity can be applied to theory and critical thought to open up alternative ways of being and knowing. Failure of this kind can disturb and challenge binary logic and produce new realms of possibility from the so-called negativity of "critique and refusal". And though I feel like I'm ultimately failing at this essay, it's nevertheless a place to start interrogating and working through my otherwise automatic musical preferences and their underlying assumptions. With the increasing number of self-aware and articulate non-binary artists, such as Christine and the Queens, Janelle Monae, Shamir and Ezra Furman, perhaps gender fluidity will slowly shift the gravitational pull of gender binaries in music into a wider, more complex constellation. And though we don't live in a post-gender world, I greatly appreciate artists like Savages who do perform a way of being a musician and artist in a more felicitous way for gender binary codebreakers like me.

Bibliography

Auslander, Philip. *Performing Glam Rock: Gender and Theatricality in Popular Music*. (University of Michigan Press, 2006).

Butler, Judith. *Gender Trouble*. (Routledge, 1990).

Halberstam, Judith. *The Queer Art of Failure*. (Duke University Press, 2011).

Holden, Madeleine. "Guys: Why Are You Fetishizing Girls Who Like Rap Music?" *Noisey*, 12 February 2014. https://noisey.vice.com/en_uk/article/why-are-you-fetishizing-girls-who-like-rap-music

Melnick, Jeffrey. "'Story Untold': The Black Men and White Sounds of Doo-Wop." In Hill, Mike (ed.) *Whiteness: A Critical Reader*. (New York University Press, 1997).

Reynolds, Simon. *Shock and Awe: Glam Rock and Its Legacy, from the Seventies to the Twenty-first Century*. (Dey Street Books, 2016).

Reynolds, Simon and Press, Joy. *The Sex Revolts: Gender, Rebellion and Rock 'N' Roll*. (Serpent's Tail, 1995).

Sontag, Susan. "Notes on 'Camp.'" In Cleto, Fabio (ed.) *Camp: Queer Aesthetics and the Performing Subject: A Reader*. (University of Michigan Press, 1999).

Where Does a Body Begin?

Frances Morgan

In February 2016, Michael Gira, the founder of the band Swans, was accused of rape by musician Larkin Grimm. Grimm wrote on her Facebook page about an incident that occurred in 2008, when she and Gira were working together on an album to be released on Gira's Young God label. Initially Gira refuted the allegation, calling it a "horrible slur"; his wife, Jennifa Gira, wrote a statement in his support, citing Grimm's mental health issues as evidence of her unreliability. A few days later, Gira posted another statement, conceding that he and Grimm had had an "intimate encounter", which had been consensual, but had been quickly curtailed. He called it an "awkward mistake". He, too, alluded to Grimm's "demons".

As the posts circulated through my network of friends I watched comment threads spill jerkily down my computer screen. I clicked on links to news stories about the incident on various music websites. On one site, in the sidebar to the right of the story, was a link to an interview with Gira that I had carried out in 2010.

At that time, Swans' first album since 1997 had just been released and Gira was about to take a new line-up of the band on tour. I was excited by what I had heard of the new material. Once best described as an anti-rock group, Swans now stretched the rock form into huge, stunning shapes that they inhabited with magisterial confidence. The dissonance of their earliest work now co-existed with a bright, strong tonality. Before the interview I was so nervous I almost puked. I had heard that Gira was a tough interviewee, courteous and articulate but taking no shit. But I called him and we talked for half an hour, and it went fine. I wrote an effusive preamble to our Q&A and submitted the piece; people liked it and I was relieved. When friends asked what he was like, I said, he seemed really nice.

My first response to reading Grimm's Facebook post was fear. I tried to shake it off by asking what I had to be scared of. Was I worried about professional reprisal for promoting the work of an accused rapist, or scared of ridicule for not realising I'd been played by a manipulative man? These concerns didn't deserve to be called fear. I told myself I wasn't in any danger. I should instead feel shame at my weakness and complicity. And yet I could not dispel a physical, wordless dread that something was at my back, on my back, telling me, as it had so many times, that I was not safe and that it was my fault. So I was scared, and I was ashamed; and I knew that I could no longer subsume these feelings into music and sound.

Shame and fear are just two of many emotional states to have been explored in the music of Swans since the group formed in New York City in the early

Eighties; but they could be said to be the ones that Swans' music most clearly faces up to and tries to face down. Sonically they're like points on a graph between which the band's dense clusters of sound swing and lurch, gathering weight until something has to give. On early albums such as *Cop* and *Greed*, through the more expansive *Children of God* and beyond, the repetitive and compulsive nature of such feelings is made literal in cyclical song structures and reiterative lyrics, with short phrases forming impossible existential demands and promises. Make me nothing. I will deny myself. You burn it, then you eat it.

Gira's band are near-contemporaries of and often associated with NYC's abrasive, experimental No Wave scene, but Swans' bringing together of affectual and sonic extremes marks them out from other rock deconstructionists such as Glenn Branca or the nascent Sonic Youth, whose experiments with repetition, dissonance and volume feel predominantly formal, concerned with psychoacoustic effect rather than psychological depths. In Swans' music, phenomena like feedback and distortion are evocative of the world's chaos and cruelty, while the crunch of voices, instruments and circuits at their limits sound out the listener's own physical and mental limits. But then something magical happens: the music reabsorbs and transmutes all this cruelty and pain, and beyond it — resulting from it — there is wonder, and the promise of transcendence, which is expressed not only in the songs' surging volume but in the ecstatic timbres that eventually emerge from within them: white-hot white noise, church bells in overdrive, a constellation of sparks spreading across the back of the skull. Everything ending, all the time, but beginning over and over again. The body transformed from guilty matter into pure sound.

This is the promise of all cathartic music and art, as well as of psychedelic experiences — that you will be changed. It is why Swans' following and mythos remained even after Gira put the group on hiatus in the late Nineties, focusing instead on his more melodic, country-inflected Angels of Light project. I had been too young for Swans' peak years and, as I've often found myself doing with cultish bands whose boat I have missed, regarded their records and the devotion they inspired with a kind of performative indifference. Then, just as I was getting too old for displays of both devotion and indifference, I got it: this music was about structure and space above all else. It was about sound as material and the song as building; as a place of worship or a fortress. Within these vibrating edifices you could house your anger, violence and sorrow. These spaces were brutal but generous. They could contain it all.

After this revelation, when writing about Swans I was careful to focus on form first, understanding their music as architectonic works inhabited (and/or demolished) by emotion. It followed then that it was possible to hear Gira's lyrics, whether prayer-like or bluntly ugly, as part of that structural process, as materials that help the listener to get there, as well as words with meaning. But where is there, and who does it belong to? Whose spaces are these, anyway? It is the question you are not supposed to ask of the psychedelic experience. In *The Art of Cruelty*, Maggie Nelson reminds us that the void is not a neutral place. She writes:

Despite their desire to catapult us into a cosmological sphere in which forces such as Artaud's "living whirlwind that devours the darkness" reign supreme, many male thinkers and artists evidence an obsessiveness with gender that can be difficult, if not impossible, to ignore, even if one is trying hard to board their post-gender transcendental train.

In her account of violent and "transgressive" art, Nelson writes mostly about visual media and theatre. I believe that music is made under different conditions of representation and abstraction and I do not believe that gender was ever meant to be ignored or transcended in Swans' music. The inescapable violence of binary gender is there in plain hearing, especially in the albums which feature vocalist and keyboard player Jarboe, who joined Swans in 1986, and who was also Gira's partner for some years. But where there is sound, gender is always malleable and its binaries can be challenged. Jarboe brought with her a shapeshifting voice which could soar or rasp, performing angel, wraith, animal, as required; she also contributed synth and electronics, creating a watery ambient ambiguity around the songs' looming shapes, further destabilising their already fractured masculinity. The gendered violence of the state and the family are also scrutinised in her contributions to Swans. The "found" tapes that you hear on the album *Soundtracks for The Blind* are from her father's desk — an FBI agent, he bugged phone lines, recording his family's conversations as well as those of suspects. After his death, Jarboe repurposed these recordings, subverting and warping their invasive aggression with altered speeds and defamiliarising effects.

Jarboe continued her father's practice of surreptitious taping to document her own domestic life. On *Drainland*, Gira's bleak solo album from 1995, the opening song "You See Through Me" includes what appears to be a recording of a phone conversation between Gira and Jarboe. He is drunk. She wants to talk about his drinking. They don't have any money. His voice is hard and flat: "Shut your mouth, get the money. We have to live."[1]

The lines and boundaries of power shift as the grind and drone of electric guitars give way to plucked acoustic strings and naive keyboard. She has recorded him unknowingly. She's in control. But he is intimidating her. It's her recording. But it's his record; his name is on the cover. It's his record label. He's sick, an addict. She tricked him. But he's fine with it. Whose narrative is this, and who gains from its telling? The point is — the point that makes the song work, if it works, as a piece of work — that you are supposed to not know. No one really knows what happened between them. If we don't know, we can't act. We are just spectators, listening to a piece of performance art; just readers on the internet, weighing up the evidence.

***

A few months after Larkin Grimm's allegations and Michael Gira's response, the editor of the same site that had published my interview in 2010 emails and asks me if I would consider reviewing Swans' new album *The Glowing Man*. The editor writes at some length about his own opinion — based on research, citing statistics — of whether or not Gira is guilty. He writes that he thinks I am a good enough writer that I could write dispassionately and professionally of the music, while also being critical of rape culture in music.

"The favorite conceit of male culture is that experience can be fractured, literally its bones split, and that one can examine the splinters as if they were not part of the bone, or the bone as if it were not part of the body", Andrea Dworkin writes in *Pornography*. I draft the beginnings of a response. My tone is calm because I don't want to upset him, but my heart is thudding and won't slow down. I feel raw and adrenalised, wiped out but with a delusional energy like when you stay up all night and think you can do everything. I pick skin off my thumbs until I feel calmer. And then I feel diminished, an old body that has had enough. It won't be transcended or separated from its mind. It's not professional. It is trying to keep it together, wondering if it has a band-aid for its thumbs. "Where does your body begin?" Gira asks on Swans' *The Great Annihilator*. And, "Now is your body you?"[2]

The editor asks, if I cannot do it, can I recommend someone who can? Someone — he does not say "a woman", but I assume that is what he means. Yet it occurs to me that, during the time it took for him to write the email, he did not think of me as a woman, which is to say, someone whose experience cannot be broken into convenient splinters. As I concurred with this characterisation and tried to write back, my body resisted. Now is your body you?

That I am being expected to write "as a woman", to give a woman's perspective, yet not somehow not be a woman, is the impossible place at which many of us arrive as music journalism grapples with an increased awareness of gendered and racialised violence in the music industry and how this reflects, or doesn't reflect, on the music produced by that industry. But while men continue to do violence, and women continue being the ones expected to write about it for magazines and websites primarily edited and owned by and marketed towards men, we allow them to make a show of acknowledging this violence without addressing their complicity in it. We make ourselves unsafe, in order that they will be safer. Safer from what, from whom? No one seems to know.

***

Like a lot of female-identified people, there have been many times when I didn't want a body. A body was trouble. Listening to Swans, I would not think of the trouble it had already caused me: of the man who told me, when I had flu, that I probably had Aids, because I had slept with so many people, or of the pregnant friend being manipulated and abused by the father of her kid. I would not think about the man who asked me, when he saw me reading Lisa Carver's book *Drugs Are Nice*, in which she describes her marriage to nihilistic musician, Nazi sympathiser and violent abuser Boyd Rice, if I related to Carver because "you're both damaged women". Instead I would recall the metamorphoses I'd experienced when I took ketamine or acid and felt that I could wrap myself around the world like an iridescent tape-loop. I would think about mystical unions and cosmic endurance. A body could be damaged, but extreme sound made me believe that I could push it to its limits and still survive; that I could strengthen it and contain it. At the very least, I could handle it. As *Village Voice* critic Lindsay Rhoades reflected, shortly after Grimm's allegation was made public, "The fact that I could appreciate this band — full of aggression and ambiguity and ugliness, things women aren't supposed to embody — made me feel somehow like my gender was incidental or unimportant. Like I was just a default human. Instead of feeling othered I could simply touch the angry, animalistic tendencies we all encounter simply because we are alive."

The woman who can handle it, whatever "it" is, is one of the few types of women welcomed in transgressive art forms such as industrial music or horror film. First, though, she has to be brutalised; hence the rape-revenge horror subgenre and the trope of the "final girl". Or songs like "When Will I Return?", on Swans' most recent album, *The Glowing Man*. Sung by Jennifer Gira, the lyrics — written by Michael — detail a violent assault on a woman by a male stranger. Michael has said in an interview that he wrote it for his wife as a tribute to her "strength, courage and resilience" after she suffered such an attack. In the song, Jennifer retaliates and survives: "Oh, I'm alive"[3], repeats the refrain. It is true that people of all genders can draw strength from narratives of violence and cruelty, and can create highly subversive ones: I have defended — often to men — my choice to consume such narratives, on the basis that they strengthen me against that which would harm me. They help me build a critique, I say. (They help me build a fort, I think.)

But we're back to buildings again. "A human present, or future, cannot be constructed in the manner of a building", Klaus Theweleit writes in his study of masculinity and fascism, *Male Fantasies*. "The problem — power as thought and intention — is contained in the very notion of 'building'." Theweleit's book is about the proto-fascist Freikorps units in 1920s Germany and the memoirs and novels their soldiers wrote, in which women are frequently, horribly obliterated in passages of hallucinatory violence. "The monumentalism of fascism would seem to be a safety mechanism against the multiplicity of the living", Theweleit notes.

When I read *Male Fantasies* I think about this imperative to separate an artist's work from their personal life, to appreciate art on "its own terms". This is not because I want to make an equivalence between the Freikorps narratives and the music of Swans, or between the people who created those works. It's because I want to think about when we should separate and when we should not and how this is not only a moral or political imperative but also an aesthetic one. If the premise for the usefulness of cathartic art is to contain and transform violence within the art, so as to help us process and challenge the violence of the real world, what does it say about the quality of that art when it is revealed that its makers are doing the very thing their work is supposed to contain or challenge? It says to me that the artist's imagination has failed, and that their art has failed: as critique, as fiction, as a political force, as art. It becomes as lifeless as the reality depicted by and wished for by Theweleit's fascists. At the very least, as Rhoades notes, "Whatever catharsis I found in [Gira's] work previously now has an asterisk next to it".

Art whose intention is to shock can easily become an amplification of, rather than a challenge to, that which it purports to critique. It is easy to blame co-option by art institutions and cultural industries for this; but what this co-option often reveals more than anything is such art's latent conservatism, or at least its creators' tangled, co-dependent relationship with the power structures they appear to work against. This is revealed yet more clearly when the artist or their work are challenged by voices whose relationship with power is even more unequal than the one which the artist thinks they have. When the extreme is met with another extreme, it flounders, lashes out; it fails. It doesn't know what to do.

I mean, I don't know what to do. This is an essay about thinking about what to do.

The website found another woman to review *The Glowing Man*. In October 2016, reflecting on the aftermath of the rape allegation, Sasha Geffen reported on MTVnews.com that, "No dates were canceled after Swans' tour was announced in April... *The Glowing Man*'s promotional cycle rolled out on schedule, seemingly without a hitch". At the time of writing, tour dates for 2017 have just been announced. They keep popping up on my Facebook feed. Meanwhile Larkin Grimm has released a single called "I Don't Believe". It says on her Bandcamp page, "This song was written for all the survivors of abuse. You are not alone."

Notes

1 Michael Gira, "You See Through Me", *Drainland* (1995), Sub Rosa/Alternative Tentacles. Copyright Michael Rolfe Gira and Young God Publishing (1995).

2 Swans, "Where Does A Body End?", *The Great Annihilator* (1995), Young God Records. Copyright Michael Rolfe Gira and Young God Publishing (1995)

3 Swans, "When Will I Return?", *The Glowing Man* (2016), Young God Records/Mute Records. Copyright Michael Rolfe Gira and Young God Publishing (2016)

She wears short skirts, I wear T-shirts: The Complicated Feminism of Taylor Swift[1]

Charlotte Lydia Riley

My relationship with Taylor Swift is complicated, which feels appropriate.

She's four years younger than me; *Fearless*, her second album, the one that really got her noticed in Britain, was released when she was almost nineteen. I was twenty-three. (Twenty-three. Wow.) Of course then I was too cool to like her or her music; I'd always been too cool for girls and girl bands. Slightly too young for Eternal, I didn't get the Spice Girls, didn't really like Destiny's Child (!). I liked All Saints, but mostly because their slightly-spoken-word tone on "Never Ever" sounded like an attempt to be "indie", which is how teenage-me identified everything that I thought was cool. So Blur were indie, Blink-182 were indie, Franz Ferdinand were indie and above all Pulp — and the skinny-hipped, corduroy-clad Jarvis Cocker — were indie. (A few years later I heard Los Campesinos sing "four sweaty boys with guitars tell me nothing about my life"[2] and thought, yeah, pretty much. Though I always did love Candida.)

So to start with, I was far too sophisticated for Taylor: her girly music wasn't for me. Girly music was pop music, and pop music was always banging on about relationships and men and love — and the women were always half-dressed — and the lyrics were saccharine and trite. I had fallen for the line that lies unspoken in so much pop cultural critique, that anything beloved of teenage girls must be stupid (because, of course, deep down, we all believe that teenage girls are stupid, too).

I'm not quite sure exactly when this changed — or if any of this was ever properly, completely true. I remember secretly sort-of loving "Love Story" and "White Horse", both on *Fearless*, with their stories of high-school love. Even Taylor's biggest critics normally admit that her songs are catchy, you know, if you like that sort of thing: her lyrics were slick enough to get caught in my head and the melodies were sweet. I definitely didn't admit to this, though. *Speak Now*, her third album, sort of passed me by at the time. But *Red* — well, *Red* was different.

Red came out in autumn 2012, pre-empted by the single "We Are Never Ever Getting Back Together", and I fell for this song so hard. I bought the album and I played it over and over again, and I bought the two previous albums, too. When *1989* came out in Britain, I'd had it pre-ordered for a month.

I decided that I'd been wrong about Taylor — she was a feminist. Of course she was! Her songs were full of clues. On "White Horse", she played with the trope of the fairytale princess, passively waiting to be rescued by her fairy prince. The song, which starts by lamenting a disappointing relationship and a romantic betrayal, ends on a hopeful note of starting something new: "this is a big world / that was a small town / there in my rearview mirror disappearing now".[3] Rather than waiting to be rescued, she reverses the trope, and sings to her former prince that "it's too late for you and your white horse / to catch me now". Her song "Fifteen" critiques the idea that teenage girls should submit their lives to boyfriends, without undermining their emotion in the moment. There are lines like "in your life you'll do things greater than dating the boy on the football team", and "Back then I swore I was gonna marry him someday / But I realised some bigger dreams of mine".[4] In "We Are Never Ever Getting Back Together", I cheered her takedown of the pretentious ex-boyfriend who tries to police her musical tastes: "you would hide away and find your peace of mind / with some indie record that's much cooler than mine".[5] And, in "Blank Space", when she sings "Got a long list of ex-lovers / they'll tell you I'm insane", she owns her sexuality and critiques the "crazy ex-girlfriend" myth.[6]

It's easy to claim that Taylor "discovered" feminism when it became fashionable to do so — that her embrace of the label and the concept was a marketing conceit, tapping into a pop cultural zeitgeist where feminism was cool and exciting. After all, her conversion was apparently encouraged by Lena Dunham and took place in the context of megastars like Emma Watson proclaiming their own feminist credentials. Being feminist seemed to be the new trend for young, female stars, no longer potentially alienating to a commercial fan-base. To which I say: a) I wish we lived in a world where feminism was universally embraced as cool and exciting, but I just don't think that's true, and b) some of the strongest feminist themes above are actually on her earliest albums. No, I felt pretty sure of my redefinition of Taylor as feminist icon. I — like many late-twenties/early-thirties women that I knew — was head-over-heels in love with her music, her style, her #girlsquad, her rose-tinted imagination of high school years that we were all at least a decade removed from, her assertion that she was the underdog who had, somehow, grown up to be the popular kid. I would defend Taylor to the death.

But slowly, after a few months of listening, I started to feel doubts creeping in. The performative feminism was all very well and good — I still enjoyed it — but feuds with other female artists, notably Nicki Minaj (whose music I also love) started to make me feel uncomfortable. The video to "Shake It Off", especially the twerking backing dancers, felt awkwardly culturally appropriative. The video to "Wildest Dreams" was worse: set in an unnamed "African" landscape, it's a nostalgic reimagining of imperial romance that doesn't feature a single person of colour. It started to feel like Taylor was just another white feminist refusing to engage with more nuanced or critical ideas of identities and oppression, ignoring intersectionality in favour of vapid assertions about "supporting other girls" as she surrounded herself by other slim, pretty, wealthy white women.

And, of course, some of her songs just don't pass the feminist test. In fact, pretty much every trope she subverts above, she embraces in other songs. Taylor loves to present herself as a Cool Girl, not like other girls, and that sits uncomfortably with any attempt to cast her as a feminist heroine. In "You Belong With Me" she contrasts herself with and belittles the girlfriend of the object of her affections, in a lyric that carries an air of slut-shaming: "she wears short skirts, I wear T-shirts".[7] There's something similar going on in "Speak Now" where she interrupts a wedding (!) to save her crush from marrying a "pageant queen" dressed in "a gown like a pastry" surrounded by her "snotty little family".[8] In "Love Story", she buys right in to the fairytale princess fantasy, asking her Romeo to "save" her, forgiving his abandonment when he proposes (after, of course, he's asked her father for permission).[9] And "Better Than Revenge" is a whole song devoted to ripping apart the reputation of another girl — and this is not a fictional tale but reputedly an attack on a real woman, an actress who is "better known for the things that she does on the mattress", who stole Taylor's boyfriend.[10]

(As a side note, it's interesting how little agency the men in Taylor Swift songs actually have. They are always passively getting into relationships that make them unhappy, or marrying women to whom they are entirely unsuited, or being "stolen" from — or, just as often, by — Taylor. Women drive all the narratives — her songs are bursting with female agency — but, as seen above, this agency isn't universally empowering.)

Taylor Swift operates in a cultural context in which the potential, affirmed or imagined feminism of all women, including Beyoncé, Hillary Clinton, Madonna, Miley Cyrus, Ivanka Trump, Kim Kardashian, Carey Mulligan or Theresa May is being constantly debated, critiqued, denied and reaffirmed. Within this context, in which young female pop stars are asked overtly about feminism in interviews and are expected to affirm their credentials enthusiastically (but not threateningly), and in which female politicians are celebrated as feminist icons regardless of their actual gender politics, it is unsurprising that Taylor's feminism is up for grabs. Much of this is legitimate critique — not all women are feminists, even if they label themselves as such, and without a focus on deeds over words the label becomes meaningless. But some of this critical analysis is merely the background hum of patriarchy made audible — the demand that women must perform their politics impeccably, in every aspect of their lives, as a baseline for being taken seriously.

My relationship with Taylor goes up and down, depending on my mood and which album I'm listening to. Sometimes now I feel like I might have outgrown her, and when I need my feminism to be firm and uncompromising, I reach for other women artists: Beyoncé, Jenny Lewis, Kathleen Hanna, Janelle Monae, not Taylor's cheerful, upbeat girl power. But I still defend her. I resent it especially when men scoff at her, dismiss her as pop music (and what, exactly, is wrong with music being popular?), tell me that I can't possibly like her, or — worse — trying to explain to me why I do. When Ryan Adams covered 1989, it felt like he was performing a particular type of gatekeeping. It's pop music, by a young woman, so it must be awful, except it isn't — and aren't I clever for realising that! Here, let me translate it for you.

It is hard, in the face of these responses, so knowing and patronising and *smug*, not to feel defensive. Perhaps the most helpful reply is a defence of the agency of female listeners, who are far more likely to be belittled and harassed about their cultural choices than men. Men are allowed to appreciate music by deeply problematic performers, and they are assumed to be capable of separating the Art from the Artist without too much trouble. Women — and girls, especially girls — are assumed to be passive empty vessels into which culture is poured unfiltered. Our choices are never allowed to be conditional or critical: whatever we listen to, we must surely be absorbing, like sponges, without critique, as if our whole lives were not a constant, exhausting attempt to filter out the barrage of patriarchal bullshit that would otherwise do us harm.

By the time we become teenage girls we already know that our role models are always, inevitably, problematic, that even the positive messages about our bodies are slyly double-edged, that the approved pathways for our lives are still fraught with danger. We spend our whole lives negotiating the patriarchy and you want to tell us how the music that we like is sexist? Believe me, we know. We've made our choices — if you need us, we'll be over here, dancing.

Notes

1 I would like to thank the editors of this volume for their sensitive and encouraging feedback on early drafts of this piece. I would also like to thank Dr. Lucy Robinson, both for affirming my (guilty) love of Taylor Swift and for asserting that, just because something is beloved of teenage girls, doesn't mean it's shit.

2 Los Campesinos, "And We Exhale and Roll Our Eyes in Unison", *Hold on Now, Youngster...*, (2008), Wichita Recordings. Copyright Alexandra Berditchevskaia, Oliver Simon Staple Briggs, Thomas Edward Bromley, Harriet Coleman, Gareth David Paisley, Neil Turner, Ellen Clare Waddell, Universal Songs of Polygram International Inc. (2008).

3 Taylor Swift, "White Horse", *Fearless*, (2008), Big Machine Records. Copyright Liz Rose, Taylor Swift, Ole Care Taker Music, Sony, ATV Tree Publishing, Taylor Swift Music (2008).

4 Taylor Swift, "Fifteen", *Fearless*, (2008), Big Machine Records. Copyright Taylor Swift, Sony, ATV Tree Publishing, Taylor Swift Music (2008).

5 Taylor Swift, "We Are Never Ever Getting Back Together", *Red*, (2012), Big Machine Records. Copyright Martin Karl Sandberg, Johan Karl Schuster, Taylor Swift, Sony, ATV Tree Publishing, Taylor Swift Music (2008).

6 Taylor Swift, "Blank Space", *1989*, (2014), Big Machine Records. Copyright Martin Max, Shellback, Taylor Swift, Sony, ATV Tree Publishing, Taylor Swift Music (2014).

7 Taylor Swift, "You Belong With Me", *Fearless*, (2008), Big Machine Records. Copyright Liz Rose, Taylor Swift,

Orbison Music LLC, Sony, ATV Tree Publishing, Taylor Swift Music, Warner-Tamerlane Publishing Corp. (2008).

8 Taylor Swift, "Speak Now", *Speak Now*, (2010), Big Machine Records. Copyright Taylor Swift, Song, ATV Tree Publishing, Taylor Swift Music (2010).

9 Taylor Swift, "Love Story", *Fearless*, (2008), Big Machine Records. Copyright Taylor Swift, Sony, ATV Tree Publishing, Taylor Swift Music (2008).

10 Taylor Swift, "Better Than Revenge", *Speak Now*, (2010), Big Machine Records. Copyright Taylor Swift, Sony, ATV Tree Publishing, Taylor Swift Music (2010).

Notes on Contributors

Eli Davies is a writer, researcher and former editor of *New Left Project*. She has written on music, politics, popular culture and literature for the *Guardian, Noisey, The Quietus* and *New Statesman*.

Rhian E. Jones grew up in South Wales and now lives in London where she writes on history, politics and popular culture. Her work has appeared in *The Quietus, Salon, McSweeneys Internet Tendency* and the *Morning Star*. She is the author of *Clampdown: Pop-Cultural Wars on Class and Gender*; *Petticoat Heroes: Gender, Culture and Popular Protest*; and co-author of *Triptych: Three Studies of Manic Street Preachers'* The Holy Bible. @RhianEJones.

Christina Newland is a journalist on film and culture for publications including *Sight & Sound, Esquire, VICE* and *Little White Lies*. She specialises in Golden Age Hollywood and boxing flicks. Find her on Twitter at @christinalefou.

Stephanie Phillips is a London-based freelance journalist specialising in music, race and feminism. Her work has been featured in outlets including *gal-dem*, Bandcamp and BFI. @stephanopolus

Nina Power teaches Philosophy at the University of Roehampton and Critical Writing in Art & Design at the Royal College of Art. She is the author of many articles on philosophy, politics, feminism and culture.

Manon Steiner is a writer, blogger and self-proclaimed vagabond. Currently she is exploring the world, learning new things every day and sharing her stories on her blog http://vagabondmanon.com/. The essay in this book is derived from her thesis "The display of satanic imagery in 1960s British youth culture on the example of the Rolling Stones" and is her third publication in this context.

Em Smith is a Proper Northern music writer wino living the breadline life in London. Turning cursive letters into knives.

Elizabeth Newton is a music writer and researcher in New York City. She studies histories of fidelity and reproduction.

Jacey Lamerton is a Margate ex-pat, fond of scooters, ska and scallywags. She learned journalism the old-fashioned, gritty way but took the content marketing shilling and now works in a collective as Killer Content.

Fiona Sturges is an arts and culture writer whose work has appeared in the *Guardian*, the *Financial Times*, the *i* and *Uncut*.

Beatrice M. Hogg is a writer, rocker and social worker, as well as a coal miner's daughter from western Pennsylvania. She now lives in Sacramento, California and is working on a collection of personal essays about long-term unemployment and homelessness during the economic downturn.

Rachel Trezise is a novelist, playwright, non-fiction and short story writer.

Kelly Robinson is a freelance writer and researcher from Knoxville, Tennessee with particular interests in history, popular culture, and early film. Her magazine bylines include *Rue Morgue*, *Smithsonian*, and *Mental Floss*. She is currently completing a book on lost horror films.

Johanna Spiers is a qualitative health researcher by day and a writer by night. She DJs hip hop and pop music wherever she is allowed, and believes that yoga is the solution to most problems. She is currently working on a mystery novel about socialists, journalists and polar bears called *Eat the Rich*.

Zahra Dalilah is a community activist and writer who has written at length on the interplay between resistance, identity and the arts. Follow her @ZahraDalilah1 to follow upcoming projects.

K. E. Carver hails from that middle-ground of the US that's not quite the Midwest but neither is it the Northeast (and is definitely not Appalachia). She is currently a researcher in Scotland, writing and teaching on popular culture, fandom studies, and shows that she probably binge-watched on Netflix when she should have been marking essays.

Jasmine Hazel Shadrack is a Senior Lecturer in Popular Music at the University of Northampton, UK. Her research fields include graphic novels, gender, feminism, performativity, extreme metal, black metal, autoethnography and esotericism.

Marissa Chen graduated from Birkbeck College with an MA in Creative Writing, and divides her time between the UK and Asia. She is currently working on two photographic series based in North Korea and Japan, as well as a collection of prose about women and trauma. www.marissa-c.com

Emily McQuade is a word herder and occasional stand-up comedian residing in London. She hopes to write some fiction one of these days.

Jude Rogers is a music critic, arts journalist, interviewer and Radio 4 broadcaster.

Alison L. Fraser is a PhD Candidate at Trent University, studying Euro-American constructions of "difference" and the implications of these constructions for people labeled as "different." Her current work investigates Canadian goth/industrial subcultures.

Amanda Barokh has dabbled in DJing and music journalism. Over the past few years she has been on the run from responsible adulthood - living in Chamonix, London, Porto and Ibiza and doing various random and often ill-advised jobs to support herself whilst she writes her first novel.

Abi Millar is a freelance journalist now living in the Netherlands. You can read more of her writing at thisisawriteoff.wordpress.com.

Dr Judith May Fathallah is a lecturer and writer in media and cultural studies, whose interests include fan cultures, new media, and convergence. Her first monograph, *Fanfiction and the Author: How Fanfic Changes Popular Cultural Texts*, is published by Amsterdam University Press.

Laura Friesen lives in Winnipeg, where she works as communications manager at the National Screen Institute - Canada. Her music writing has appeared in *The Quietus*, *Shameless Magazine*'s blog and Winnipeg's *Stylus Magazine*.

Anna Fielding is the editor of *Emerald Street*, a daily lifestyle email for women published by ShortList Media. She has worked as a journalist for over seventeen years, starting out as a staff writer at *Mixmag* and going on to contribute to many titles including the *Evening Standard*, the *Times*, *NME* and the *Face*. Anna also curates The Emerald Street Literary Festival.

Larissa Wodtke is the Research Coordinator at the Centre for Research in Young People's Texts and Cultures at the University of Winnipeg and the Managing Editor of the academic journal *Jeunesse: Young People, Texts, Cultures*. She is a co-author of *Triptych: Three Studies of Manic Street Preachers'* The Holy Bible and has published research on architecture, MP3s, crowdfunding, and affective labour in popular music.

Frances Morgan is a critic based in London. She is the former editor of *Plan B* magazine and a contributing editor of *The Wire*, and has written on music and film for publications including *Sight & Sound* and *Frieze*.

Charlotte Lydia Riley is a lecturer in twentieth-century British history at the University of Southampton. She writes about the British Empire, the Labour Party, gender politics and women's history, and is on Twitter as @lottelydia

Acknowledgements

For advice and enthusiasm about the project in its early stages, thank you to Richard King, Tamar Shlaim, Emma Jackson, Laura Snapes and Dan Hancox.

Thanks also to Rory Macqueen, Laurence Scott, Kate Bradbury, John Davies, Máire Messenger Davies, Zoe Kemp, Agata Pyzik and Sinead Mulready for support, interest, encouragement and inspiration throughout the process of putting the book together.

Thanks to Josh, Tamar, Phoebe, Johnny, Tariq and all at Repeater.

Finally, thanks to everyone who shared the initial call-out for submissions, enabling such a range of distinct voices to be represented in this collection, and to everyone who contributed their thoughts and experiences.

Repeater Books

is dedicated to the creation of a new reality. The landscape of twenty-first-century arts and letters is faded and inert, riven by fashionable cynicism, egotistical self-reference and a nostalgia for the recent past. Repeater intends to add its voice to those movements that wish to enter history and assert control over its currents, gathering together scattered and isolated voices with those who have already called for an escape from Capitalist Realism. Our desire is to publish in every sphere and genre, combining vigorous dissent and a pragmatic willingness to succeed where messianic abstraction and quiescent co-option have stalled: abstention is not an option: we are alive and we don't agree.